BUDGETING
A GUIDE FOR LOCAL GOVERNMENTS

Robert L. Bland
University of North Texas

Irene S. Rubin
Northern Illinois University

International
City/County
ICMA
Management
Association

06 05 04
7 6 5
05-114

To Bob and Helen Bland:
Your inspiration helped make this possible
—RLB

To Dotty Sharp:
I hope she was as proud of me as I was of her
—ISR

International
City/County
ICMA
Management
Association

The International City/County Management Association is the professional and educational organization for appointed administrators and assistant administrators in local government. The purposes of ICMA are to enhance the quality of local government and to nurture and assist professional local government administrators in the United States and other countries. To further its mission, ICMA develops and disseminates new approaches to management through training programs, information services, and publications.

Local government managers—carrying a wide range of titles—serve cities, towns, counties, councils of governments, and state/provincial associations of local governments. They serve at the direction of elected councils and governing boards. ICMA serves these managers and local governments through many programs that aim at improving the manager's professional competence and strengthening the quality of all local governments.

The International City/County Management Association was founded in 1914; adopted its City Management Code of Ethics in 1924; and established its Institute for Training in Municipal Administration in 1934. The institute, in turn, provided the basis for the Municipal Management Series, generally termed the "ICMA Green Books."

ICMA's interests and activities include public management education; standards of ethics for members; the *Municipal Year Book* and other data services; urban research; newsletters; a monthly magazine, *Public Management*; and other publications. ICMA's efforts toward the improvement of local government management—as represented by this book—are offered for all local governments and educational institutions.

Foreword

Local government budgeting decisions vary with local preferences, resources, and needs, but all budgets are designed to answer the same basic question: What is the best way to allocate community resources? Whether the concern is blacktopped versus concrete road surfaces, line-item versus program budgeting, or managerial discretion versus financial control, local government budgeting gives rise to technical and policy issues that require thoughtful evaluation and open, deliberate discussion and debate.

Budgeting: A Guide for Local Governments provides a comprehensive, straightforward look at this fundamental local government activity. The extensive coverage of basic budgeting functions details the advantages and disadvantages of various approaches to revenue projection, the collection and review of departmental proposals, the development of capital budgeting policy, and other essential budgeting tasks. Budget implementation, accounting, and financial reporting are given detailed consideration, as are a variety of methods for maintaining budgetary balance, preventing overspending, and dealing with contingencies.

Beyond the basics, the volume addresses the evolving role of the budget. Once primarily an instrument of financial control, the budget is now widely used as a tool for management and communication. Particularly when a program or performance format is used, the budget has become central to productivity, performance measurement, and management improvement efforts. The budget also plays a key role in addressing demands for governmental accountability: citizens and elected officials alike expect budgets not only to be complete and accurate, but also to be accessible to the nonspecialist reader.

As the role of the budget has changed, so has that of the budget office. Formerly the "bottleneck" in the budgeting process and the adversary of departments, the budget office has taken on the role of educator and communicator, assisting departments to prepare requests and helping frame trade-offs for the chief executive. Changes in the role of the budget office reflect, in turn, a number of gradual shifts in the "openness" of local government budgets and budget processes: indications of these shifts include efforts to increase citizen participation; to balance managerial discretion and financial control; to address—rather than to avoid—conflict in budgeting; and to develop budget formats that show not only what the local government does, but why and how well.

Budgeting: A Guide for Local Governments addresses issues every local government has to face. Using information gathered from communities across the country, the book clarifies alternative approaches to common budgeting problems and explores a range of developments and reforms. From monitoring budgetary balance to conducting public hearings to dealing with conflict on the council, this volume offers tested approaches that can be tailored to local opportunities and needs.

ICMA is grateful to the authors, Robert L. Bland and Irene S. Rubin, for their thoughtfulness and hard work during the development and writing of this volume and for their unfailing responsiveness during the editorial phase. A number of other individuals who assisted in this project are acknowledged in the preface.

William H. Hansell, Jr.
Executive Director
International City/County
   Management Association
Washington, D.C.

Preface

We gratefully acknowledge the assistance of a number of people in the development, writing, and publication of this book.

Because we intended the book as a resource for both public managers and students of public administration, we sought the advice of both academics and practitioners in the field. We wish to thank two colleagues in particular, whose thoughtful reviews of a draft manuscript helped us better focus the content of the book: John Forrester, associate professor, Department of Public Administration, University of Missouri-Columbia; and Michael A. Pagano, professor, Department of Political Science, Miami University of Ohio. We are also grateful for the assistance of Larry A. Maholland, director of finance/administration, St. Charles, Illinois. His reviews of an early draft demonstrated what all budget directors know: that the devil is in the details.

During 1989, 1990, and 1991, we visited a number of local governments, attending council meetings and budget work sessions and interviewing current and former council members and staff. We wish to thank the following jurisdictions and individuals for their generous assistance with this fieldwork, which became the basis for significant portions of the material in this volume: Boston, Massachusetts—Bob Ciolek, Barbara Gottschalk, and Mary Nee; Dayton, Ohio—Ted Bucaro and Paul Woodie; Dekalb, Illinois—Mark Stephens; Phoenix, Arizona—Alan Brunacini, Frank Fairbanks, Pat Manion, Barry Starr, and Andrea Tevlin; Rochester, New York—Al Sette; St. Louis, Missouri—Gerry Osborn; Tampa, Florida—Al Desilet, Mike Salmon, Jim Stefan, and Roger Wehling.

The creativity shown in the design of budgets, budget manuals, and other supporting documentation is truly remarkable. We wish to thank the many budget directors in cities, counties, school districts, and special districts whose willingness to share such documents was of immense benefit in our research for the book.

We also benefited from the research assistance provided by a number of graduate students at the University of North Texas: Jon Fortune, Kim Hoffman, MaryEllen Miksa, Marisol Trevizo, and D'Arlene Ver Duin.

The editorial guidance of the ICMA staff, under the direction of Barbara Moore, is unparalleled in our experience of working with publishers. We wish to thank Barbara Moore for her invaluable assistance during manuscript development. Sandy Chizinsky has no equal when it comes to editorial scrutiny; her assistance during the editorial phase enabled us to translate our thoughts into a much more coherent work. We also wish to thank Julie Butler, publishing assistant; Jane Gold, production editor; and Dawn M. Leland, production director; for their contributions to the final product.

Our deepest appreciation goes to these and many other people who have made this book possible.

Robert L. Bland
University of North Texas

Irene S. Rubin
Northern Illinois University

About the authors

Robert L. Bland is professor and chair of the Department of Public Administration at the University of North Texas, where he teaches classes on the economic aspects of government, governmental accounting, and budgeting in the public sector. He is the author of *A Revenue Guide for Local Government* and of a number of articles on the municipal bond market, property taxation, and the impact of capital spending on municipal operating budgets. He has also conducted two workshops in Poland on revenue sources for local governments. Professor Bland received his Ph.D. degree from the Graduate School of Public and International Affairs at the University of Pittsburgh, his M.P.A. and M.B.A. degrees from the University of Tennessee, and his B.S. degree from Pepperdine University.

Irene S. Rubin is a professor in the public administration division of the political science department at Northern Illinois University. Her published work deals primarily with the politics of budgeting, with a particular emphasis on municipal funding problems. Professor Rubin is the author of *Running in the Red: The Political Dynamics of Urban Fiscal Stress* and *The Politics of Public Budgeting*, and coauthor (with Charles Levine and George Wolohojian) of *The Politics of Retrenchment*. Professor Rubin is editor of *Public Administration Review* and past editor of *Public Budgeting & Finance*. She received her Ph.D. from the University of Chicago, her M.A. from Harvard, and her B.A. from Barnard.

Contents

1/26

2/9

2/3

2/3

2/16

2/2

Figures

Table

1 The context of local government finance

Governmental versus private sector budgeting

Budgeting at the local level

Substituting for market mechanisms
Supply
Demand
Price

Conflict in the budget process
Advocates versus guardians
The battle over information
Accuracy versus political expediency
Bureaucracy versus democracy
Special versus collective interests
Public will versus public welfare

The environment of public budgeting
Economic influences
Social and demographic change
The legal and intergovernmental context

Summary

The context of local government finance

Governmental budgeting allocates resources to public services and projects. Because it determines the total amount of taxes levied and on whom, governmental budgeting also allocates the burden of taxation. Budgeting balances the resources drawn from the public against the demand for services and projects, keeping taxes within acceptable limits and ensuring that services are sufficient to allow economic growth and social stability. Budgeting helps policy makers set goals, assists program managers and department heads to improve organizational performance, and ensures that both elected and appointed officials are accountable to the public.

This chapter first details the differences between public and private sector budgeting, then distinguishes between local and state and national budgeting. Because local government activities are founded on the public interest rather than on profit, local governments use a number of measures to substitute for market control of supply, demand, and price; the chapter examines these mechanisms in detail. Finally, the chapter considers sources of conflict in the budget process and the economic, social, and legal context of local government budgeting.

Governmental versus private sector budgeting

Governmental budgeting is legitimately and necessarily different from the sort of budgeting undertaken by individuals and companies. First, governments have a broader set of responsibilities than private individuals or businesses. For example, government provides services that the private sector cannot or will not provide at a reasonable cost. Moreover, government services and programs are expected to address social problems, although agreement on which problems should be addressed and at what cost is difficult to achieve. In short, government action derives from a public mandate that promotes community interest, whereas the actions of individuals and businesses are not subject to such strictures.

In capitalist economies, private individuals are free to act in their own interest, even when self-interest clashes with community interests. Businesses rarely concern themselves with facilitating the economic health of other businesses, especially competitors. Government, in contrast, must protect citizens' interests as well as provide the minimal conditions necessary for business activity. For example, local governments in some states regulate weights and measures, employing staff to inspect scales in supermarkets and meters on gasoline pumps. Unless consumers are confident that a pound is a pound and a gallon is a gallon, they cannot make choices on the basis of price, and basic market mechanisms cannot function efficiently. Society thus has an interest in protecting the integrity of weights and measures and uses government regulation and inspection to do so.

Another major difference between governmental and private sector budgeting is that governmental budgeting takes place in a public forum.

Governmental budgeting	Private sector budgeting
Protects the interests of citizens and promotes business activity	Is based on self-interest: goal is to maximize net income, without concern for facilitating economic activity of other businesses
Depends on finding agreement among decision makers on the existence and importance of societal problems	Depends on market considerations to guide budget decisions
Requires that budgeting decisions be made in a public forum open to taxpayers and the media	Is conducted on the basis of formulas by professionals who work in private
Incorporates extensive financial controls designed to prevent financial mismanagement, excessive borrowing, inordinately high tax rates, and deficit spending	Is conducted according to financial practices that are controlled by the market and by accounting standards
In the context of accountability to citizens, pursues goals of efficiency and effectiveness by balancing short-term and longer-term community interests.	Is insulated from the public and accountable only to shareholders; goal is to maximize profits in the short term.

The budget decisions of individuals and businesses, in contrast, are made in private. Developers of private budgets need not concern themselves with the process used to create the budget; nor do they have to take advice. When Uncle Charlie prepares his household budget, he can choose to ignore Aunt Letitia's suggestion that he buy a used rather than a new car. But both Uncle Charlie and Aunt Letitia have a legitimate right to influence the local government's **budget**, as does every other resident who may have an opinion about what should be done, at what cost, and at whose expense. In addition to occurring in a public forum, governmental budgeting decisions must be explained, almost inevitably angering those whose opinions did not prevail. Developers of private budgets worry less about being second-guessed or publicly embarrassed if they make a mistake.

Public budgeting would perhaps be easier if it could be insulated from the demands of competing interest groups and carried out by technicians according to a formula—but it would be much less democratic. Public budgeting processes reflect the openness of democracy, balancing the various interests and priorities in the community. The public—taxpayers and their elected representatives—is thus a legitimate actor in the budget process.

Because a public budget results from negotiations among groups who want different things, budget implementation must be visibly consistent with the agreements reached. Once a government passes its budget, there are practical limitations on the number of amendments allowed during the budget year or biennium. In contrast, private entities can change their budgets whenever they wish and for whatever reason.

In the public sector, the ideal is to make only unavoidable technical changes during the year. Too much effort goes into soliciting opinions and mediating among competing demands to revise the budget extensively during the year. Moreover, substantially redoing parts of the budget out of public view threatens the legitimacy of the process. Implementation of public budgets must be rigid enough to maintain the public's confidence in agreements arrived at in open proceedings, yet flexible enough to deal with unexpected events.

Another major difference between public and private sector budgeting is that government is burdened with a greater number of financial controls to prevent mismanagement, excessive borrowing, inordinately high taxes, and overspending. In the private sector, the market exerts control over financial decisions. For example, as debt burdens increase, the market responds by making additional borrowing more expensive. A firm that overextends itself and is unable to recover will go out of business. Because governments—especially general-purpose governments, such as counties and municipalities—provide services that are considered essential, their continued existence is not optional; in other words, governments cannot go out of business. In extremely rare cases, they may declare bankruptcy if they are unable to meet their debt obligations, but they must still continue to function, funding daily operations and arranging for a new schedule of debt payments. The consequence is that each time a state or local government makes an error or exceeds public tolerance, new controls are imposed that reduce the chances that such events will recur. These controls sometimes come with strict oversight that lasts for decades or even centuries. In some states, for example, laws and regulations specify the precise accounting and budgeting systems that local governments may use. In New Jersey, local budgets must be reviewed by a state agency before they can be implemented.

Financial controls—such as debt limitations, rate limits for property taxes, limitations on how cash can be invested, and requirements to use fund accounting—make public budgeting different from and often more difficult than private budgeting. Moreover, with time, financial controls on government have tended to accumulate rather than to be eliminated once the original problem faded. For example, the prohibition that forbids local governments in most states from investing in the stock of private companies dates from the days of railroad expansion, when cities, eager for growth, were lured into excessive and risky levels of investment in railroads. When railroad companies went bankrupt, cities were left with worthless stock and no cash with which to meet their obligations.

Virtually all governments in the United States are required to use fund accounting, which breaks the budget into separate funds (like piggy banks), each with separate rules about what money goes in and how it can be spent. Most important, each **fund** must balance revenues with expenditures. Unlike businesses, which have a single bottom line, governments must contend with multiple bottom lines, one for each fund. Even if there is enough revenue in another fund to cover a shortfall, a deficit in any fund is still a deficit. These requirements make public budgeting different from, and often more difficult than, private budgeting.

Rigid and sometimes excessive controls have been compounded at the local level by **mandates**—requirements from the state and federal governments that specify which services local governments must provide and at what level; furthermore, mandates typically contain regulations with which local governments must comply, often at great expense. State governments may legislate the cost of local police pensions, regulate who may work overtime, and require local governments to provide water that meets a particular standard of purity. Some of the requirements reflect the effectiveness of lobbying groups that find it more efficient to deal with state governments rather than with hundreds or thousands of local governments; other requirements reflect efforts to deal effectively with collective problems such as pollution of the water supply.

Regardless of the source of the mandate, local governments must comply, often within revenue constraints mandated by the state. The combination of controls and mandates was less problematic when intergovernmental **grants** partially covered costs, but as the flow of grants slowed, many local governments were left with less ability to respond to local priorities. Mandates in public budgeting have some parallel in businesses that must adhere to government regulations, but the constraints are far more extensive in the public sector.

Budgeting at the local level

Budgeting at the local level differs from budgeting at the state and national levels. Local governments have to bear a larger number of mandates from above, but they generally do not have to worry about the implications of their actions for the local economy, because municipalities and counties typically do not spend enough to affect a complex and porous economy. (*Porous* refers to the fact that money spent in one jurisdiction spills over into surrounding communities—where workers live, where owners of businesses reside, or where the local government purchases goods or services.)

Unlike the federal and state governments, most local governments are not responsible for **entitlements**—benefits such as social security or unemployment compensation, which are awarded to individuals according to eligibility criteria defined in law. Entitlements are open-ended grants: the amount of funding depends on the number of people or governments that meet the eligibility criteria. For example, unemployment compensation is a benefit to which unemployed workers are entitled under certain conditions. The demand for entitlements usually goes up during recessions—just when slow economic growth causes government revenues to lag. Because they are not responsible for funding entitlements, local governments are usually not squeezed this way during recessions; this makes it somewhat easier (though it is never easy) for local governments to balance the budget during an economic downturn by cutting or delaying expenditures.

Local governments are organized differently than the national and state governments. At the national and state levels, there is usually a sharp division between executive and legislative responsibilities with respect to the budget: in the system of budgeting that has evolved over time, the chief executive receives and examines budget requests from departments and puts together a budget proposal that is then scrutinized by the public and approved, rejected, or modified by the legislature. This process, when it works, provides some element of public accountability.

At the local level, the roles of the executive and legislative branches in budgeting are often blurred. In the increasingly rare form of government known as the commission form, department heads (executive branch) and the council (legislative branch) are the same people. Historically, many local governments used a board composed of members of both the executive and legislative branches to handle budgeting; a few local governments retain this procedure. Today, many municipalities, counties, and special districts hire a professional manager as the chief executive officer. The manager is an appointee of the legislative branch and serves at its pleasure. While the manager normally prepares a budget and presents it to the council or board for approval, the degree of independence exercised by the manager may vary widely, depending on the council or board. In local governments that do not have a manager, the mayor may be so dominant in the budget process that the governing body has neither the knowledge to scrutinize the executive's proposal nor the power to change it.

Because of the structural differences between local governments and those at the state and national levels, accountability at the local level is less effectively provided by the division of responsibilities between the executive and legislative branches. At the local level, the budget document itself is a much more important tool of public accountability than it is at higher levels of government.

For one thing, citizen participation in budgeting is easier at the local level. Residents can follow local budget stories in the newspaper and attend council meetings to express their views. Chief executives and council members can present budget proposals to citizen forums and obtain responses directly from voters. This level of participation is much more difficult to achieve in a large state and nearly impossible at the federal level, because of the complexity of the budget and budgetary issues, the size of the country, and the difficulty of attending even a regional hearing. Despite, however, the potential importance of citizen involvement as a source of accountability and control, public participation is often underutilized.

Substituting for market mechanisms

Governments, including local governments, are economically different from private firms. In the private sector, the market regulates supply, demand, and price (holding quality constant). By contrast, there are limited competitive markets for the goods and services that local governments produce. A citizen who has been assaulted does not stop to decide whether to call a private police company or the city. Nor do citizens pay for police services on a per-call basis. As a result, demand for police protection is not regulated by price. If the supply of police services is not regulated by price, what determines supply? In the case of public services, various mechanisms substitute for the market to regulate supply, demand, and price.

Supply

For some public services, supply depends roughly on demand. That is, when citizens call the police department for assistance, they are making a demand for services; within limits, the more calls they make, the more service is provided. The same is generally true for ambulance, fire, and many social services. Citizens also make implicit demands for education; generally speaking, the more children attending school, the more schools and teachers provided.

To the extent that these services are funded through taxes, citizens do not pay for them every time they use them. Presumably, if citizens had to pay the full cost of ambulance service every time, they would hesitate to call—or even avoid calling—a public ambulance. If they had to pay directly for schooling, some residents might not send their children to school because the cost would seem prohibitive. Some economists claim that many public services are overused because of the absence of a direct cost that citizens can associate with the services. Others argue that it is in the public interest to see that certain services—education or alcohol rehabilitation clinics, for example—are readily available.

Demand

The level of demand influences the supply of services, but sometimes "demand" comes from professional government staff in response to anticipated problems. On the basis of projected population growth, for example, the town planner may recommend that additional roads be constructed and that schools and sewage facilities be expanded. These technical evaluations serve as proxies for demand, under the assumption that citizens will not want to be caught in traffic gridlock and will assuredly not want sewage backups. Because it is less expensive to plan and install extra capacity before it is needed, local governments are likely to take steps to satisfy expected demand.

Sometimes, however, professionals' assessments of needs may diverge from the public's willingness to pay to meet those needs. When a business tries to fill a perceived need, but actual demand does not materialize, the product or project is dropped. Governments may proceed for some time trying to satisfy what staff (and elected officials) perceive as a need, even when the demand does not develop or when it is limited to a small group of beneficiaries. Perceived need in government can substitute for demand in the market, but it falls short of a perfect fit.

While perceived need influences the level of public services produced, the supply of services ultimately depends on available revenue. At the state and local levels, revenue (tax) burdens are not likely to be driven by spending requirements; instead, revenue availability generally determines spending. Public officials seldom say, "We need a new road—let's go get more taxes to pay for it." They are more likely to say, "This is the amount of revenue available: how much road can we get for that amount of money?" A national study of 171 municipalities showed that spending was revenue driven: past revenue changes helped predict current expenditures.[1] Similarly, a study of the Massachusetts state budget found that previous revenue levels helped predict current state expenditures.[2]

Funding for operating budgets is limited because citizens resist tax increases and politicians find it politically difficult to raise taxes. At the local level, the supply of services can increase only up to the level of revenues set in the approved budget. Where demand exceeds these ceilings, local governments must ration—that is, either curtail service provision (e.g., serve only the first thirty patients or reduce office hours in some locations or facilities), or prioritize services (e.g., rank emergency calls). Although governments generally do not increase taxes to reduce demand, they may use demand management in the case of fee-supported services.

If a local government chooses not to increase prices to curtail demand, consumption will inevitably exceed capacity, much to the frustration of public officials. Reducing services to match revenue levels would not be nearly as difficult or painful if demand could be curtailed at the same time, but that seldom happens. Cutting back on drug rehabilitation programs does not reduce the number of citizens needing rehabilitation; cutting back on road crews does not reduce the number of potholes or slow the deterioration of roads. Local officials continually strive to stretch limited—and sometimes diminishing—resources by various means, such as improving productivity and privatizing service delivery; but sometimes, no matter how hard they try, they cannot meet demand.

The budget plays a central role in limiting spending to the amount of available revenue and allocating limited funds among services and projects. Over time, the budget's allocation of services should follow public demand—or, where demand is unclear, some measure of need. That is, within the constraints of revenue, budgets normally allocate more to those services for which the need is clearly demonstrated and that are widely accepted by the public. When crime is seen as a problem, local budgets tend to allocate more resources to police services. When demand for prisons increases, states budget more for prisons and less for roads and education.

At the local level, there is not a one-to-one relationship between demand and changing budget allocations. First, the cost of some existing services may increase without any change in demand; second, rigidities in budgets, such as long-term contracts, make it difficult to reduce some expenditures or increase others. Third, national or state-level funding may be cut in areas of intense need, contributing to imbalances between demand and resources at the local level. Fourth, the budget process itself may not be open and sensitive enough to reflect changing needs. Fifth, increased demands from one group may compete with those from another, and the result may not be a single, clear set of demands. Finally, tax limits may make it difficult to respond to new demands without cutting current, popular services. These obstacles to rapid changes in public budgets often contribute to the public's perception that government is unresponsive. Unfortunately, only one of these factors—the design of the budget process—is under the control of the mayor or manager.

Price

As a substitute for market signals on both the cost and the mix of services, managers may rely on prior history (the town has always provided police escorts for funerals); on technical determination of need (traffic flow through the intersection warrants a stop light); on studies of community problems (homeless people wandering the streets downtown or accosting passersby); and on public opinion as expressed during the budget process. Tax protests, public hearings, complaints, and demands made by citizens to elected or appointed officials help provide the missing information that would otherwise be provided by the market. The fact that the various pieces of information may not all point in the same direction turns budgetary decision making into an adjudicatory process.

When a service is financed by taxes, the community bears the burden because the presumption is that everyone benefits. Because residents are not charged every time they call for police assistance, a local government does not have to decide what to charge for police services. However, government-owned **enterprises**, such as utility services, operate on a fee-for-service rather than a tax-paid basis. In the case of enterprises, governments must determine how much to charge—again, in the absence of a competitive market. A local government does not raise water rates simply because the demand is high: the local government's mandate is not to maximize profits, but to supply necessary services that cannot (or could not, at some point in the past) be provided satisfactorily or at a reasonable price by the private sector.

One issue in setting prices for government-produced services is the proportion of costs to be recovered from user fees and the proportion to be subsidized by general revenues. When those who purchase the service are the sole beneficiaries, they should pay a *pro rata* share of the full cost. Sometimes, however, those who consume a service are not the only beneficiaries. When people use public transit, for example, those who drive their own vehicles have less traffic to contend with and less difficulty finding parking. Everyone benefits from the reduced pollution, and the reduced dependence on imported oil helps the economy. In situations like this, local governments may recover part of the cost of the service from riders and the remainder from general taxes. Because nonriders pay part of the cost, the price for riders is lowered. The subsidized price of public transit has the further advantage of increasing demand among potential riders, which has additional positive effects on the collectivity.

While purely economic considerations may suggest that those who benefit from a service should pay in proportion to the level of benefits they receive (the **benefits received principle**), social and political concerns may also enter into the price-setting process. In the case of water rates, for example, a local governing body may establish a multitiered rate structure to accommodate the poorest of the jurisdiction's residents. The lowest rate for water consumption enables poorer households to afford a basic level of service; residents who use more pay higher rates as usage increases. Water rates structured in this way have the additional benefit of discouraging wasteful consumption.

Politicians may also support a scheme that lowers water prices for large industrial users. The argument for such subsidies is that they contribute to the profitability and stability of local companies—and hence to the stability of jobs and, ultimately, to the community's prosperity. Such pricing schemes are not necessarily inappropriate as long as rates are determined in a public setting and the price breaks serve an obvious public purpose and are available to all who qualify.

The benefits received principle, under which users pay for the cost of services consumed, cannot necessarily be used to determine who should pay for service expansion. If expanding a service is desired as a matter of public policy, and the cost of extending the service is high, current users may share in the cost, thereby subsidizing new users. If public policy is to limit expansion or to make it pay for itself, then the true cost of expanding the service is charged to those who will benefit from the expansion. The cost of adding one more resident or company is called the **marginal cost**. Sometimes the marginal cost is negligible—and sometimes it is prohibitive. A local government that charges very high prices for expanding a service (because that is how much it costs to extend the service) may cut off growth. Because economic growth is generally viewed as desirable, the pricing of service expansion is seldom based on marginal costs.

While governments use a variety of mechanisms to substitute for the competitive market, they rely increasingly on the market itself. Many municipalities and counties, for example, contract with the private sector for services such as road repair, snowplowing, and garbage pickup. Provided that there is competition among private providers and that the contract periodically comes up for rebidding, market forces can help contain service costs. However, many local government services cannot be privatized or otherwise subjected to market competition, and jurisdictions that are located outside major metropolitan areas may find competition limited. Contracting out does not guarantee lower costs over time, but it may be useful if local government management has grown slack and the budget's growth is out of sync with citizen preferences.

Since performance by both the public and the private sector can become slack, there is merit to a model that periodically pits public departments or services against private providers of the same services. This model is used especially with internal services, those functions that support other units within government rather than provide services directly to the public. For example, a county vehicle-maintenance facility may compete with private repair shops for the same service contract. Competition with the private sector should be conducted cautiously, however, because private companies may "lowball," offering unrealistically low prices or promising to meet unrealistically high service standards in order to get a contract.

Conflict in the budget process

Conflict is endemic to public budgeting, in part because of the budget's role in airing community concerns and building agreement on government's role in meeting perceived public needs. The budgeting process attempts to balance many competing and legitimate claims. The chief executive's task is not to rid the process of conflict, but to mediate conflict, ensuring that those with a stake in the budget have an opportunity to present information and question budget recommendations.

Figure 1–2 depicts some of the sources of conflict that must be managed: tensions between advocates and guardians, between the budget office's need for information and the departments' reluctance to provide it, between accuracy and political expediency, between the goals of democracy and those of bureaucracy, between special and collective interests, and between public welfare and perceptions of public will.

Advocates versus guardians

The conflict between advocates and guardians consumes much of the deliberation during the budget preparation stage.[3] Advocates such as department heads may request more funding than they know will be approved, in hope of gaining a budget increase to meet growing demand. Other advocates include clients or interest groups benefiting from particular services and the council or board committees overseeing various agencies.

Guardians, or conservers, form the neck in the budgetary hourglass. Because the budget office must balance revenue considerations with departmental spending requests, it is often at odds with departmental advocates. Such conflict is particularly noticeable in budget deliberations involving general-fund departments—those that receive funding from general tax sources such as the property, general sales, and income taxes. Because spending decisions are made separately from taxing decisions, most general-fund department heads have little incentive to concern themselves with revenue availability: they ask for whatever they need or want, and the budget office bears the burden of cutting these requests to a level that matches revenue estimates. One strategy chief executives use to mitigate this conflict is to provide departments early in the budget preparation phase with the government's forecasted revenue figures, noting the implications for each department. Some executives go further and specify a target budget for each department, within which its request must be prepared.[4]

(continued on page 14)

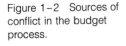

Figure 1–2　Sources of conflict in the budget process.

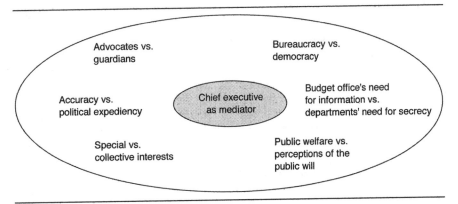

Advocates vs. guardians

Bureaucracy vs. democracy

Accuracy vs. political expediency

Chief executive as mediator

Budget office's need for information vs. departments' need for secrecy

Special vs. collective interests

Public welfare vs. perceptions of the public will

Budget types and budget reform

Like any field, budgeting has been shaped by a series of innovations. Particularly at the local level, the tendency has been to retain those elements of an innovation that work well for the community and to discard those that are less suitable. The result is that local budgets are often layered with elements of various innovations that have been merged over time.

Budget reforms have generally fallen into one of two categories: (1) innovations designed to improve budget format—i.e., the type and organization of budget information and (2) innovations designed to improve the budget preparation process. In practice, these categories overlap, since changes in the process inevitably affect the information that is collected and reported in the budget document.

Generally speaking, budget formats have evolved from line-item, to performance budgeting, to program-based budgeting. Not surprisingly, these three basic formats parallel the development of the budget process, characterized by Allen Schick—a noted scholar in public budgeting—as evolving from (1) a control orientation to (2) improving the management of operations to (3) improving the assignment of priorities to public programs.[1]

The line-item (or object-of-expenditure) budget, the format most often associated with budgeting, collects and reports information on inputs used in the production of government services. Line-item budgets include lists, some rather lengthy, of the goods or services to be purchased—labor, supplies, utilities, capital items, and miscellaneous. The line items represent the objects of expenditure allowed for each department or agency; once the council appropriates the funds (i.e., approves the proposed budget), department heads can then begin to acquire the objects authorized in the line-item budget.

It is clear why a line-item budget format is associated with a control-oriented budget process: the more detailed the objects of expenditure, the greater the governing body's control over administrative agencies. In fact, the line-item budget originated in the late nineteenth century in response to the excesses of the political machines that controlled many state and local governments: this format was ideally suited to shifting power away from political bosses and toward legislative bodies, which were more accountable to voters.

While line-item budgets are effective at controlling expenditures, they provide no information on outputs—how much work gets accomplished or with what level of efficiency. Although a number of local governments had already experimented with performance budgeting, the approach gained popularity in the 1950s, following a report by the Hoover Commission that recommended collecting and reporting output measures in the federal budget. In the 1990s, performance budgeting experienced a significant resurgence as a result of such innovations as management by objectives (MBO) and total quality management (TQM), and as a consequence of the national performance review undertaken by the Clinton administration. Both in its original and more recent incarnation, the purpose of performance budgeting was to improve program efficiency, to better evaluate the results of program operations, and to provide decision makers and the public with better information on the quality of public services.

Performance budgets typically include a statement of a program's goals and objectives, plus (1) measures of the amount of work to be accomplished (number of clients served, number of arrest warrants issued), (2) the efficiency with which work will be completed (cost per client, cost per warrant issued), and (3) the effectiveness of the program (citizen satisfaction, length of waiting period for clients, recidivism rate). Goals provide a general statement of a program's purpose and basic values; objectives are measurable results that the program expects to achieve in the forthcoming year. In other words, objectives move a program incrementally toward achieving its goal, but both goals and objectives suggest measures for evaluating a program's effectiveness.

The procedural reforms associated with performance budgeting focused attention on improving the management of public programs. More recent variations on performance budgeting, such as entrepreneurial budgeting, shift the focus from reporting on performance to increasing flexibility in the use of funds at the agency or departmental level.[2] One of the inefficiencies arising from traditional budgeting is year-end spending: because any unused appropriation authority lapses at the end of the year, department heads have a powerful incentive to use all appropriations, regardless of whether the funds are needed. Some variations of entrepreneurial budgeting place the department head more in the role of an entrepreneur who is charged with the task of deciding how best to use appropriated funds; an added incentive is the opportunity to retain some or all year-end savings for expenditure in future years.

Performance budgets focus attention on efficiency and effectiveness, but they do not address more fundamental questions—such as whether a program is necessary at all, or how best to allocate limited resources among competing purposes. The quest to develop a budget format that would help decision makers choose among alternative programs began in the 1960s, with the introduction of planning-programming-budgeting systems (PPBS). Program budgeting organized government activities into programs (activities or services with a common goal), identified alternatives for achieving each goal, determined the costs and benefits of each alternative, and selected the alternative that maximized net benefits. In short, it sought to interject more formal economic analysis into fundamental budgetary decision making—i.e., how much to allocate to activity A as opposed to activity B.[3]

While the level of analysis demanded by the full-scale version of PPBS quickly overwhelmed budget offices ("paralysis by analysis" became budget analysts' characterization of PPBS), local governments continue to use many of its features—for example, developing goals for each program and reporting budget information by program rather than according to traditional departmental lines.

In the 1970s, an alternative approach to determining spending priorities—zero-base budgeting (ZBB)—was developed in the private sector (by Texas Instruments) and quickly spread to local governments in Texas; it was then popularized at the federal level by the Carter administration.[4] ZBB organizes information into decision packages—incremental spending levels that reflect varying levels of effort and costs. In theory, each department (or decision unit, which is the lowest level in the organization at which budgetary decisions are made) prepares at least three packages: a base level package, which would meet only the most basic service needs; a current services package, which would ensure delivery of services at the current level; and an enhanced package, which would allow the decision unit to extend its services to currently unmet needs. Decision units can prepare more than one enhanced package, each representing a different level of expanded effort. Packages from all the decision units are then ranked according to the perceived need for the package. Unlike PPBS, which uses more objective criteria, ZBB relies on the subjective judgment of decision makers in ranking packages.

There is a "zero" in ZBB because, in theory, decision makers conduct an annual evaluation of each program's purpose and priority, weighing it against all other spending possibilities; as a consequence of this evaluation, decision makers may decide not to renew funding for an existing program, choosing instead to fund an enhanced spending package for another decision unit or even to provide base level funding for an entirely new initiative. In fact, such reallocation rarely occurs.[5] Even more significant, chief executives quickly found department heads unwilling to provide estimates of the base package; their argument was that they were already at the minimum level, and any further reductions would make it difficult to continue providing service. Vestiges of ZBB still persist in a number of local governments, particularly in the use of enhancement packages, which receive separate and more thorough scrutiny from decision makers. The base level (or minimum) package, however, has all but disappeared from the scene.

Target-based budgeting (TBB), which entered the picture in the 1980s, reversed the trend toward increasingly complex budget preparation. TBB was viewed as a means of simplifying budget preparation, mitigating interdepartmental conflict, and reducing gamesmanship in the preparation of budget requests. Under TBB in its simplest form, the budget office gives each department a maximum dollar figure for its budget request.[6] The budget office bases its targets for each department on revenue estimates for the forthcoming fiscal year and on any changes in priorities (e.g., more for public safety, less for park maintenance) that have been communicated by policy makers.

The more complex part of TBB involves estimating each department's current services budget, which is defined according to rules that are sometimes rather elaborate. Generally, the current services budget is the department's appropriation for the current year, unless it happens to contain funding for one-time purchases or for a position that was filled well into the fiscal year. Once the current services budget is established, the target is typically set at some percentage of that level—for example, 95 percent if the program has a lower priority in the current year or 105 percent if it has a higher priority. Although TBB includes some elements of ZBB, it greatly reduces the level of conflict and the role of subjective judgment found in ZBB, because departments know from the outset their likely level of funding for the forthcoming year.

Budgeting in the 1990s represents a rich blend of all these innovations. Especially at the local level, where budget format and process are substantially shaped by the chief executive's management style, the budget is likely to contain some combination of line items, performance measures, and even enhancement packages for new spending initiatives—and departments are likely to be given target funding levels at the outset of budget preparation.

1   Allen Schick, "The Road to PPB: The Stages of Budget Reform," *Public Administration Review* 26 (December 1966): 245–56.
2   Dan A. Cothran, "Entrepreneurial Budgeting: An Emerging Reform?" *Public Administration Review* 53 (September/October 1993): 445–54.
3   Verne B. Lewis, "Toward a Theory of Budgeting," *Public Administration Review* 12 (winter 1952): 43–54.
4   Peter A. Phyrr, *Zero-Base Budgeting: A Practical Management Tool for Evaluating Expenses* (New York: John Wiley, 1973.)
5   Thomas P. Lauth, "Zero-Base Budgeting in Georgia State Government: Myth and Reality," *Public Administration Review* 38 (September/October 1978): 420–30.
6   Irene S. Rubin, "Budgeting for Our Times: Target-Base Budgeting," *Public Budgeting & Finance* 11 (fall 1991): 5–14.

(*continued from page 11*)

By contrast, **enterprise fund** agencies, such as a water department, generate their own revenue through the sale of services, and that revenue directly affects spending levels. The water department's income depends on the projected demand for water and the unit price at which it will be sold. The roles of departmental budget advocates and budget office guardians are thus less relevant for services financed through enterprise funds.

The battle over information

Conflict over information contributes to the tension between general-fund departments and the budget office. The budget office may need information that a department head wishes to withhold, especially if it is potentially harmful. Under **target-based budgeting**, the budget office needs less detailed information, because it is the departments' responsibility to reduce spending requests to fit within the target, usually without intervention from the budget office. When financial conditions require the budget office to cut back departmental requests, it will inevitably use information provided by the departments to make those cuts.

Zero-base budgeting (ZBB) was one way to help provide the budget office with information on which to base cuts. However, some of the difficulties that occurred in implementing ZBB illustrate the tension that develops over the amount and type of information departments are willing to reveal. ZBB typically required departments to make three expenditure estimates for each service or program: one for a minimal, stripped-down version; one for roughly the status quo; and one or more proposals for an enhanced level of service. The minimum services package was defined as that level of effort that would meet only the most urgent needs. Understandably, department heads resisted disclosing their estimates of the cost of minimum service levels, because to do so virtually invited the budget office to cut that deeply, in the event that spending had to be reduced. Department heads typically contend that their departments are already at the minimum level and that any further reduction in funding would be catastrophic. Thus, departmental budget strategies—to protect current funding and to obtain increased funding if at all possible—are contradicted by the very notion that a level of service below the current one would be other than disastrous.

To minimize damage to efficiency and effectiveness, a budget office that has to cut departmental requests needs detailed information. Even when major cuts are not being made, a budget analyst must have accurate and timely documentation to make fair and responsible budget recommendations. However, the budget office sometimes asks for more information than it needs, and department heads sometimes resent the time required to prepare the documentation. When the budget office requests additional information, department staff have to spend time tracking down the information—time they would otherwise have spent filling potholes, apprehending criminals, or creating constructive activities for at-risk youth. If departments have a trusting relationship with the budget office and depend on it to support their interests, they may be more than willing to document those needs. But if they see the budget office as exclusively concerned with balancing the budget, cutting requests without much concern for departmental needs, department staff may resent the budget office's demands on their time. Understandably, department staff will be resentful if the information they are asked to provide is used against them or is not used in budget deliberations at all.

The chief executive and the director of the budget office can help moderate conflict over information by (1) making clear what information is essential to decision making; (2) recruiting professional budget examiners who have good interpersonal as well as analytical skills; (3) promoting automation of the budget preparation process; and (4) annually reviewing the budget manual's instructions to the departments and budget request forms for unnecessary or duplicative requests. Often, the instructions can be simplified and unnecessary forms eliminated.

Accuracy versus political expediency

Another conflict common to public budgeting is the tension between accuracy and political expediency. Public administrators' preoccupation with budgetary realism often clashes with politicians' concern for their image and that of the city or county. Technical concerns for accurate revenue projections may duel with political requirements for a positive budget picture. Budget offices generally provide conservative estimates of revenue, while council members sometimes pressure forecasters to raise revenue estimates in order to ease the task of balancing the budget. Sometimes policy makers manipulate **cash flow** to make a budget look more balanced than it is: for example, they may authorize the acceleration of tax payments or defer payment of liabilities to the next **fiscal year**.

Accounting legerdemain is especially tempting in a political atmosphere that makes raising taxes unthinkable to elected officials.[5] For example, the Texas legislature authorized the state comptroller to temporarily transfer over $1 billion from various special funds to the **general fund**, so that the comptroller could certify that the proposed budget was indeed balanced. The money reverted to the funds of origin on the following day, but on the day the comptroller needed to warrant that the general fund budget was balanced, it was technically balanced.

If the financial problem is temporary, such expedients as accelerating revenue collections or holding back expenditures may prevent cuts that hurt efficiency and morale. Over the long run, however, such measures obscure deficits and prevent the kind of action necessary to rebalance the budget. They also sap the budget's credibility in the financial markets and raise the cost of borrowing capital. Moreover, many of these short-term expedients actually make matters worse for the future. For example, if a government accelerates revenue collection from the next fiscal year into the current one, then the next fiscal year will be short.

The chief executive should generally oppose financial gimmicks, while understanding their purpose, and try to develop alternatives that help the government over the tight spots without substantial tax increases or service reductions. **Rainy day funds** and **fund balances**, which are explicitly designed for these purposes, can balance politicians' concerns with the need for honest numbers. Keeping such funds intact until they are needed can introduce a different tension to budgeting, but one that poses considerably less danger.

Bureaucracy versus democracy

The budget process is also characterized by a tension between the goals of democracy (citizen participation and public accountability) and those of bureaucracy (efficiency, centralization of power, and control). Prominent theorists in public administration have examined and evaluated broad strategies for keeping bureaucracy (the executive branch) accountable to democracy (the people and their elected representatives).[6] The introduction of governmental budgeting in the United States represented a significant contribution to the quest for democratic control of the bureaucracy.

Modern governmental budgeting began at the municipal level during the late nineteenth century as an outgrowth of Progressive Era reforms; it culminated in 1921, with the passage of the Budget and Accounting Act at the federal level. Prior to the adoption of a formal budgeting process, public financial management practices—accounting, budgeting, and auditing—were at best informal and often ad hoc. At the federal level, for example, departments presented their budget requests directly to the appropriate congressional oversight committee, without any review by the president or any effort by the executive's office to scrutinize requests for waste or relevance to policy. Beginning in the late nineteenth century, however, reformers in government and academia recognized the need for improved financial management systems, beginning with improved accounting procedures. These reforms were quickly extended to the development of more formal budgetary methods.[7]

Early budget reforms in the United States blended concerns for democracy and efficiency by exposing political machines, reining in departments that had become independent fiefdoms, and opening the budget process to public scrutiny and control. High on the reformers' agenda was the introduction of an **executive budget**, an innovation that was drawn largely from the experiences of a few reform-minded cities in the United States and from the national governments of western Europe. Under executive budgeting, the chief executive proposes a spending plan based on departmental requests, which is then subject to legislative revision and approval. One of the earliest descriptions of executive budgeting was the National Municipal Leagues' model city charter of 1899; this was followed in 1907 by New York City's introduction of a formal budgeting process.[8]

By concentrating budget power in the hands of the chief executive, the reforms made it possible to hold one official responsible for the budget. Although a side effect of this restructuring was a weakening of the budgetary power of the legislative branch, this shift of power was rationalized as democratic because the chief executive was said to represent all the people—and because the defeat of political machines gave government back to the people. Indeed, one of the purposes of the executive budget reforms was to protect the budget from the influence of political machines. Jesse Burkhead, a leading scholar of budgeting, summarized the thinking of this early period:

The budget was conceived as a major weapon for instilling responsibility in the governmental structure: the budget system rests on popular control; the budget will publicize what government is doing and make for an informed and alert citizenry; the budget will destroy the rule of invisible government—the party bosses who are responsible to no one.[9]

In the early years of executive budgeting, the chief executive was to report to the public on the budget from time to time, choosing to tell the public whatever he or she thought appropriate. The Progressive Era reformers were concerned that citizens have a more direct and meaningful voice in determining expenditures and in shaping public policies.[10] **Public hearings** thus became a routine part of budget preparation and adoption, but public participation in budget preparation faded in importance as the Progressive Era ended. Instead, budgetary reporting became more important: rather than allow the executive to decide what and when to report, budgeting reforms began to specify what information would be collected and reported and how frequently. Requirements for hearings prior to budget adoption were retained, but were often implemented in a pro forma manner.

Thus, the tension between democracy and bureaucracy was resolved by strengthening the chief executive's power over executive agencies and by holding the chief executive responsible for budget preparation and outcomes. Bureaucracy was to some extent tamed and democracy to some extent protected. As direct citizen involvement in budgeting faded in importance, the budget document and year-end accounting reports increased in importance as instruments of public accountability. It may be that democracy did not get enough out of the compromise, and pressures in the 1990s have been in the direction of increasing direct public control over budget preparation.

The early reformers had emphasized chief executive control over the departments, but that shift may also have gone too far over the years. The balance between central control and departmental responsibility is now being renegotiated in many governmental settings. In 1993, *The National Performance Review* suggested that overcentralization leads to inefficiency.[11]

The tension between bureaucracy and democracy is still very much alive. When these values clash, public officials need to be cautious about siding too strongly with efficiency and bureaucratic control. The risk is not only that democratic values will be seriously slighted, but also that overcentralizing control will decrease, rather than increase, efficiency.

Special versus collective interests

Budgetary decision making often pits the wishes of special interests against those of the community as a whole. Interest groups inside and outside government may press for increased funding for their own benefit—for increased spending for recreation, highway construction, or police, or for special tax favors to relocate a business venture. Politically, it may be difficult for members of a local council or board to refuse the requests of special interests, especially those of well-organized groups.

If funding comes from the general fund, the cost of meeting a demand from a special interest is borne by all taxpayers (the collectivity) at a negligible and presumably unnoticeable cost to any one taxpayer. If policy makers oppose the interest group's request, they risk losing the group's electoral support; on the other hand, they are unlikely to win collective support by opposing interest-group requests. Particularly influential petitioners, such as those representing large developers, major realty firms, or businesses with large payrolls, may gain concessions or benefits that are then sought by others who have less influence. It is difficult to deny benefits to one group or individual that have already been granted to another.

While special interests have a decided advantage, they are not invulnerable or immune to influence. Some special interest groups are poorly organized; internal quarrels may also weaken their ability to sway government. If interest group members agree on only a few matters, competing interests may be able to play them off against each other. Moreover, there are limits to how much special interests can claim before a conflict with the collective interest becomes obvious. For example, special interests may successfully claim tax breaks. After a while, the cumulative effect of multiple tax breaks reduces the revenue stream, either producing deficits or creating pressure to cut spending and increase taxes. Such counterpressures help control the level of tax breaks.

Special requests come not only from organized groups, but also from individuals or firms that make specific claims for services or for exemptions from rules. For example, when a city is repaving a street, individual homeowners may ask to have their driveways paved at the same time.

If the city complies with these requests, the cost of the project will increase, as will the time for completion. The continuous tension between what individuals request and what is best for the collectivity inevitably surfaces in budget deliberations.

Public will versus public welfare

Budgeting often reveals a major tension between the public will—what the public demands or says it wants—and public welfare—what public officials think the public really needs. To be sure, both elected and appointed officials must be attuned to public opinion and the will of the majority. Effective leadership depends on the ability of the chief executive and the council to accurately read public attitudes on sensitive issues facing the community. Yet the community's long-term well-being may not be best served by policies derived from public opinion. For example, although the public may support a tax abatement to enable a local manufacturer to expand its existing facilities, it may be in the county's best interest to use the abatement to attract other types of industries and diversify the local economy.

To resolve this tension, public officials must become educators. If, for example, a local government manager has access to information on the potential effect of a given policy, he or she must explain the issue to policy makers, the media, department heads, and citizens, sharing the evidence that led to a particular conclusion. In a democratic society, neither elected nor appointed officials have the right to simply impose their views. The only reasonable solution is for officials to argue convincingly for what they perceive as the long-term public good, backing off when necessary to collect more evidence and reevaluate their original position.

When public officials cannot convince the public to adopt what they feel is the wiser strategy, a compromise position may help. Such a compromise should take into account the nature of citizens' objections. For example, if the objections to a long-term plan that maximizes the public interest are financial, providing some financial assistance may reduce opposition. Requiring every resident to connect to the town sewer and water system may make the most sense financially, but the cost to individual households may create obstinate disapproval no matter how logical the plan. A cost-sharing arrangement, reflecting the benefit to the collectivity as well as the benefit to individual households, may help change residents' opinions. Ultimately, managing the conflict between public will and public welfare requires some flexibility.

The environment of public budgeting

The demands that local government budgets face depend, in part, on the community's changing social and demographic composition. A government's ability to respond to emerging problems depends (1) on the economy and (2) on the legal environment, which allows or forbids changes in tax burdens and the assumption of new functions. In short, both the problems that governments face and the options available to deal with those problems depend on the environment.

Governmental budgeting is extremely sensitive to its economic, social, and legal environments. Economically, both the revenue and expenditure sides of budgets are sensitive to recessions and booms and to competition for residents and business investment. Changes in inflation and in interest rates can tear apart the best-laid financial plans. Socially, budgets are sensitive to factors such as in- and out-migration, the age distribu-

The economic environment is affected by	The social environment is sensitive to	The legal environment is affected by
• Recessions and booms • Inflation and changes in interest rates • Competition for business investment and residents.	• Population change • Age distribution • Personal income.	• The extent of home-rule powers • Requirements for budgetary balance • Mandates.

Figure 1–3   The economic, social, and legal environments of public budgeting.

tion of the population, and problems such as drug use, homelessness, and crime. Legally, governments have to work within laws that require a **balanced budget**; limit debt; specify legal revenue sources; mandate particular activities, procedures, or spending levels; and forbid some activities. Local governments are subject to a host of restrictions and rules, many of which affect public budgeting.

Economic influences

A number of factors can affect the economic environment of local government budgeting: economic downturns, inflation, interest rates, and competition among local governments. The four sections that follow examine each of these sources of economic influence.

Economic downturns   Economic downturns affect local budgets in two main ways. First, revenues may decline somewhat, especially if the local government levies (such as a sales or income tax) are sensitive to economic cycles. Second, during a recession, state revenues are often hard hit, and states have to deal with increasing unemployment and welfare costs, which means that state aid to local governments may drop.

Economic slowdowns are also troubling to budgeters because their onset, severity, and duration are nearly impossible to predict: thus, any revenue projection, no matter how carefully prepared, is likely to be off if the economy takes an unexpected turn. Because of this irreducible source of uncertainty and the widespread requirement for a balanced budget at the state and local levels, budget planners must build in some flexibility—some way of adjusting during the year if revenues fall below expectations or expenditures are greater than predicted. A variety of mechanisms are used to help budget planners adjust to such uncertainty: for example, prohibiting departments from spending all their allocations; holding back on permission to hire new staff or to make other contractual commitments; building reserves or rainy day funds; and authorizing the chief executive to make small cuts in existing allocations without seeking council approval.

Inflation   Inflation, another economic factor that influences budgeting, complicates budget planning by creating uncertainty in revenue and expenditure forecasts. For example, a budget that had been completely worked out in Tampa, Florida, had to be revised at the last moment because of sharp increases in gasoline costs. Since gasoline use could be only marginally curtailed, other expenditures had to be reduced to compensate.

If inflation affects revenues and expenditures roughly proportionately, governments should not experience increased fiscal stress. Indirect evidence suggests, however, that the public sector suffers from a relative price effect: that is, because government is more labor-intensive than the private sector, inflation of expenditures occurs at a more rapid rate.[12]

When the cost of living increases rapidly, governments may experience considerable pressure from organized labor to keep wages current with inflation. Moreover, revenues do not always increase in proportion to inflation. For example, Cook County (which includes the city of Chicago) and its surrounding counties are under a tax cap that allows property taxes in non–home-rule communities to increase by the inflation rate or by 5 percent, whichever is lower. If inflation rises above 5 percent, this revenue source will not keep pace with inflation.

Interest rates   Changes in interest rates can also affect the budget, although the effects are not as great at the local level as at the national level, where the de_.cit has required continual borrowing. Local governments can usually time long-term borrowing to take advantage of more favorable interest rates, but higher interest rates may still adversely affect their budgets. For example, if short-term borrowing rates go up, borrowing for cash flow can become expensive because local governments typically cannot defer borrowing until short-term rates are lower. And if long-term interest rates remain high for long periods, local governments may be forced to borrow at high interest rates rather than delay needed projects indefinitely.

Competition among local governments   Because it affects taxation decisions, competition among local governments for new residents or business investment is another source of economic influence on local budgeting. One way to obtain a competitive advantage over other jurisdictions is to export taxes—that is, to shift the tax burden from residents to nonresidents. Exporting taxes lowers the burden on residents and allows service levels to be maintained; the combination of low taxes and high service levels further augments the community's attractiveness to new businesses and residents.[13] One example of tax exportation is a levy on hotel and motel occupancy, which is paid by visitors rather than by residents. In a community that is home to a regional mall, the general sales tax also serves as a form of tax exportation.

Intergovernmental competition seems to influence expenditure levels as well as taxation decisions. At the state level, for example, one study of the forty-eight contiguous states found that a state's spending increased by $.70 for every $1.00 increase in spending by its neighbors.[14] By increasing spending—albeit at a somewhat lower rate—to keep pace with expenditures in nearby states, a state can continue to provide services that are at least somewhat competitive and still keep taxes lower than they are in surrounding states. Local governments display a similar awareness of their neighbors' service levels. Improvements in the quality and range of library services in one jurisdiction, for example, often induce surrounding municipalities to follow suit.

Critics of government often argue that competition forces inefficient businesses into bankruptcy, but that there is no comparable mechanism for weeding out inefficiency in government. Competition between governments, however, helps improve management and keeps taxes down without resulting in bankruptcy. Moreover, while businesses are unlikely to share the secrets of their success—because the failure of their competition is part of their goal—governments regularly share innovations and improvements. Local governments do not benefit from the financial failures of other jurisdictions; in the eyes of the public, one city's failure is likely to redound to the disadvantage of all. The competition among local governments is not zero-sum, except in the case of businesses' locational decisions. While that narrow form of competition can be costly and destructive, it seldom affects the more positive forms of competition, which encourage local governments to seek out and imitate good management and budgeting practices.

Social and demographic change

Studies show that changes in three social factors particularly affect public budgets: population, age distribution, and personal income.

Population change   Basic economic principles suggest that as population increases and fixed costs are divided among more households, the resulting **economies of scale** will mean lower per-unit costs. However, in a study of 103 Massachusetts cities and towns, Helen Ladd found that expenditures were U-shaped with respect to population changes.[15] Per capita expenditures were lowest for jurisdictions experiencing moderate rates of growth (3 to 4 percent per annum) in population. Municipalities experiencing extraordinary rates of population decline (more than 4 percent per annum) or growth (more than 8 percent per annum) had the highest per capita expenditures. Thus, this study suggests that public services cost the least in cities and towns experiencing moderate rates of growth. This information should serve as a warning to communities that view rapid growth as a way to reduce costs and taxes.

Because financial obligations do not decline in proportion to population loss, communities with declining populations have difficulty reducing spending. Pension commitments and **debt service** payments must now be borne by fewer taxpayers. The same amount of **infrastructure** (roads, streets, lights, traffic signals, storm drainage) must be maintained. Similarly, in communities experiencing inordinate population increases, any excess capacity in public services will be quickly exhausted. Streets, recreation facilities, and public school classrooms will become congested. Demand for water and sewer services and waste disposal may exceed capacity, requiring major investment in expanding the physical plant.

The cost of local services appears to be affected not only by the rate of population growth, but also by absolute size. Studies have repeatedly found that as jurisdictions grow beyond some minimum threshold, the same services cost more per capita. Table 1–1 shows that the number of employees per 10,000 population tends to increase with city size, too. There are many possible explanations for this phenomenon, including the greater likelihood of crime in large cities, increased fire risks associated with greater population density, the greater power of unions when the workforce is large, and the difficulty of maintaining adequate oversight in multiple locations, such as garages, lockups, and housing facilities. The level of complexity of operations may also increase as the population grows. In cases where larger cities have higher unemployment rates, city government may be more likely to become an employer of last resort, hiring more people than absolutely necessary in order to reduce unemployment.

The age of the city may also explain budget variations. Many of the largest cities are old and reflect the traditions of the time and place of their founding.[16] Older housing stock, often built before modern fire codes, may be subject to more frequent and more costly fires. Older cities also have aging infrastructure, which may need costly replacement. Water pipes may last eighty or even a hundred years, but at that point the city has to begin again. Communities experiencing rapid growth now will at some future point face the daunting task of replacing their infrastruc-

Table 1–1 Municipal employment per 10,000 population by city size, 1992.

Service	Population (in thousands)							
	All cities	>1,000	500– 999	300– 499	200– 399	100– 299	75– 199	<75
Police protection	27.6	43.6	33.8	30.3	26.7	25.0	23.8	23.5
Fire protection	13.1	15.6	17.5	16.8	16.4	15.7	14.7	10.4
Highways	8.5	7.5	7.8	8.8	7.0	7.4	7.6	9.3
Parks and recreation	8.0	7.4	11.1	12.3	11.6	9.6	8.8	6.5
Libraries	2.9	4.7	4.3	3.1	3.7	3.2	2.7	2.2
Sewage treatment	5.0	5.2	6.3	6.4	4.1	5.0	3.8	4.7
Solid waste collection	5.5	10.9	6.6	5.0	5.3	4.8	3.5	4.4
Water supply	6.8	7.6	7.6	8.6	7.0	6.2	6.1	6.3
Government administration	13.5	16.9	19.1	15.5	13.4	11.3	11.1	12.3
FTE employment per 10,000	152.9	302.0	222.7	166.8	160.2	147.8	130.3	107.3
Average October earnings of full-time employees	$2,723	$3,157	$2,931	$2,659	$2,823	$2,752	$2,810	$2,315

Source: U.S. Bureau of the Census, *City Employment: 1992*, series GE/92-2 (Washington, DC: GPO, 1994).

ture all at once—by which time the tax base (property values) will most likely have peaked and started to decline.

Age distribution   Spending for education and police protection are the budget categories most likely to be affected by the age distribution of the population.[17] Younger families with children push up the costs of schooling; crime, particularly violent crime, is concentrated among persons between the ages of fourteen and twenty-four.[18] The number and proportion of elderly residents may also be relevant, not only in terms of service needs, such as visiting nurses or in-home assistance, retirement homes, or ambulances staffed by emergency medical technicians, but also in terms of residents' ability and willingness to pay property taxes. Many states provide circuit breakers or freeze property tax liability for elderly citizens with low incomes. Despite these tax breaks, however, local governments that have a large percentage of retirees on fixed incomes may have difficulty gaining support for programs that benefit young families.

Personal income   Research consistently shows that growth in personal income significantly affects the size of local government budgets. This relationship holds despite the fact that wealthier people use fewer local government services. Nevertheless, people who are wealthier often demand more and better services from government—despite the fact that many wealthier people endorse conservative ideologies that argue for limited government. The answer to this apparent contradiction may lie in the relative homogeneity of wealthier communities, where community preferences are easier to identify and satisfy. In fact, one study found that more homogeneous communities—*regardless* of income—are more likely to support school referenda.[19] Governing and budgeting seem to be much more complex in heterogeneous communities, possibly because it is more difficult to negotiate the level of agreement required to determine service levels and budget allocations.

The legal and intergovernmental context

The legal and intergovernmental context of local government budgeting is shaped by three principal factors: home rule, balanced budget requirements, and mandates. The next three sections examine each of these factors in detail.

Home rule   As legal creations of state government, local governments are permitted to do only what state law specifically permits, unless the state grants them home-rule powers. **Home rule** gives municipalities and counties limited (and usually specific) additional powers besides those already granted by the state—for example, the ability to decide what services to offer, what taxes to levy, and how much to borrow.

Until the early 1900s, states controlled local financial and budgetary practices through legislation and constitutional provisions that gave local governments little, if any, autonomy. Beginning around the turn of the century, states granted limited home rule to their local governments, but home rule was accompanied by administrative supervision to ensure that home-rule discretion was being used appropriately. For a number of years, the principles of home rule clashed with state administrative supervision—especially during the Depression, when state administrative controls over property taxes sometimes obscured home-rule powers entirely. Gradually, states eased off on the more extreme forms of administrative control: instead of substituting state policy making for local decisions, they merely reserved the right to examine local government decisions for compliance with state laws.

In the 1970s, a new push toward home rule developed that had its roots in post–World War II spending increases. During the Depression, capital projects other than those funded by the federal government had often been delayed; during World War II, those same projects were further delayed to allow capital to flow into the war effort. Nor were local governments allowed to accumulate cash to deal with the inevitable, pent-up, postwar needs: after the war, long-delayed capital projects had to be funded through long-term debt.

The postwar increase in debt-funded projects combined with war-induced inflation to push up local government expenditures; at the same time, suburbanization pushed up service demands. Local officials complained that they lacked the broad tax bases of the state and nation and could not produce the revenues required to satisfy the growing demand for services; thus, local governments pressured the states for more home rule—particularly for control over new nonproperty tax revenues.[20] In the 1960s, struggling with urban unrest, local governments further pressured the states to facilitate local efforts to address urban problems.[21] This pressure often took the form of demands for more home-rule power. Where such demands were successful, the result for local governments was the opportunity to increase property tax levies, which had in many cases been low—and stable—since the early years of the Depression.[22]

Ultimately, the post–World War II increases in property tax levies and spending levels—and the suburban growth that made it easier for middle-class families to own their own homes—stimulated the tax limitation movements of the 1970s and 1980s. Recessions and increased economic uncertainty added to the public's unwillingness to pay additional taxes. Proposition 13 in California, Proposition 2½ in Massachusetts, and the Hancock Amendment in Missouri were among the most stringent of the tax limitation measures.

Even in states in which stringent tax limitation measures have not been passed, the tax limitation movement has had major effects on local government budgeting. Because local officials perceive the public as being opposed to property taxes (and, to a lesser extent, opposed to tax increases of any kind), local governments have greatly increased their use of service charges; where permitted by law, local governments have also shifted to greater reliance on nonproperty taxes, especially the sales tax. In addition, local governments have held constant or even modestly increased expenditures on highly visible services such as police and fire protection, while reducing spending in areas such as general government, public works projects, parks and recreation, and libraries. At the same time, many local governments have significantly expanded income-producing activities such as utilities and other enterprise services.[23] Finally, the notions that government is wasteful and that voters' hard-earned money should not be spent on those who are presumably working less also continue to shape local government budget allocations: research has shown that voters who support tax limitations often want less spending on social services.[24]

Iowa granted home rule constitutionally in 1969; Illinois granted municipal home rule in 1970; Pennsylvania granted a home-rule option to counties and municipalities in 1972; Indiana strengthened and codified its home-rule provisions in 1980 and 1981; and Montana offered a home-rule option in 1976. Nevertheless, home-rule powers have yet to be fully achieved and defined. Many home-rule laws do not increase local discretion over finances. The laws themselves may be ambiguous or ignored, often evolving through court cases and new legislation. Many states constrain the scope of home-rule powers by limiting property taxes—and sometimes other tax sources as well—and by continuing to mandate service and benefit levels.

Virtually the first question any local official must ask when considering a new or increased revenue source is, "Is this legal?" The answer may not be all that clear. Despite gains in home-rule powers, local officials facing public demands for property tax relief, court- and referendum-mandated upgrading of assessment practices, and increasing state restrictions on local tax and spending powers continue to ask for more discretion over policy making.[25]

Budgetary balance The legal environment in which state and local budgeting operates usually includes a requirement for budgetary balance. On the one hand, this requirement shapes the entire budget process: it makes the budget revenue driven and exaggerates the impact of tax limits and spending mandates. On the other hand, like the definition of home rule, the definition of balance is less clear in practice than it may appear on paper.

At the state level, 49 states have some kind of balanced budget requirement. (Vermont, the lone exception, requires the governor to propose the elimination of any deficit in the following year's budget.) The definition of a balanced budget, however, is highly variable, and is much looser in some states than in others (see Figure 1–4). For example, the governor must submit a balanced budget in 47 states, but in only 35 states must the legislature adopt a balanced budget; and only 34 states require that the budget be in balance at the end of the fiscal year.[26] Fewer than half the states apply the balanced budget test to all funds.

At the local level, the requirement for balance is widespread but varies in stringency. A study of the 100 largest cities showed that 99 require a balanced budget; most such requirements are found in statutes or in city charters, and sometimes in both. Of the 99 cities, 84 are required to

Figure 1–4   Variations in state balanced budget requirements.

Number of states	Requirement for balance
49	Balanced budget required
47	Governor's proposed budget must balance
35	Legislature must adopt a balanced budget
34	Budget must be balanced at the end of the fiscal year

Source: U.S. General Accounting Office, *State Balanced Budget Practices*, GAO/AFMD-86-22BR (Washington, DC: U.S. GAO, 1985).

balance the budget when submitted, 86 are required to balance the budget when adopted, but only 35 are required to balance the budget at the end of the year.[27]

Requirements for budgetary balance are further complicated by a technical question: whether a balanced budget is defined by the cash on hand (**cash basis**) or on a more comprehensive accounting basis, which assigns expenditures to the period in which they were incurred (**accrual basis**).[28] Many governments measure deficits or surpluses on a cash basis because it is easy to understand and explain. Cash balances, however, can be easily manipulated: to make the budget look more balanced than it is, payments can be delayed until the following fiscal year and revenue collections accelerated for credit to the current year.

Mandates   As noted earlier, mandates are requirements that specify the particular services to be provided and the level of service. Both the federal and state governments can mandate services or service standards for local governments. The problem is that unless the federal or state government also provides full funding to implement the mandates, local officials may have to cut current services to comply. Federal and state priorities may thus preempt local ones.

As long as the level of federal and state funding to local governments continued to grow, mandates did not impose a severe problem, but the level of federal funding peaked around 1978 and then began to decline, and the level of state aid to local governments has not kept pace with the growth in the cost of mandates. As reliance on property taxes decreased and reliance on sales and income taxes increased, local governments became more vulnerable to recession, exacerbating the difficulty of complying with mandates. Communities suffering the effects of recessions have sometimes been struck simultaneously by unfunded mandates and cutbacks in state spending.

In response to pleas from local governments, states have tried to curtail unfunded mandates. The most common response has been to add a **fiscal note** to proposed mandating legislation; the note estimates the cost of the mandate to local governments. By forcing state policy makers to calculate the costs imposed on local governments, fiscal noting exposes the real cost of mandates, which may deter lawmakers from initiating unfunded mandates. By 1979, 25 states had adopted some form of fiscal noting for mandates, and others were considering such action.[29] By 1991, the number that had adopted fiscal noting had increased to 28.[30] As of 1993, 16 states (many of which also use fiscal noting) had adopted some form of reimbursement to local governments for mandated costs.[31] By 1995, at least 17 states had either amended their constitutions or passed legislation limiting the ability of the legislature to foist unfunded mandates on local governments.[32]

Neither fiscal noting nor reimbursement legislation, however, has been particularly successful in curtailing state mandates. The legislation is too easy to bypass, and costs to local governments are difficult to measure accurately, especially before the legislation passes. Florida's constitutional amendment to control unfunded mandating, passed in 1990, has been somewhat more successful than other state legislative controls. A spokesman for the Florida League of Cities felt that the number of expensive unfunded mandates had been reduced since passage.[33] Nevertheless, the Florida amendment is still relatively easy to evade (lawmakers need only declare an important state interest in the provision), and it has been difficult to track the financial impact of many bills.[34] In 1993, for example, Florida passed 45 laws that imposed mandates on local governments and 21 laws that created new or expanded revenue opportunities for cities and counties. With respect to the first group of laws, the state Advisory Council on Intergovernmental Relations (ACIR) found that fiscal notes had been prepared for only six of the laws; of the second group, the ACIR found that fiscal notes had been prepared for only seven of the laws.[35]

Other states have had markedly less success than Florida. A 1978 Rhode Island law curtailing unfunded mandates has largely been ignored. In 1978, Michigan changed its constitution to forbid unfunded mandates, creating a state review board to determine the impact of the mandates and provide for reimbursement—but the review board was never implemented.[36] Illinois passed a 1981 law forbidding unfunded mandates but regularly exempts legislation from the law.[37] At the national level, Congress passed 1995 legislation forbidding the federal government from issuing unfunded mandates. Given the experiences of the states, however, this legislation is likely to be difficult to enforce.

To summarize, the legal and intergovernmental environment of budgeting has been highly restrictive—forbidding particular revenue sources, constraining tax increases, requiring balance, and mandating services and service levels. The unpopularity of the property tax has led to increasing dependence on the general sales tax, which is more **income elastic**—sensitive to growth or decline in the economy. Income elastic revenue sources tend to exaggerate the impact of recessions. This combination of factors has created enormous fiscal stress at the local level during the past two decades. Local governments have made a number of efforts to free themselves of some of the restrictions imposed by the legal environment—by seeking additional home-rule powers, by meeting requirements for balance in principle but not in spirit, and by pressing for an end to unfunded mandates. However, none of these strategies has been an unqualified success.

Summary

Because public budgeting in the United States occurs in a political environment that requires public accountability, and because local governments are controlled by their state governments, public budgeting is more complex and subject to more constraints than private sector budgeting. So that governmental budgeting can take account of public interests, budget processes must provide for public participation and public accountability; the budget document must be comprehensible to citizens as well as elected officials; and the budget must comply with a variety of laws, including those that specify the basis of fund accounting and the definition of budgetary balance.

Earlier in the twentieth century, reform movements altered local government structure to make it more efficient. In many cases, efficiency was increased at the expense of accountability; in fact, accountability was sometimes reduced to a level comparable to that in the private sector—a level that is inadequate for a democracy. Government should be efficient and effective, but it cannot be run like a business. Businesses are fundamentally nondemocratic, and their decision making is insulated from public scrutiny. Businesses are accountable only to owners and shareholders—and only for the level of short-term profits. Government, in contrast, has no profit incentive and makes decisions in public forums attended by the media, individual citizens, or representatives from well-organized interest groups. Government must balance the quest for efficiency with responsiveness to diverse community needs; consequently, decisions are usually made through compromise rather than fiat. Thus, private sector measures of accountability have little utility in the public sector.

Faced with the complexity and constraints of public budgeting, some people—including public officials—long for the simplicity of personal and business budgeting. However, one cannot generalize from individual, family, or business budgeting to understand local government budgeting or to make recommendations for reforms. The beginning of wisdom is the recognition that governmental budgets are legitimately different and necessarily more complicated. The goal should be to improve efficiency and effectiveness in public budgeting while strengthening, rather than weakening, the role of citizen participation and public accountability. This book explores a range of mechanisms for achieving this goal within the context of current local government structures.

This first chapter described the differences between public and private budgeting and outlined the economic, social, and legal context of local budgeting. Chapter 2 focuses on organizing the budget process, assigning responsibility for decision making, and coordinating decisions. Chapter 3 explores the role of the departments and the budget office in the request process, the winnowing of requests to achieve balance, and the steps involved in adoption of a budget proposal. Chapter 4, which deals with policy making in the budget process, focuses on (1) the kinds of policy decisions that are made during budgeting and (2) ways to handle the controversy that often results from explicit consideration of policy issues. Chapter 5 describes how to use the budget as a management tool, and Chapter 6 considers budgeting as a tool for financial control. Chapter 7 focuses on the capital budget and long-term investment decisions. Chapter 8 provides guidelines for the budget document—from ensuring legal compliance to framing policy decisions and designing a readable, interesting budget.

1   Douglas Holtz-Eakin, Whitney Newey, and Harvey S. Rosen, "The Revenue-Expenditure Nexus: Evidence from Local Government," *International Economic Review* (May 1989): 415–29.

2   David Joulfaian and Rajen Mukerjee, "The Government Revenue-Expenditure Nexus: Evidence from a State," *Public Finance Quarterly* (January 1990): 92–103.

3   Anthony Downs, *Inside Bureaucracy* (Boston: Little, Brown, 1967), 96–103.

4   Irene S. Rubin, "Budgeting for Our Times: Target-Base Budgeting," *Public Budgeting & Finance* 11 (fall 1991): 5–14; and Thomas Wenz and Ann Nolan, "Budgeting for the Fu-

ture: Target-Base Budgeting," *Public Budgeting & Finance* 2 (summer 1982): 88–91.

5   Businesses also manipulate cash flow and distort balance sheets—especially when the company is in trouble financially—to make themselves look better. See Kevin Delaney, "The Organizational Construction of the 'Bottom Line,'" *Social Problems* 41, no. 4 (November 1994): 497–518. Businesses' distortion of their record keeping is a problem that has been with us for a long time. It was particularly prevalent in the early railroads and was of concern to Frederick Cleveland, one of the major contributors to public budgeting in the United States. See Frederick Cleveland and Fred

Wilbur Powell, *Railroad Finance* (New York: D. Appleton and Co., 1912).

6 See Dwight Waldo, *The Enterprise of Public Administration* (Novato, CA: Chandler Publishers, 1980), 81–98; and Frederick C. Mosher, *Democracy and the Public Service*, 2d ed. (New York: Oxford Univ. Press, 1982).

7 Irene Rubin, "Who Invented Budgeting in the United States?" *Public Administration Review* 53 (September/October 1993): 439.

8 Ibid., 441–43.

9 Jesse Burkhead, *Government Budgeting* (New York: John Wiley, 1956), 14.

10 Frederick A. Cleveland, *The Growth of Democracy in the United States, or the Evolution of Popular Cooperation in Government and Its Results* (Chicago: Quadrangle Press, 1898); and William H. Allen, "The Budget Amendment of the Maryland Constitution," *National Municipal Review* 6, no. 4 (1917): 485–91.

11 National Performance Review, *Creating a Government That Works Better and Costs Less* (Washington, DC: Office of Vice President Al Gore, September 1994).

12 Robert T. Deacon, "State and Local Government Expenditures," in *Essays in Public Finance and Financial Management*, ed. John Petersen and Catherine Spain (Chatham, NJ: Chatham House, 1980), 32.

13 Robert L. Bland, *A Revenue Guide for Local Government* (Washington, DC: International City Management Association, 1989).

14 Anne C. Case, James R. Hines, Jr., and Harvey S. Rosen, *Copycatting: Fiscal Policies of States and Their Neighbors*, Working Paper No. 3032 (Cambridge, MA: National Bureau of Economic Research, 1989).

15 Helen F. Ladd, "Municipal Expenditures and the Rate of Population Change," in *Cities Under Stress*, ed. Robert W. Burchell and David Listokin (New Brunswick, NJ: Rutgers Univ. Press, 1981), 351–67.

16 Roland Liebert, *Disintegration and Political Action: The Changing Functions of City Governments in America* (New York: Academic Press, 1976).

17 Thomas Muller, "A Demographic Perspective," in *Public Sector Performance*, ed. Trudi Miller (Baltimore: Johns Hopkins Univ. Press, 1984), 132.

18 Ibid., 144.

19 Corliss Lentz, *Citizen Decision Making in the Context of School Financial Referenda: The Illinois Experience* (Ph.D. diss., Northern Illinois Univ., 1995).

20 For Kansas, see Jack F. McKay, *Recent Trends in City Finance: A Survey of Ten Cities in Kansas* (Lawrence, KS: Bureau of Governmental Research, Univ. of Kansas, 1950), 7.

21 For Indiana, see James Owen, "A Decade of Reform," in *Politics and Public Policy in Indiana: Prospects for Change in State and Local Government*, ed. William P. Hojnacki (Dubuque, IA: Kendall/Hunt, 1983), 146.

22 For Kansas, see McKay, *Recent Trends*.

23 Gary J. Reid, "How Cities in California Have Responded to Fiscal Pressures Since Proposition 13," *Public Budgeting and Finance* 8 (spring 1988): 20–37.

24 Helen Ladd and Julie B. Wilson, "Why Voters Support Tax Limitations: Evidence from Massachusetts' Proposition 2½," *National Tax Journal* 35 (June 1982): 137–40.

25 Maurice White, "ACIR's Model State Legislation for Strengthening Local Government Financial Management," *Governmental Finance* 8 (December 1979): 22.

26 U.S. General Accounting Office, *State Balanced Budget Practices*, GAO/AFMD-86-22BR (Washington, DC: U.S. GAO, 1985), 27.

27 Carol W. Lewis, "Budgetary Balance: The Norm, the Concept, and Practice in Large U.S. Cities," *Public Administration Review* 54 (November/December 1994): 515–24.

28 Robert Albritton and Ellen Dran, "Balanced Budgets and State Surpluses: The Politics of Budgeting in Illinois," *Public Administration Review* 47 (March/April 1987): 144.

29 White, "Model State Legislation," 23.

30 Janet M. Kelly, *State Mandates: Fiscal Notes, Reimbursement, and Anti-mandate Strategies* (Washington, DC: National League of Cities, 1992), 20.

31 Janet M. Kelly, "Mandate Reimbursement Measures in the States," *American Review of Public Administration* 24 (December 1994): 353.

32 Keith Schneider, "Many States Are Limiting the Power to Pass the Bucks," *New York Times*, 5 February 1995, 13.

33 Ibid.

34 Florida Advisory Council on Intergovernmental Relations (ACIR), *1991 Report on Mandates and Measures Affecting Local Government Fiscal Capacity* (Tallahassee, FL: Florida ACIR, 1991).

35 Florida ACIR, *1993 Intergovernmental Impact Report* (Tallahassee, FL: Florida ACIR, 1993), 27.

36 Schneider, "Many States."

37 Kelly, "Mandate Reimbursement," 363–64; U.S. General Accounting Office, *Legislative Mandates* (Washington, DC: U.S. GAO, 1988).

2 Designing the budget process

The budget cycle

Designing the budget process

Constraints on the design of the budget process

Three broad policy issues
  The chief executive and the governing body
  Centralization versus decentralization
  Citizen participation

Assembling the pieces
  Managing timing
  Information and training
  Framing decisions

Budget policy statements

Elements of a budget policy statement
  Operating budget policies
  Revenue policies
  Budget implementation policies
  Debt policies

Summary

Designing the budget process

The budget process frames decisions and organizes decision making so that budgeters can make timely choices with sufficient information. The process also defines and monitors budgetary balance and influences the scope of governmental services and the distribution of the tax burden. The budget process determines whose opinions will be solicited and how they will be weighed. It also structures the level of competition among budget participants, programs, and parts of the budget.

To create a context for the design of the budget process, this chapter first considers the general outlines of the budget cycle. Factors that chief executives need to consider when designing the budget process are then examined in detail. These factors include legal and historical constraints, the form of government, the degree of centralization, and the level of citizen participation. The chapter offers a number of recommendations for managing the timing of the budget cycle, providing participants with adequate information and training, and framing budgetary decisions. Finally, the chapter presents guidelines to assist in the development of budget policy statements, which provide a specific, agreed-upon basis for routine financial practices.

The budget cycle

The budget process shapes decision making throughout the **budget cycle**. The four main stages of the budget cycle are preparation of budget requests, legislative approval of the budget requests, budget implementation, and summary reporting on actual budget transactions. Figure 2–1 depicts a simplified version of the budget cycle.

The preparation stage begins with the budget office giving instructions to departments or agencies, which then prepare requests and return them to the budget office. If there is an **executive budget** process, the chief executive and the budget office review these requests, cut them back, ask for modifications, or do whatever is necessary to prepare a proposal that balances available revenues with expenditures for the following **fiscal year** (two years for a **biennium budget**). This executive proposal is then presented to the governing body.

Many smaller governments do not have an executive budget process, in which case the comptroller or other financial officer gathers the departmental requests, trims them to meet revenue estimates, and hands

Figure 2–1 Phases of the budget cycle.

Phases of the budget cycle	End product of each phase
1. Preparation of requests	Proposed budget
2. Legislative adoption	Appropriations
3. Implementation	Encumbrance and disbursement of funds
4. Summary of transactions	Audited financial report

the requests to the council for review and adoption. Alternatively, the requests may go directly from the departments to council committees for examination.

After reviewing and revising the budget proposal, the governing body adopts the budget, often subject to a **veto** by the chief executive if the government has an elected executive. Local legislative bodies approve the budget by passing an **appropriation** ordinance, which sets the legal spending limits for each department and agency for the forthcoming fiscal year.

After the budget has been approved, department heads and program managers responsible for budget implementation can enter into contracts and issue **purchase orders**. These obligations to spend money are usually treated as **encumbrances**; that is, before the good or service is delivered and before the invoice is actually received, the amount of the purchase order is subtracted from the department's appropriated balance. The accounting section of the finance department (sometimes called the comptroller's office) records encumbrances and authorizes the subsequent **disbursement** of funds once the goods or services contracted for are delivered.

At the end of the fiscal year, the chief accountant or comptroller prepares a **financial report** that, among other things, compares each department's appropriation with actual expenditures. An **independent auditor** then reviews the financial report and compares it with a sample of financial transactions, in order to certify that the report represents accurately the fiscal condition of the local government.

The budget process applies to both the **operating** and **capital budgets**. The operating and capital budgets may be prepared separately during the fiscal year, or they may be prepared concurrently, as shown in Figure 2–2. The operating budget serves as the spending plan for ongoing services such as police and fire protection, parks and recreation, and water and sewer service. Information is typically organized by department, providing details on line items such as personnel, supplies, contractual services, travel, utilities, and office equipment. Financing for the operating budget comes from current revenues such as property, sales, and income taxes; service charges; fees and fines; and grants.

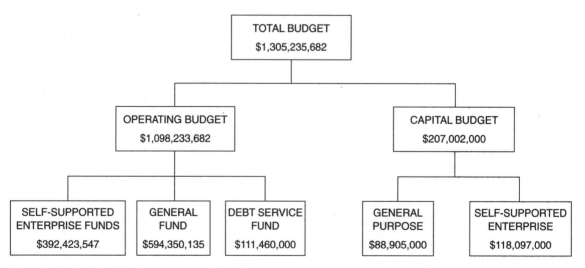

Figure 2–2 Combined budget summary, Dallas, Texas.

Source: City of Dallas, Texas, *1996–97 Annual Budget,* ix.

The capital budget represents a spending plan for the acquisition of **fixed assets**, such as highways and buildings, water and sewer pipes, and open space. This budget is usually part of a comprehensive **capital improvements plan (CIP)** that projects the construction needs of the jurisdiction for a five- to eight-year period. Funding for the capital budget usually comes from the sale of bonds or other long-term obligations, supplemented by funds from grants and current revenues. Information in the capital budget is usually organized by project. Although the processes for preparing an operating and capital budget have some similarities, the rest of this chapter focuses on the decision-making process for the operating budget cycle; Chapter 7 examines capital budgeting in detail.

Designing the budget process

The chief executive should first decide what he or she wants the budget process to accomplish, then design a process to accomplish the selected goals. If, for example, timely decisions have been a problem, then a change in the **budget calendar** may be in order. If the problem is that the budget is balanced when approved by the governing body, as required by law, but later during the year becomes unbalanced, giving departments an incentive to come in under budget may solve the problem.

The chief executive's active involvement in the design of the budget process is important because there are inevitably conflicts among the goals the budget process is intended to achieve, and it is part of the chief executive's job to set priorities when goals clash. For example, the goal of making the budget more open and interesting may increase the level of conflict and delay decisions. Creating more opportunities for citizen participation may subject the council to a barrage of contradictory advice—which may in turn give way to deep conflicts within the community and on the council.

In addition to ensuring that the budget process will achieve certain goals, the chief executive will want to select a process that is compatible with his or her leadership style. Some chief executives are detail oriented: they want to know, for example, exactly what the departments promised in the way of service levels, what they actually delivered, and the reasons for any discrepancies. Others are less interested in the details of departmental operations and more interested in achieving responsiveness—soliciting public opinion and translating it into policy goals. Whatever the leadership style of the chief executive, it is important that he or she avoid overwhelming departmental staff with requests for budgetary information. Chief executives who identify the central issues to be resolved in the budget process and determine what information they really need can reduce the frustration that often accompanies budget reforms.

One of the principal issues that the design of the budget process must address is participation by interested parties. The chief executive, policy makers, budget analysts, department heads, citizens, and interest group representatives should all participate in budget decision making: the goal is to allow potentially contradictory demands on the budget to be expressed and resolved rather than suppressed or ignored, while at the same time ensuring that conflict does not overwhelm the process or render decision making impossible.

The "openness" of budget deliberations is a key factor in the level and quality of participation. If the process is too "closed," only the initiated will be able to follow the issues. If citizens—and even council members—have difficulty understanding basic budget proposals ("Are we increasing the authorized strength of the police department by two, or are we just replacing staff lost through resignations?"), something is wrong with the process. Clearer and more timely information is necessary; perhaps the printed agendas should include more detailed information for those who have less background, or perhaps the text of the budget requires more explanatory detail. Another option is to circulate the budget document more widely or to distribute a simplified version.

The forum in which budget deliberations occur is another factor affecting their openness. For example, if contact between citizen groups and council members or staff tends to occur one-on-one, it may be better to create opportunities for citizens' opinions to be solicited in the open. For many years, Wheaton, Illinois, has had a Saturday morning coffee-with-council, an open meeting that gives anyone in the community an opportunity to talk with council members and provides council with a setting in which to hear citizens' concerns.

In addition to determining how open or closed budget deliberations are, the design of the budget process can be used to regulate the level of conflict that accompanies those deliberations. If the level of conflict is so high that the goal of participatory—but effective—decision making is not being served, changes in the process can tone it down. If the level of conflict is so low that budgeting brings yawns to council members and the public alike, the process may need to be altered so that issues are presented more clearly and policies are discussed more fully and publicly.

Finally, the design of the budget process can be used to address specific problems facing the community. For example, if the economy has slowed or significant sources of tax revenue have moved away, the priority may be to cut expenditures. The requirement for a balanced budget may need strengthening. Efforts to reduce the public's expectations may also be needed, and citizens and department heads may need stronger messages about the limits on spending requests. To emphasize total limits on spending requests and to compel program managers to assign priorities, it may be necessary to shift to target-based budgeting. Or a more radical scheme may be required such as some form of zero-base budgeting to set priorities and better ration limited resources.

If one of the problems confronting a community is resistance to tax increases, then it may be appropriate to increase the openness of the budget process and encourage greater participation by interest groups. The more citizens understand the community's financial situation and the quality of services that they receive for their dollar, the more likely they are to support tax increases. The more local officials solicit and implement citizens' opinions, the more favorable public attitudes toward taxation and fees are likely to be.

Where conflict has arisen over equity issues—for example, if downtown and the surrounding neighborhoods are competing for capital investment—then district-based council members may need to be more actively involved in setting budget priorities. In one approach, council members bring the manager's or mayor's budget proposal to their districts for discussion, then return with citizens' responses in the form of proposed amendments. Funding for such amendments comes from money that has been withheld from departments. This approach may help neighborhoods and community groups feel more engaged in the budget process and more optimistic about getting their projects funded.

In summary, a chief executive should not expect a budget process to work merely because it is popular or because the private sector uses it. The process chosen should be suited to the basic requirements of local government budgeting, should address specific problems the local government faces, and should complement the leadership style of the chief executive.

Constraints on the design of the budget process

Some local governments may have complete freedom to design a budget process and a budget document, but most local officials are constrained to some degree by state laws and local charters. State statutes may require, for example, that the budget be prepared by the chief executive, that the budget document be prepared on forms provided by the state— or, in the case of New Jersey, that the state review the proposed budget before final implementation. State law typically requires local governments to balance their budgets, although the meaning of *balance* may be left unspecified. The state of Washington goes even further, requiring local governments to prepare **program** and **performance budgets**. Municipal charters may have executive budget processes written into them, may require the budget to include personnel summaries (a listing of all positions and salaries), or may specify that the budget be presented in a line-item format. Laws commonly include specific dates for the completion of documents, for adoption of the budget, and for determination of the property tax rate required to support it.

Rather than merely ordering local governments to do their budgets in a particular way, states may set up committees composed of both state and local representatives to sift through proposals and recommend legislation for reforming the budget process. For example, in 1969, when Iowa adopted a constitutional home-rule provision, legislation implementing the constitutional amendment set up an oversight committee composed of both state and local government representatives. This committee is empowered to implement legislative mandates, including requiring program performance budgeting and capital improvements programming. The committee can specify budgetary formats, provide rules for **interfund transfers** and budget amendments, and establish uniform accounting practices. Thus, while still maintaining much of its central control, the state delegated the creation of further regulation to an administrative unit composed of both local and state officials.[1] The clear implication was that legislation would not be formulated or presented to the legislature unless local governments had examined and agreed to it. A pattern that had been state centered and authoritative thus became more consultative, giving local governments a larger role in determining the requirements for budgeting.

Even local charters may not be as constraining as they initially appear. Frederick Clow, an early scholar of local finance, argued at the turn of the century that

the precise location of decision making power depends on the personality of the officials, rather than [on] the charters. Each system has someone who runs things, a controlling mind, though often not the nominal head. In financial matters, this is sometimes the mayor, sometimes the controller, sometimes the treasurer, often the chairman of a council committee, and most often the head of the accounting department or his chief assistant. Reality can go some distance beyond charters, in an informal law.[2]

Clow's insight remains equally true today.

Both state laws and local charters are often considered minimums rather than rigid requirements. Local governments may even be formally authorized to go beyond the state-mandated formats. While some charters require a line-item format or the inclusion of the number of employees by position category, they do not limit what may be in the budget document or require that only one budget document be prepared. One document may satisfy legal requirements in the charter, and another may meet decision-making requirements. In some local government budgets, different formats are interleaved, the legally required line-item format alternating with the more readable program format. Moreover, the laws or charters can sometimes be changed. For example, St. Louis changed one of the budget provisions in its charter to deal with delays caused by the council's failure to act on the proposed budget before the beginning of the fiscal year.

A third source of constraint, in addition to state laws and local charters, is the form of government. Each of the principal forms of local government—mayor-council government and council-manager government—is associated with particular patterns in the budget process and in the distribution of budgetary power. Mayor-council government, which came into being in the 1890s, was viewed, in part, as a means of reforming legislative budgeting, which had been the dominant form throughout the century. Under **legislative budgeting**, council committees reviewed proposals that came directly from the departments (this was analogous to the pattern at the federal level). With respect to the budget, mayor-council government gave the mayor more power and the council less.

Council-manager government, first adopted in 1908, was characterized by smaller councils, whose members were elected at large rather than by district, and by the presence of a professional manager who served at the pleasure of the council. The council-manager form gave the council a greater role in budgeting than did the mayor-council form. In many council-manager jurisdictions, the at-large council has yielded over the years to a mix of at-large and district seats, but the council continues to take a comparatively active role in budgeting.

While the form of government influences the location of budgetary power, it does not lock it in. Indeed, some extremely disempowered councils are now searching for ways to express themselves on budget matters. Although legal constraints are powerful limits on the role of the governing body, informal grants of power from the chief executive may successfully get around such limits. It is, in fact, often in the interest of the chief executive to rely on the governing body as a source of information and support.

Thus, while there are real constraints, shaped by history and by law, they are generally not immutable; local officials normally have considerable discretion in reshaping the budget process.

Three broad policy issues

Whether the chief executive is designing a budget process from scratch or altering an existing one, three policy questions must be addressed: (1) the relationship between the executive and the governing body; (2) the level of centralization; and (3) the role of citizens and interest groups.

The chief executive and the governing body

With respect to the budget, the relationship between the executive and legislative branches ranges between two extremes. In the rare case of a legislative budget, a council or board committee receives requests from the departments and pares them back; the role of the executive branch is minimal. (A comptroller may provide an estimate of revenues and collect the departmental requests.) At the other, more common, extreme—

executive budgeting—the chief executive, in cooperation with the budget office, prepares a budget calendar, collects expenditure proposals, examines and pares them back, then submits a recommendation to the council—which, by charter, may be permitted to make only limited changes.

There are many variations between these extremes. The balance of power between the executive and council depends on a number of factors, including the strength of the chief executive's veto and how frequently it is used; the council's freedom to add to the chief executive's proposal or to move expenditures; the council's ability to use delay to extract concessions from the executive branch; and the degree of discretion granted to the executive to change appropriations after they have been approved by the council. The balance of power also depends on whether the form of government is mayor-council or council-manager.

Form of government and the balance of power   Generally speaking, the budgetary role of the council in mayor-council communities is more circumscribed than it is under the council-manager form. In mayor-council communities, moreover, the relationship between the executive and the legislative branches has an additional layer of complexity, because every council member is a potential mayoral opponent. If, for example, a council member is planning to run against the mayor, the mayor may be reluctant to provide the council with budget information that may weaken his or her chances of reelection. In council-manager communities, the manager is not an elected official but a council appointee who can be fired at will; thus, politically motivated tension between the manager and the council is unlikely to occur.

According to a Boston official, council members' degree of involvement in budgeting depends on whether the chair of the ways and means committee has mayoral ambitions:

The ways and means chair has done a good job of learning about the budget and getting involved. He views himself as a potential candidate for mayor, and the position gives him some visibility, so there is some motivation to get involved.

Despite potential electoral challenges, it is unwise for the mayor to keep budgetary information away from the council: depriving the council of budget information also deprives the press and the public. A better strategy may be for the mayor to give the council, the press, and the public the fullest possible budget information, taking the initiative to explain any potentially embarrassing decisions. If council members can ask the mayor detailed questions during budget hearings, the mayor may be able to back away from unpopular or unwise decisions before they become policy. The result may be not only improved budgetary decision making, but a more interesting and absorbing mayoral campaign that can help restore public confidence in government and the electoral process.

Although the governing body should ideally help set policy, it does not always fulfill that role in mayor-council jurisdictions. At the very least, the council should serve as a sounding board, assisting the chief executive to determine what the problems are, what can be improved, and what needs to be explained to the public. An interested council will ask questions that bring problems to light that the local government can then correct.

The council can also act as a check against decisions that make financial but not political sense. A Boston official observed that the council members' level of involvement depends on the financial condition of the city:

The council gets involved in bad times, not in good times. But the council does not have much real power. If the financial situation deteriorates, it will meddle more, but the relationship won't change fundamentally.

A council's increased involvement in decision making may be a nuisance, especially for administrators trying to balance the budget during periods of fiscal stress, but warnings from the council may be extremely important in alerting the chief executive to the danger of exceeding public tolerance for service reductions. A Boston political appointee noted that the council

sometimes forces restoration of cuts. It was the library budget last June. We may have overcut. The council is a real-time check on the cuts we have made. Council gets complaints from constituents. Council addbacks are not problematic—as long as spending desires are reasonable. We have a $1.3 billion budget, so $1 million here or there should not be rejected out of hand.

In council-manager governments, the manager may bring the council into the budget deliberations from the earliest stages of preparation and keep members informed of budget decisions as the proposed spending plan reaches its final form. In some jurisdictions, however, the manager may prepare a budget proposal independently and present it to the council for approval without prior consultation. This may be acceptable if the manager already knows what the council wants or major policies are simply being continued.

In council-manager jurisdictions, the council normally plays a large role in setting the priorities that are reflected in the budget. In Phoenix, for example, the staff makes many decisions in consultation with the manager, then presents a package for the council to evaluate; that is, the manager and staff frame the decisions that council members make. Issues taken to the council are rated on a six-point scale that assigns priorities for cuts.

The form of government is not, however, the sole determinant of the relationship between the two branches; it merely influences it. In Boston, for example, after many years in which the council had been virtually without budgetary power, a ways and means committee was created, over the initial objections of the mayor. Although the power the council could exercise remained limited, its ability to examine the budget and ask pertinent questions was improved.

Informal adjustments   Whatever the form of government, some elements of the balance between the chief executive and the governing body are informal and can be altered as necessary. One important factor is the council's ability to obtain additional information on budget requests.

In the early years of this century, budget reformers were concerned that councils would ask for too much money and tried to curb their budgetary power by emulating the British parliamentary system, under which executive-branch officials appear before parliament to respond to detailed questions; this power of inquiry is virtually the only authority legislators have over the budget. Some reformers in the United States went even further, making it difficult for council members to get any backup information about the budget.

In a democracy, such extreme limits on the power of the council are inappropriate—the council is, after all, a representative body. Regardless of the form of government, the council should be free to ask for any relevant information about the budget, and the chief executive should willingly provide that information. At the very least, the council should be given a chance to examine budget requests and ask questions about them. That may mean making budget requests more easily understandable, or it may mean making staff available to the council to explain technical portions of the budget.

The difficulty of securing adequate information for council members' decision making has been exacerbated by recent trends toward contracting out services. Contractors may be unwilling or unable to provide detailed information on the cost of delivering services. The lack of detailed information makes it difficult for both the chief executive and the council to justify budgeted expenditures for contracted services. In such cases, staff may have to make additional efforts to collect and interpret data, especially when the decision to contract is a politically hot issue.

Other informal adaptations can strengthen the council's power in the budget process. For example, in Phoenix, even though the charter limits the legal power of the council, the manager and the budget office consult extensively with council before presenting the budget for approval. The charter prohibits the council from raising the manager's estimates—but by tradition, council members are able, within the limits of projected revenue, to add specific projects. Similarly, in Boston, where the council's budgetary powers are severely circumscribed by law, council members express their views during executive-branch decision making; as one official noted,

pressure from the council is generally exerted before the budget is completed. We watch council preferences and try to accommodate them. They requested a supplemental appropriation for a crime watch: it was a good idea and we did it. We attempt to be responsive. The legislative branch isn't initially interested in financial impact. Sometimes the money isn't there, and we'll tell them. A council member wanted a security system for low-income and elderly housing units. It's a good idea, but we can't afford it.

While the executive branch has enough power in these circumstances to ignore the council, it rarely does. Using the little power it has for political grandstanding, the council can embarrass the administration if it chooses to. A Boston mayoral appointee commented that even though the mayor doesn't have to yield to the council, the mayor wants the budget in place by 1 July, so he compromises with the council to get the budget in on time.

Increasing council participation What is the best balance between executive and legislative power in budgeting? In many jurisdictions, the balance was worked out many years ago, and the situation may have changed dramatically since then. Although power tends to be more evenly distributed in the council-manager form than in the mayor-council form, both forms tend to concentrate authority in the chief executive, sometimes radically disempowering the council.

Given current levels of citizen disillusionment with government, it may be appropriate to ask whether citizens feel adequately represented under current arrangements—and if not, how the situation might best be improved. As long as total costs are kept within reason (the total cost of satisfying council requests is normally affordable), there are advantages to giving councils a larger role in setting spending priorities. First, increasing council participation improves executive-branch access to citizens' views. Failure to use the council as a source of information on citizens' views may leave citizens feeling underrepresented and may ultimately lead to structural changes. In Phoenix, for example, excessive cuts during the recession of the early 1980s contributed to changes in the structure of the council and a shift to district elections. In the city manager's view, one of the factors that contributed to changes in the budget process was the citizens' level of trust in city hall: when the level of trust dropped, citizens responded by expanding the role of the council.

Concern that the council will use its influence to add too many expenditures appears to have been dealt with effectively by a number of jurisdictions, which put aside a reasonably small sum for council projects, then scrutinize the projects to ensure that the money is not wasted. In communities that have such arrangements, local officials noted that when funds are insufficient to implement council projects, staff makes an extra effort to explain the constraints to council members and gain their cooperation.

Centralization versus decentralization

The second dimension of the budget process that can be adjusted by local officials is the degree of centralization in decision making. When public budgeting was in its early days, executive agencies were extremely decentralized. One of the intentions of executive budget reforms was to bring the departments under greater executive control—in fact, budget reform became almost synonymous with centralized control. Under executive budgeting, the chief executive was held politically accountable for agency actions. Departments would submit estimates of their funding needs to the budget office, which would then reduce requests—sometimes at a level of great specificity.

In more recent years, decentralizing the decision-making process has been a major focus of reform. To ensure that balance is achieved and that the laws governing budgeting are observed, revenue estimates are still usually made in the budget office, but departments have often been given greater freedom to set priorities for expenditures and to make any necessary reductions in their own budgets.

The level of centralization should avoid the extremes and should be appropriate to the problems currently facing the government. At one extreme is a budget office that micromanages departments, denying legitimate departmental requests and demanding reams of information and justification. At the other extreme is the nearly autonomous department whose every request is funded because no one has the expertise to question it (or whose requests are automatically cut on the basis of an across-the-board percentage). Ideally, the budget process should ensure that the budget office is able to maintain budgetary balance and compliance with the appropriation legislation, while allowing departments to manage their budgets without the burden of an enormous system of prior controls.

Overcentralization carries a number of risks, including micromanagement—excessive budget office involvement in departmental budgeting. If most budgeting decisions are taken out of the hands of department heads and placed in the hands of the budget office, budget analysts must have detailed knowledge of departmental operations in order to make managerially sound decisions. This poses two problems: First, budget offices are unlikely to have sufficient information—and may, as a consequence, make decisions that impair management and reduce efficiency; second, developing and delivering the amount of information required by the budget office occupies staff time that would otherwise be spent delivering services—which damages service delivery and creates frustration among department heads. A second risk of overcentralization is that employees will simply evade controls. Because monitoring and enforcing a plethora of controls is extremely difficult, staff are provided with the opportunity to select the controls that they will follow and ignore the others.

Although trends toward performance budgeting and outcome rather than input controls have burdened departments with even greater information and reporting requirements, these requirements are only indirectly linked to budget allocations and have not subjected departments to micromanagement by the budget office. One of the advantages of outcome-oriented budgeting, in fact, is that it maintains a sufficient level of managerial autonomy while increasing the level of accountability. Boston, for example, adopted its program and performance budget with a view to making the departments more responsive to the mayor's policy directives. The shift toward a reduction in controls and an increase in accountability may ultimately recentralize control over departments under a different guise, by requiring them to be more sensitive to the policy directives of elected officials.

A government that is attempting to decentralize the budget process by shifting from controls on inputs to performance- or outcome-based budgeting may run into legal problems. For example, when revenue is **earmarked** for specific funds or projects, it is difficult to shift money between projects, even if doing so would be more efficient; requirements for line-item budgeting and prohibitions on changing the budget during the year may make it difficult to adjust to changing circumstances or political priorities. A performance or outcome orientation requires a budget that is broken into programs, a shift that may be difficult to achieve if state or local laws require line-item budgets.

Union agreements or professional staffing standards that limit flexibility in the use of staff may further exacerbate the difficulty of shifting to performance- or outcome-based budgeting. Where personnel and capital are controlled separately, program managers may be unable to make trade-offs between personnel and equipment. Another potential problem is that governments experiencing fiscal stress tend to rely more on "rules," eroding the autonomy of lower-level units at precisely the time that initiative and innovation from department heads and program managers are most needed.

Although such problems may constrain efforts to decrease centralization, compromises are sometimes possible. By combining line-item and program formats, for example, a local government can follow the law yet maintain an outcome orientation. If rules imposed by the budget office prevent managers from making trade-offs between capital and labor, perhaps the rules can be suspended, leaving the budget office to handle only egregious cases of abuse (e.g., a department that proposes no capital spending in order to maximize staffing, then pleads the following year for unusual amounts of capital because it had received none the previous year). If a jurisdiction is under fiscal stress and wants to encourage efficiency, it may be wise to substitute incentives for rigid rules. For example, a department that does not spend its entire annual **allotment** may be allowed to keep a portion of the savings, a strategy that may help prevent overspending or wasteful end-of-year spending. Such an approach saves money without reducing the autonomy of program managers and department heads.

Budget offices may also be able to create some flexibility for program managers by complying with laws in the aggregate but not applying them in each circumstance. For example, where line items are relatively fixed for a year, the budget office may develop a system of line-item swaps, which effectively "zeroes out" the balances in each line item at the end of the year: those who need more funding can get it, and those who need less are compelled to give it up. Of course, such a system would have to be legal—or at least not illegal—to work. Generally, a good strategy for preventing overcentralization is to handle individual problems as they arise, rather than to impose rules throughout the organization, regardless of whether they are needed.

In summary, the "right" place for a particular local government may be almost anywhere on the centralization-decentralization continuum. If departments have too much independence, some form of centralization is likely to occur. In jurisdictions that are already highly centralized, some decentralization may be energizing.

Citizen participation

The third major dimension in the design of the budget process is the degree of citizen involvement. Statutes favor such participation, but general practice has, if not ignored the law, often evaded its intent. There are virtually no legal barriers to citizen participation, but there may be attitudinal hurdles on the part of both citizens and government. Attendance at public budget hearings—one of the principal forums for citizen participation in the budget process—is generally low; citizens are more likely, however, to attend tax hearings, where their immediate interests are involved. The literature on local government budgeting has never questioned the appropriateness of citizen involvement in budget preparation in a democracy; nevertheless, it has long questioned the value of **legislative budget hearings** as a means of gathering public opinions.

The concept of public hearings developed during the Progressive Era, which was marked by widespread sentiment that political machines were corrupt and nonrepresentative, and that government therefore needed to be controlled by the public. Direct participation in the formation of the budget offered citizens a means of bypassing political machines and exerting direct control over government. In addition, Progressives viewed government as a means of solving community problems, and budget hearings afforded citizens an opportunity to tell their elected representatives about their needs and to call attention to problems that the government needed to address.

When the Progressive Era ended, around 1910, it was followed by a more conservative period. The conservatives argued against government's role in solving public problems and regarded direct public participation in budgeting as anathema. The chief executive was given much more authority over the budget and was accountable to the public after the fact, through periodic financial reports to the governing body. These changes were colored on the one hand by a fear of "the masses" and on the other by the apparent failure of public hearings to draw large crowds or stimulate much public interest.

In 1917, the Progressive and conservative points of view clashed head-on in the proposals for a budget amendment to the Maryland state constitution. William Allen represented the Progressive point of view, and Frederick Cleveland represented the conservative point of view. Cleveland had helped design the budget amendment for Maryland, which simultaneously disempowered the state legislature with respect to budget matters and omitted any requirement for public hearings. William Allen took issue with the proposal:

Frankly, I am among those who believe that the right of the taxpayer to be shown legislative proposals and to be heard regarding them is among the bedrocks of democracy's fundamentals. Taxpayers have a right to stay away from taxpayer's hearings. They have a right to be foolish and unreasonable at hearings. They also have the right to come before city and state and national appropriators of public money, armed with constitutional and statutory rights to be informed and to be heard before their money is spent.[3]

Cleveland argued that hearings were fruitless because "almost no one except the few parties interested have attended." Allen responded, "believers in taxpayers' hearings answer those who consider them unnecessary and fruitless: 'The majority, no matter how large, has no right to take from a minority of even one, the right to be told what budget alternatives are and to be heard regarding them before it is too late.' "[4] Allen argued further that even when only a few interested parties show up, they may be well informed and present important arguments that are picked up in the press, widely discussed, and ultimately influence decisions. The upshot of this clash of beliefs is that many local governments retain requirements for public hearings but expend little effort to encourage citizens to attend.

In many communities, the citizenry either does not know what the local government does, disapproves of the way it is done, or views the local government's financial management as inept and wasteful. Especially where this is the case, it may be useful to increase citizen involvement in the budgeting process, so that residents can learn what local government does, why it does it, and how well it carries out its tasks. Citizens who have an opportunity to directly influence government are less likely to think that their money is funding activities of which they disapprove. Although some local officials may think of budget hearings as a nuisance, they have tremendous potential to build consensus for the spending plan. Even where there is no apparent lack of citizen support, budgeting in a democracy requires a substantial amount of public discussion and direction.

Options for increasing citizen participation in the budget process include more informative and citizen-friendly budget hearings and the creation of citizen committees—for example, bond advisory committees, planning committees to recommend priorities for new initiatives, and budget advisory committees to review departmental budget proposals as well as the executive budget.

Where the openness of budget deliberations has been a mere formality, citizens may feel unwelcome, and the local government may have to find ways to communicate the importance of public participation. This sometimes means attending to symbolic issues—for example, scheduling budget meetings in advance and publicizing the schedule to both residents and the press; timing meetings so that citizens can more conveniently attend; avoiding arguing with citizens during hearings intended to solicit their opinions. The same sessions that educate the council can be used to educate interested citizens. In addition, it may be necessary to make budget hearings more interesting—by, for example, publicizing in advance potentially divisive issues and using graphics to display alternative budget scenarios.

An added advantage of increasing citizen participation (particularly through increased attendance at budget hearings) is that it provides residents with a more realistic view of the complexity of the budget process: citizens have the opportunity to see that their opinions are competing with those of others, and that city hall is not simply being stubborn by refusing to meet all their demands immediately and in full. Of course, excessive openness can cause the entire budget process to get out of hand—subject to special pleading and excessive influence from interest groups.

Although it may be tempting under such circumstances to make the budget process less open, reducing access to interest groups may limit legitimate public input. One strategy that balances the values of openness and equity is to appoint citizen committees, determining their composition carefully in advance to balance interests and force compromises or to structure consideration of individual interests in the context of community interests.

Another approach is to ensure that all contact between interest groups and council members occurs in public; many illegitimate or inappropriate requests would never be implemented if they were publicized first. Interest groups have the right to express their views about the budget, but they do not necessarily have the right to disproportionately influence the process in a way that automatically overrides community interests.

The accompanying sidebar is a self-test for communities to determine their degree of public participation. If the responses indicate that the local government has not been making a sufficient effort to obtain and use citizens' views, and lack of public support has been a problem, then staff should develop ways to increase public participation.

Assembling the pieces

The roles of the executive and legislative branches in the budget process reflect the larger issues of accountability, managerial effectiveness, democratic participation, and representativeness; the level of centralization reflects the need to balance fiscal control with managerial expertise and initiative; and the degree of citizen participation reflects the trade-off between being vulnerable to demands and judiciously responsive to public interests. These are the basic values that the budget process addresses; the process must also deal with more mundane issues—timing decisions, training participants, and framing decisions.

Managing timing

Part of the responsibility for managing the timing of budgetary decision making falls on the chief executive and part on the budget director. The

---

Public participation self-test

1. Is public opinion sought concerning the budget?

2. If public opinion is sought, is it sought before or after major decisions are made?

3. Are citizens' opinions regarded as advisory and often ignored, or do citizens' views have some authority?

4. How open are budget processes? How many budget planning and evaluation sessions are held? How far ahead is notice given of these meetings? Is the notice printed in the newspaper? Are the meetings held at a time when citizens could attend?

5. How much explanation of the budget is given at meetings and in documents? Is the language understandable to an ordinary citizen?

6. How much effort does the jurisdiction make to involve citizens or make the budget process interesting to them?

7. How much publicity is there about the proposed budget?

Figure 2–3 Sample budget calendar.

Preliminary development memo distributed	3/04
Budget manual and budget preparation packets distributed	4/01
Rolling stock proposals due no later than	4/01
Personnel/Support Services/Office Automation requests due no later than	4/08
Group I budgets due on or before	5/02
Group II budgets due on or before	5/05
Group III budgets due on or before	5/10
Group IV budgets due on or before	5/13
Group V budgets due on or before	5/18
Group VI budgets due on or before	5/25
Budget available for chief executive review on or before	5/31
Departmental budget reviews begin	6/07
Revenue sharing proposed use hearing	6/14
Departmental budget reviews end	7/19
Budget delivered to city council	7/29
City council work session (tentative)	8/13–14
Public budget hearing	8/22
Budget adopted	9/12

manager, mayor, or head of the board must ensure that the process begins early enough to allow sufficient time to review proposals, yet not so early that participants lose interest in the process. The chief executive should verify that a **budget calendar** has been prepared that is in accordance with law and that will ensure timely preparation of the budget. A calendar of due dates and hearings is normally issued by the budget director and included in the **budget manual** sent to department heads (see Figure 2–3).

The budget calendar may be fixed in law or charter. Sometimes legal provisions sound antiquated, for example: "The committee will continue to meet daily until they have examined and approved a budget." Such a provision does not say how long the process will take, but it does ensure that time will be devoted to the task—and that all committee members will be motivated to finish the task as soon as possible so that they can get on with other matters of governance.

Even when all the appropriate dates are not included in law, the end point is usually defined—namely, the point at which the governing body must adopt the budget into law. A budget planner can work backward from that date to determine the following dates:

When the budget must be delivered to the governing body for review and approval

When the budget office must receive spending proposals from the departments (in order to review them and prepare a budget proposal for the chief executive)

When the departments must receive the forms or budget guidelines to follow in preparing their requests.

Experience dictates how much time each step takes—from the preparation of forms for the departments to the final council or board decision and the beginning of the new fiscal year.

This schedule should be adjusted from time to time to reflect changes in needs. If, for example, the request process is computerized, this will shorten the time necessary for preparation. If the local government has adopted a target-based budget, then the decentralization of decision making should shorten the amount of time that the budget office needs to examine departmental requests. For citizens' opinions to receive timely consideration, it may be appropriate to initiate citizens' involvement at the beginning of the budget process—or even before it begins. Such a shift is in keeping with the structure of most local government organizational charts, which place citizens at the apex of the pyramid. It may also make sense to solicit citizens' views at several points in the process.

Information and training

The budget process is unlikely to work smoothly or to produce good decisions unless key participants understand their roles and have information appropriate to the decisions being made. The budget director, who is almost always responsible for training department heads in budget procedures, conducts the training by (1) preparing a budget manual and (2) holding individual and group meetings. At these meetings, department heads discuss the step-by-step preparation of budget requests and work out any problems. The budget director may also be responsible for explaining to the council the current year's limits and possibilities. The manager or mayor may share the role of educating the governing body, providing information not only on revenue estimates but also on impending federal or state actions or other legal and environmental changes that may influence the current budget.

The chief executive and budget director are also responsible for educating citizens about the budget process. Even if citizens come to a hearing just to express their views, officials should make available handouts explaining what is happening. The earlier in the process citizens become involved and the more authoritative their input, the more important it is to educate them about their role, to explain the legal and financial constraints on the local government, and to clarify the specific issues on which citizens' views are being sought. Technical matters must be conveyed without the implication that this is a matter only for experts. Training must be conducted in such a way that it does not preclude participation or open expression of opinion. Constraints must be presented realistically and convincingly, or citizens may view them as manipulative.

As a means of educating the general public, the chief executive is also responsible for educating the press. While some reporters have a good understanding of the budget and the key issues, some do not view budget stories as being of much interest to readers. Local officials may have to explain various aspects of budgeting in order to get the press to take note of an important story. Coverage should improve if the manager or mayor takes responsibility for educating the press about important issues. If the press presents these issues in a compelling way, more citizens are likely to participate in budget hearings.

Framing decisions

Although it is the governing body that ultimately passes the budget, adoption is preceded by a series of choices originating in the earliest phases of budget preparation. How those choices are framed can affect both the timeliness and the quality of the decisions that are made.

In designing the budget process, the chief executive should consider a number of factors that can affect decision making. First, unless budget participants are asked the right questions, they cannot make the best possible contribution to the budget process. Second, the executive should consider how the budget format and the presentation of options may affect decisions. Finally, the manager or mayor should ensure that decisions being presented are policy issues rather than managerial concerns.

The right questions   To make sound contributions to the budget process, budget participants need to be asked the right questions. Department heads should be asked about the details of service delivery—how much it costs to put an officer on the street, or how much it would cost to begin snowplowing after a three-inch snowfall versus a four- or five-inch snowfall. Citizens should be asked what the local government should be doing: What collective problems need to be addressed during the next five or ten years? Which problems are most urgent? Key questions for citizen review boards may be, "Does this make sense? Can you understand what we are doing here? Should we be doing it?"

Elected officials should be consulted about their priorities for the coming year—for example, should the community focus on flood control projects or street reconstruction? Or should both projects be begun at the same time and stretched out over several years? Council members should be asked about specific priorities for services, about funding increases or decreases, and about possible tax changes. Council advice should also be sought on capital projects—especially those that could be seen as neighborhood or district projects, if council members are elected from districts.

The budget office should be asked for revenue estimates by source and for estimates of the effects of changes in taxes or other revenues. The budget office may also provide advice on borrowing and guidance on the legality of various budgetary actions. As a department head, the budget director may also be asked questions about departmental operations.

Issues presented to the chief executive will include, for example, questions about granting various departmental budget requests and about the design and funding of new programs. The chief executive's decisions on budget matters will be based on his or her sense of community goals, tempered by perceived public opinion and council preferences.

Budget format   Because the budget format shapes the information requested from various participants, it also determines the information available for decision making. For example, if budget forms ask departments to delineate the impact of cutting a service or program, then decision makers can compare various proposals and choose the one that provides the greatest benefit at the least cost. Some budget formats allow for comparison among programs and program requests, while others do not.

In a **line-item budget**, department heads express their financial needs in terms of inputs—costs of staff, benefits, contractual services, travel, automobiles and gasoline, and the like. (Figure 2–4 provides an example of such a format.) Line-item budgets typically compare last year's actual expenditures with the amounts budgeted for the current year. Citizens or council members examining a line-item budget will focus on the information that is available to them—namely, the change in funding between last year and this year. A line-item budget does not provide information on goals or accomplishments or on the impact of increasing or decreasing a line item. Thus, decisions will necessarily deal with justifications for increases or decreases from last year rather than with overall policy issues (e.g., What is the program trying to accomplish? Is it effective?).

Performance budgets, in contrast, require department heads and program managers to indicate the extent to which departments have achieved goals and objectives. Such budgets provide decision makers

Figure 2–4   Line-item budget, Alice, Texas.

	City of Alice, Texas		
20 – GENERAL FUND			CITY OF ALICE
226 – SWIMMING POOL			1986-1987 BUDGET
ACCOUNT	1984-85 ACTUAL	1985-86 REVISED	1986-87 PROPOSED
501.00 SALARIES - WAGES	23,393	24,000	25,008
501.10 EXTRA HELP & OVERTIME	387	63	
501.20 SALARY RESERVE			
501.30 TAXES - SOCIAL SECURITY	1,676	619	1,788
501.40 INSURANCE			
501.50 RETIREMENT			
501.60 LONGEVITY			
TOTAL PERSONAL SERVICES	25,456	24,682	26,796
502.00 OFFICE SUPPLIES	150	59	100
502.20 WEARING APPAREL		200	200
502.40 TOOLS			50
502.50 DISINFECTANT AND CHEMICALS	1,167	1,500	2,000
502.90 OTHERS	4,705	2,763	3,000
TOTAL SUPPLIES	6,022	4,522	5,350
503.00 BUILDING MATERIALS	50	200	200
503.90 OTHER - MATERIALS	691	631	600
TOTAL MATERIALS	741	831	800
504.00 FURNITURE & FIXTURES			
504.40 DISTRIBUTION SYSTEM	330	1,500	1,500
504.90 OTHER - POOLS	1,024	1,000	1,000
TOTAL MAINTENANCE OF EQUIPMENT	1,354	2,500	2,500
505.00 COMMUNICATIONS	753	801	800
505.30 SPECIAL SERVICES AND LEGAL	1,344		
505.60 GAS AND LIGHTS	2,016	2,200	2,400
TOTAL CONTRACTUAL SERVICES	4,113	3,001	3,200
509.90 OTHER EQUIPMENT		900	
TOTAL CAPITAL OUTLAY		900	
TOTAL SWIMMING POOL	37,686	36,436	38,646

Source: City of Alice, Texas, *Annual Budget, 1986–87 Fiscal Year*, 52.

with information on a program's workload, efficiency, and effectiveness over time.

Presentation of options   Like the budget format, the presentation of options can affect the budget process and budgetary decisions. Sometimes, staff may choose to consider a number of alternatives but to give decision makers only the option that staff regards as the best. Decision makers then consider this option from all sides and decide whether to accept it. For example, in an extremely complicated situation involving many interests, putting forward one alternative may be the best solution: otherwise, the number of alternatives—each of which would favor some interests over others—may simply be overwhelming.

In other situations, it may make more sense to provide several options, with a clear description of the costs, benefits, and policy implications of each: "If you want to accomplish this goal, then pick this option; if you want to accomplish that goal, pick that option." Presenting and costing out options with this degree of clarity takes effort and creativity, but it facilitates decision making. (Because it is very difficult to thoroughly compare four or more alternatives at one time, decision makers are rarely presented with more than three.)

Managerial versus policy decisions   Recognizing that some decisions will inevitably fall into gray areas, staff should ensure, when framing options, that the council and the public are free to offer advice on policy but that they do not interfere with what should be managerial decisions. For example, during a budget hearing with a citizen advisory board, the issue was whether the city should drill a well or build a water storage tower. A citizen noted that the grant being used to fund the project required only a well and questioned why a tower should be built at four times the cost. A staff member answered angrily that this was a technical question and was therefore under the staff's jurisdiction; staff proceeded to deal with the issue on technical grounds. But the debate as framed— water tower versus well—obscured an underlying policy issue that ought to have been presented to citizens: namely, whether water services should be expanded to attract new business to that part of town.

In short, budgetary decision making has to be managed. The timing of decisions, the information available to participants, and the framing of decisions must be thought through and implemented so as to ensure that the key actors know their roles, are asked the right questions, and are given enough information to come up with thoughtful responses.

Budget policy statements

Although it is not uncommon for the budget process to proceed from year to year with little or no examination of assumptions, routines, or policy implications, lack of prior agreement on policy can pose problems.[5] For example, a local government may have gone along for years without any explicit policy on borrowing to balance the budget. If a financial problem develops and someone proposes borrowing to solve it, there is no guidance on what to do. To avoid such difficulties, it is useful to develop specific, agreed-upon policies as the basis for the local government's routine financial practices.

It is much easier to formulate a policy and come to agreement when a local government is not facing a financial emergency. When there is no deficit confronting them, officials are more likely to agree that the government should not borrow to cover a deficit. Having a policy in place will not always prevent unwise decisions, but it may eliminate particularly poor options or make them look less attractive—because the consequences of these options will already have been widely discussed, and prudent financial practice will have become more institutionalized in the jurisdiction's decision-making framework. In addition, by making budget policies public (publishing them in the budget document or elsewhere), the local government effectively creates a compact with citizens and the press. Unwritten policy is vulnerable to compromise, but deviations from written policy are likely to be closely scrutinized.

The principal benefit of a written policy is that it provides a standard of budgetary performance that all participants—both the executive and governing body—have endorsed. If, as a matter of policy, a government will not incur a general-obligation debt burden that exceeds 15 percent of **assessed property value**, then any proposal to exceed that limit places the burden of proof on those seeking to exceed the limit. The written policy becomes the conscience of the organization by reducing—although never eliminating—incentives to make imprudent financial decisions in the interest of political expediency. The more specific the policy statement, the more effective it will be in furthering financially responsible budget actions.

A formal statement also provides budgetary decision making with greater continuity, reinforcing the core financial values of the organization and preserving them for successive administrations and legislative bodies. Although policies may be amended as community needs or standards of financial prudence change, any amendment will require extensive executive and legislative deliberation before it becomes effective.

A written policy statement may also reduce the number of technical issues open to debate during budget preparation and adoption, freeing up time to discuss substantive issues—for example, how much money should be allocated to street repair and how much should be spent on outreach programs for troubled teens. By taking some of the technical issues off the table, budget policies can sometimes expedite budget deliberations, a prospect likely to be greeted warmly by anyone who has ever prepared a budget.[6]

Finally, the overarching goal of a budget policy may be to preserve a particular distinction of the local government. The budget policy of Fairfax County, Virginia, for example, includes the following statement: "The Board of Supervisors endorsed a set of policies designed to maintain the 'triple A' bond rating awarded to the County."[7] The strategic financial plan of Glendale, Arizona, requires a sufficient fund balance to ensure both a stable spending level and a stable tax rate whenever revenues fall.[8]

Elements of a budget policy statement

1. **Operating budget policies**
    a. How comprehensive is the budget? What funds should be included in the operating budget? Should the operating and capital budgets be prepared concurrently or separately?
    b. What constitutes a balanced budget?
    c. What kinds of budget reserves should be maintained? How much money should be maintained in each? Under what conditions should money be withdrawn?
    d. Who is responsible for budget preparation, and what are the critical tasks for which they are responsible?

2. **Revenue policies**
    a. How much change in the property tax rate is acceptable in a given year?
    b. How will one-time revenues, such as grants or tax windfalls, be used?
    c. How frequently should service charges and fees be reviewed?

3. **Budget implementation policies**
    a. To what extent should enterprise funds balance themselves with revenue they have produced?
    b. What policies should govern the transfer of money across accounts or funds?
    c. Under what conditions should governments authorize interfund borrowing or interfund payments in lieu of taxes?
    d. When should the chief executive be empowered to prevent approved spending?
    e. Who should be held responsible for expenditures exceeding appropriated amounts?
    f. What standards should govern accounting, financial reporting, and auditing?

4. **Debt policies**
    a. What is the maximum long-term debt burden that the government will incur?
    b. What mix of long-term debt and current revenues, if any, will be the basis for financing capital improvements?
    c. How will bond proceeds be used?
    d. Under what conditions will short-term debt be issued?

Elements of a budget policy statement

As part of the criteria used to recognize governments with distinguished budgets, the Government Finance Officers Association (GFOA) recommends that each budget document include "a coherent statement of budgetary policies. These may take the form of goals and objectives, strategies or other mechanisms."[9] Several municipal and county governments have adopted formal policy statements to establish the financial goals of the organization and the principles that govern budget deliberations. The following four sections draw on the experiences of such local governments to provide recommendations on policies for the operating budget, revenues, budget implementation, and debt. The accompanying sidebar summarizes the issues that a budget policy statement should address.

Operating budget policies

Operating budget policies address the budget's scope, definitions of balance, maintenance of reserves, and the assignment of roles to various budgetary actors.

Budget scope The comprehensiveness of the operating budget has been debated since the inception of formal budgeting in government. The issue is twofold: (1) To what extent should the operating and capital budgets be integrated? (2) What funds should be reported in the operating budget? Because of the different planning processes and financing sources involved, municipalities and counties usually prepare their operating and capital budgets separately. Capital projects require long planning periods because of the large, up-front investment and because any design errors are costly to correct once construction has begun. Although practice varies among local governments, capital improvements are usually financed with long-term debt, whereas operating budgets are financed from current taxes, grants, and service charges. An operating budget policy should specify whether the two budget cycles will proceed concurrently or separately and briefly explain the reasons for the choice.

To better assess the impact of a capital improvement on annual operating costs, some local governments prepare their capital budgets concurrently with their operating budget. (Although a capital acquisition— e.g., new computer hardware—may reduce operating costs by increasing efficiency, most capital spending increases operating costs.) Another benefit of concurrent preparation is that it concentrates budget deliberations—and decision makers' attention—in a single period of time.

On the other hand, many local governments prepare an operating budget first and a capital budget later. The primary advantage of this approach is that it spreads out over a longer period the workload and intensity associated with budget deliberations. Providing more opportunity to educate participants on the merits of a proposal may result in more careful deliberation, which may in turn reduce the likelihood of errors in judgment.

Budgetary balance At the simplest level, if current revenues equal current expenditures, then the budget is balanced. Unfortunately, there is more to defining budgetary balance. For example, should revenues left over from last year be treated as current revenues, and can they be used to balance this year's budget? When does the budget have to be balanced: when the executive proposes it, when the governing body adopts it, or at the end of the fiscal year? Which revenues or expenditures can be counted toward the current year's balance? Does borrowing balance the budget?

Legal requirements for balance are often set at the state level, but a local government may set even more stringent requirements if it so chooses. If the accounting basis for balance is not established by the state, it is especially important to establish policies that determine which particular dollars of revenue and expenditure will count toward the current year's balance. The main choice here is between the **cash** and the **accrual** bases of accounting.[10]

Because it is easy to understand, measure, and explain, the cash available at the end of the year is one widely used indicator of budgetary balance. However, a cash balance is easy to manipulate: payments can be delayed until the following fiscal year, and revenue collections can be accelerated for credit to the current year. Thus, a cash balance may not accurately depict the government's financial condition.

Because of the possibility of manipulating cash balances, the **Governmental Accounting Standards Board (GASB)** recommends that budgets be prepared and reported on an accrual basis.[11] Briefly, accrual involves accruing (or assigning) to a fiscal year all the expenditures (or claims) incurred in that year, regardless of when the cash payment is made, and crediting all revenues to the year in which they are received. (Chapter 6 explains the accrual basis more fully.)

Whether a local government uses cash or accrual, it must avoid manipulating the amount of money left over at the end of the year. The budget of San Luis Obispo, California, has a useful policy statement on this topic:

The city will make all current expenditures with current revenues, avoiding procedures that balance current budgets by postponing needed expenditures, accruing future revenues, or rolling over short-term debt.[12]

Budget reserves To protect against unforeseen events or to accumulate money for future purposes, governments establish reserve accounts in various funds, then earmark the money for some specified purpose. The most common types of reserves are for

Cash flow requirements

Revenue stabilization (rainy day funds)

Unforeseen contingencies

Equipment replacement

Building repair or other improvements

Debt service.

Because the inflow of revenues never precisely coincides with the outflow of payments, governments must maintain sufficient cash on hand to satisfy **cash flow** needs. The amount reserved for this purpose depends on the timing of tax and utility payments. For example, most cities in Texas begin their fiscal year on 1 October, but property taxes are not due until the following 31 January. Sufficient cash must be reserved in a fund balance to cover disbursements during the intervening period. A government should first examine its cash flow needs and the margin of protection required, then specify in its budget policy the size of the cash flow reserve it wishes to maintain. One rule of thumb is to maintain enough cash on hand to cover disbursements for sixty days.

As a result of the deep recession in 1981–82, many state and local governments established **revenue stabilization reserves**, or rainy day funds, to provide resources when revenues decline because of an economic recession. Although recessions can be anticipated to some extent, their length and severity are much more difficult to forecast. Whenever their assumptions about the economy's future are inaccurate, state and local governments risk making similarly inaccurate revenue projections.[13] In a study of revenue forecasting by the state of California, half of the forecasting errors were caused by inaccurate assumptions about the course of the state's economy, and the other half were caused by random statistical errors inherent in revenue models.[14]

Governments creating **budget reserves** must resolve two policy issues: (1) the size of the reserve and (2) the conditions that must be met before the reserve can be tapped. In a study of California, Jon Vasche and Brad Williams found that a reserve equal to 10 percent of the state's general-fund revenues would be necessary to provide "full coverage" against revenue shortfalls in a worst-case scenario.[15] However, they characterize a 5 percent reserve as adequate. Because Glendale, California, depends heavily on the notoriously unstable (income-elastic) sales tax, the city has established a stabilization **account** equal to 10 percent of its sales tax revenues. Another approach sets the reserve according to the maximum change in the property tax rate the government is willing to adopt. Milwaukee, Wisconsin, sets its reserve with a goal of avoiding an annual increase of more than 3 percent in its property tax rate.[16] In the final analysis, the appropriate size for a reserve depends on the stability of a local government's revenue stream and on the strength of its political resolve to protect against budgetary instability.

When to tap the reserve is generally left to the discretion of the governing body, on the recommendation of the chief executive. Some governments—Milwaukee, for example—require an extraordinary (three-quarters) majority of the council before money can be transferred from the reserve to the operating budget. An alternative approach links access to the reserve to an economic indicator, such as a decline in the gross state product or an increase in the regional unemployment rate. Whatever mechanism is used, the budget policy should specify the criteria and procedures for drawing from the reserve.

Reserves for unforeseen contingencies provide funding for nonrecurring, unanticipated expenditures, protecting the government from issuing short-term debt to cover such needs. For example, Tempe, Arizona, maintains a contingency reserve equal to 2.5 percent of the revenue in the general fund. Governments often establish a separate contingency reserve for each major fund (e.g., one for each enterprise fund—water, sewer, sanitation, etc.—and for large capital improvements funds). Such reserves provide funding for extraordinary purchases or cost overruns not anticipated during the budget process. For example, a particularly cold winter may result in higher utility payments than had been appropriated in the operating budget.

Equipment replacement and **building improvement reserves** are two other types of reserve accounts occasionally used by local governments. The advantage of an equipment replacement reserve is that operating equipment and vehicles can be replaced immediately as they become obsolete or unusable. Sometimes governments establish a separate reserve for building improvements, which accumulates funds for deferred maintenance, renovations, and repairs to government-owned facilities. Funding for both types of reserves usually comes from charges assessed to each department on the basis of its pro-rata share of equipment used or building space occupied.

Finally, governments establish **reserves for debt service payments**, usually as a condition of their bond agreements with private investors. Debt service constitutes the annual or semiannual payment of principal and interest that governments must make on outstanding indebtedness. For **general obligation bonds**, a **debt service fund** is created to account for the taxes levied and payments made to service this type of debt. For **revenue bonds**, separate accounts are created in an enterprise fund to track revenues and payments for debt service. In the case of revenue bonds, the **bond covenant** may require reserves of 10 to 25 percent of the annual debt service payment as protection to bondholders against **default**. The exact amount of the reserve varies, depending on the instability of the revenue stream from the project financed by the bonds. Less frequently, governments establish a small reserve for their general obligation payments, but this is usually more to maintain cash flow than because of any requirement in the bond covenant.

Assigning responsibility   The budget policy statement should broadly outline key duties in the budget process. For example, the budget policy should specify who is responsible for budget preparation (either the chief finance officer, or, if a separate budget office exists, the budget director) and should describe in general terms the authority of this officer—for example, the authority to standardize budget documentation, to prepare the budget calendar, and to review departmental budget requests for accuracy and conformity to **budget guidelines**. The policy should specify who is responsible for forecasting revenue and the frequency with which forecasts will be prepared. Finally, the policy should clearly assign to the budget director the responsibility for overseeing budget implementation. Duties in this phase include preparing and reviewing **interim financial reports**, monitoring revenues, reviewing departmental expenditure requests for conformity with the budget, authorizing **transfers** across accounts or departments, and reviewing supplementary appropriation requests.

Revenue policies

Revenue policies address three issues: (1) the stability of tax rates, (2) the use of one-time revenue sources, and (3) review of service charges and fees.

Tax rates   Tax rates are politically sensitive: a considerable increase in the tax rate may make compliance difficult for taxpayers and cause citizens to resent government. Although lowering tax rates may be politically popular during a period of economic growth, such a move may pave the way for larger increases later, as the economy slows down.

To avoid the consequences of fluctuations in tax rates, some local governments have established policies designed to maintain relatively stable tax rates. Montgomery County, Maryland, for example, has a policy of maintaining a property tax rate that avoids "wide annual fluctuations as economic and fiscal conditions change."[17] As part of its strategic financial plan, Glendale, California, schedules the sale of general obligation bonds so as to ensure a stable property tax rate. (Since these bonds are usually repaid with property taxes, local governments often have to increase tax rates to meet annual debt service requirements.) To avoid pushing property tax rates up and down, some local governments have an informal policy that requires level contributions to pension plans.

One-time revenue   Most local government revenue is recurring—that is, it comes in month after month, year after year, in a reasonably predictable way. Some revenue, however, occurs only once, or comes in for a few years and then declines or disappears. If the local government sells land or a building, the sale brings in one-time revenue. If a town wins a competitive grant for a pilot project, the grant may bring in money for a couple of years and then stop.

The risk is that one-time revenue will be spent on continuing expenditures rather than on one-time outlays. A local government that becomes dependent on one-time revenue or on a source of revenue that will soon disappear can, in essence, create deficits for itself. To protect against this eventuality, some local governments establish a policy requiring that temporary revenues be used to obtain **capital assets** (equipment, buildings, land) or to make other nonrecurring purchases. An alternative policy, used by Glendale, is to earmark temporary revenues for deposit in the revenue stabilization account.

Review of fees   Since the mid-1980s, local governments have reduced their dependence on the property tax and significantly increased their dependence on service charges and fees. Although officials ordinarily review these fees only when there is a budget crisis, an appropriate policy might call for these fees to be reviewed annually or every other year, regardless of the local government's fiscal condition. With regular and more frequent reviews, fees are likely to reflect more closely the actual cost of service delivery.

Budget implementation policies

Balancing the need for flexibility with the need for accountability requires that a number of policy-laden technical decisions be made during budget implementation. These decisions concern (1) enterprise funds and the circumstances under which revenue may be transferred into or out of them; (2) changes to the budget, either through budget amendments or at the discretion of the chief executive; (3) the prevention of overspending; and (4) the frequency and nature of financial reports.

Enterprise funds   Before the beginning of the fiscal year, a policy decision should determine which enterprise funds are expected to balance themselves—and, of those that are not expected to balance, what proportion of costs should be subsidized by the general fund. In Fort Collins, Colorado, for example, all enterprise funds (cemeteries, golf, light and power, water and wastewater, and storm drainage) are required to recover 100 percent of their costs through the five-year projection period; the long-term goal of all enterprise accounts is self-sufficiency.[18]

In general, enterprise funds should be self-supporting if (1) the benefits largely accrue to users of the service, (2) collecting a fee from users is administratively feasible, and (3) pricing the service at its full cost will not cause users to take actions that are more costly than the revenues obtained through service charges. For example, charging full cost for residential use of a landfill may increase illegal dumping of trash along roads and in vacant lots.[19] In such cases, subsidizing the service through general tax revenues is more efficient than trying to make it self-supporting.

Related issues are interfund **payments in lieu of taxes** (PILOTs) and **interfund borrowing** by local government-owned utilities. Under legislation governing PILOTs, an enterprise fund would be required to make an annual payment to the general fund to take the place of property taxes that would have been received if the service had been provided by a private firm. In Fort Collins, the water and wastewater fund and the light and power fund transfer to the general fund 5 and 6 percent of their operating revenues, respectively. In some jurisdictions, such transfers are justified as returns on investment or as overhead charges assessed to the enterprise activity for the indirect costs incurred by the general fund in administering the **activity**.

Interfund borrowing, which occurs frequently during the budget year as a cash management measure, allows a surplus in one fund (often an enterprise fund) to be used to offset a shortfall in another (often a tax-supported fund). From a policy perspective, it is important to keep interfund borrowing to a minimum: First, so that anyone reading the local government financial report can understand what spending is being funded by what revenue source; and second, to prevent the local government from using interfund borrowing to hide deficits. One helpful policy is to require all interfund borrowing, even that which is intended to be repaid during the year, to be approved by the council in public session. Generating a public record increases the likelihood that money borrowed internally will be repaid. A second helpful policy is to set a percentage standard for PILOTs and to make that standard public. Because it provides a basis for evaluating the amount of money being transferred, a publicly announced standard will make it more difficult to use surpluses in one fund to hide deficits in another.

Budget flexibility   A budget policy statement should specify the procedures for amending the budget during the fiscal year. Due to unanticipated economic changes, revenues may be greater or less than the budgeted amounts, and the operating budget may need to be amended to reflect these changes. The budget may be formally amended by a simple majority of the council, or an extraordinary majority may be required. Kersey, Colorado, requires an extraordinary majority of two-thirds to approve any expenditure in excess of the budget.

The budget policy may also detail the circumstances under which the governing body may amend the budget. For example, Fort Collins amends the budget (1) to pay for encumbrances (outstanding purchase orders and contracts) carried over from the preceding fiscal year, (2) to allocate unanticipated revenues, such as a grant or a **bond** issue, or (3) to allocate reserves when the balances are greater than those required by budget policy or when an emergency or unusual circumstance has occurred. Other reasons for budget amendments include union settlements that occurred after the budget was drawn up and retroactive approval of a transfer made by the chief executive. Such amendments align the operating budget with actual spending levels.

If a chief executive needs to transfer money within accounts or funds, such a transfer may or may not need to go back to the council for formal approval. A useful policy is to set some limit on the amount that can be transferred on executive authority before the consent of the council is required. Most local government policies specify not only the amount but also the kinds of transfers that require council approval. The policy of Denton, Texas, is typical:

1. Budget transfers between accounts *within* a department or agency require only the city manager's authorization.
2. Budget transfers between departments but within the same fund require the city manager's recommendation and the city council's approval. Such transfers may be made only in the last three months of the fiscal year.
3. Budget transfers between funds (for example, from the general fund to a **capital projects fund**) require city council approval.

Legislative approval is almost always required for transfers of appropriations between capital project funds.

Preventing overspending   There are several approaches to preventing overspending; one is to **impound** budgeted authority, thereby restricting spending, and the other is to grant departments only a portion of their spending authority at a time. Local government policy may grant the chief executive the power to impound; Fort Collins, for example, gives the city manager authority to move line items to a "frozen appropriation" status when economic developments dictate. Such a move may be appropriate in the event of an economic slowdown, if revenues fail to keep pace with requirements.

Granting departments only a portion of their funding at a time prevents them from spending their entire budget in one quarter, then coming back and arguing for more. If overspending by departments and programs is a problem, a local government may wish to make department heads personally responsible for overspending. An alternative approach is to subtract this year's overspending from next year's allocation.

Reporting   A local government's budget policy should specify the nature and frequency of budget status reports. Governments normally prepare interim financial reports (shown in Figure 2–5) that compare budgeted with actual amounts of revenues and expenditures to date. These reports, which alert decision makers to impending shortfalls in revenues or overruns in expenditures, should be prepared at least quarterly—monthly for larger governments. (Reporting is discussed more fully in Chapter 6.)

Finally, budget policies frequently include a statement on the accounting, financial reporting, and auditing standards to be used by the government. Dayton, for example, has the following statement:

1. An independent audit will be performed annually.
2. The city will produce annual financial reports in accordance with generally accepted accounting principles (GAAP) as outlined by the GASB.
3. The city will maintain a strong internal audit capability.[20]

Such policies commit the government to professional standards of financial management and auditing and reassure investors in government bonds.

Debt policies

Budget policy statements often include requirements for debt issuance and administration. Such policies may specify, for example, the maximum long-term debt burden the local government may incur, the mix of debt and current revenues in capital improvements financing, the use of bond proceeds, and the conditions under which short-term debt will be issued.

Limitations on the amount of debt a local government may incur take

General fund: Interim statement of actual and estimated revenue
for the month of September 19X6 and the nine months ended September 30, 19X6

	Total 19X6 estimated revenue	September 19X6 actual revenue	Year-to-date actual revenue	Unrealized revenue	Year-to-date actual as percentage of estimated revenue	
					Current year	Prior year
Taxes						
General property taxes—current	$ 880,000	$ —	$ 865,000	$ 15,000	98.3	95.8
Penalties and interest on delinquent taxes—general property	2,500	—	2,100	400	84.0	85.0
Total taxes	882,500	—	867,100	15,400	98.3	95.7
Licenses and permits						
Business licenses and permits	105,500	8,600	72,500	33,000	68.7	67.7
Nonbusiness licenses and permits	20,000	1,900	18,000	2,000	90.0	81.5
Total licenses and permits	125,500	10,500	90,500	35,000	72.1	70.3
Intergovernmental revenue						
Federal grants	55,000	—	55,000	—	100.0	100.0
State grants	145,000	45,000	130,000	15,000	89.7	85.1
Total intergovernmental revenue	200,000	45,000	185,000	15,000	92.5	89.0
Charges for services						
General government	40,000	3,100	27,000	13,000	67.5	68.1
Public safety	10,000	800	8,100	1,900	81.0	73.6
Highways and streets	8,000	750	6,275	1,725	78.4	80.0
Sanitation	12,000	1,100	9,200	2,800	76.7	75.9
Culture—recreation	20,000	1,400	11,900	8,100	59.5	71.4
Total charges for services	90,000	7,150	62,475	27,525	69.4	70.9
Fines and forfeits						
Fines	27,500	2,110	22,050	5,450	80.2	77.3
Forfeits	5,000	480	3,850	1,150	77.0	80.0
Total fines and forfeits	32,500	2,590	25,900	6,600	79.7	77.9
Miscellaneous revenue						
Interest earnings	1,500	90	980	520	65.3	74.7
Rents and royalties	18,000	1,650	14,000	4,000	77.8	75.0
Total miscellaneous revenue	19,500	1,740	14,980	4,520	76.8	74.9
TOTAL REVENUE	$1,350,000	$66,980	$1,245,955	$104,045	92.3	87.6

Figure 2–5   Sample interim financial report.

Source: Paul Glick, *How to Understand Local Government Financial Statements: A User's Guide* (Chicago: Government Finance Officers Association, 1986), 47. Reprinted by permission of the Government Finance Officers Association, Chicago, Illinois.

two forms: (1) a limit on the percentage of operating revenue spent for debt service and (2) a limit on the amount of outstanding direct debt as a percentage of the full value of assessed property. Tempe, Arizona, for example, has a ceiling on annual debt service of 15 percent of total general revenue and a limit on long-term debt of 5 percent of assessed value. These percentages will vary among local governments, depending on state law and local circumstances.

Budget policies sometimes address the mix of cash and debt to fund capital projects. For example, under the policy in San Luis Obispo, California, a minimum of 40 percent current revenues and a maximum of 60 percent debt may be used to finance capital improvements. Ideally, the mix should be determined by the proportion of the benefits of the project that will go to future residents as opposed to current ones—although such a proportion should probably be treated as a target rather than as a rigid constraint.

Another common provision in budget policy statements is a stipulation on how bond proceeds can be used. For example, Dayton's policy restricts bond money to "capital improvements and moral obligations." San Luis Obispo has an even more restrictive policy, in which debt may be used

only for one-time capital improvement projects and only under the following circumstances: (1) when the project's useful life will exceed the term of the financing and (2) when project revenues or specific resources will be sufficient to service the long-term debt.[21]

Governments that issue short-term debt should carefully assess their needs, then develop a policy that protects them from excessive use of this type of debt without undermining their ability to meet cash flow needs. Dayton permits notes to be issued only for bond anticipation purposes. Other governments are more permissive, allowing the issuance of notes to meet cash flow needs. The policy in Glendale, California, simply states that short-term debt cannot exceed 5 percent of general revenues or 20 percent of the city's outstanding debt.

Summary

Mayor-council and council-manager jurisdictions have traditionally been characterized by different distributions of budgeting authority, but both forms of government have found the council useful for community outreach and as a check to ensure that the local government is being sufficiently accountable to citizens. The legal structures that limit council participation can be altered, but informal patterns of consultation can evolve even within the existing structures. The executive branch can provide budgetary information to the council throughout the budget preparation process, can request policy guidance, and can include council priorities in the executive budget. Even when the council has relatively little legal power, failure to consult with its members can, in the short run, delay the budget and create public embarrassment. In the long run, failure to consult can undermine public support.

In designing the budget process, local government officials are constrained by laws, charters, and precedent, but there is considerable latitude within these constraints to shape a process that matches the management style of the chief executive and fits the political conditions of the community. A redesign of the budget process can be used to address a number of problems, including overcentralization, delayed decisions, lack of adequate information for policy making, and anger or alienation on the part of citizens. In addition to helping to resolve specific problems, the design of the budget process can influence the level of governmental accountability and the level of citizen control over government and taxation. As early budget reformers in this country argued, the budget process combines concerns with efficiency with concerns for democracy. Current practices should be evaluated from both perspectives.

A budget policy statement can be a useful way of garnering support for fiscally wise practices and setting up expectations that these practices will be observed. Such a policy statement provides a standard of budgetary performance that both the chief executive and the governing body have endorsed. The more specific the budget policy, the more effective it will be in promoting financially responsible budget decisions.

1　Council of State Community Affairs Agencies, *Department of Community Affairs Roles in Local Financial Management: Ten State Profiles* (Washington, DC: U.S. Department of Housing and Urban Development, Office of Policy Development and Research, December 1978), 3–4.

2　Frederick Clow, *A Comparative Study of the Administration of City Finances in the United States, With Special Reference to the Budget* (New York: MacMillan, 1901).

3　William H. Allen, "The Budget Amendment of the Maryland Constitution," *National Municipal Review* 6, no. 4 (1917): 488.

4　Ibid.

5　Michael J. White, "Budget Policy: Where Does It Begin and End?" *Governmental Finance* (August 1978): 4.

6　Ibid.

7　Fairfax County, Virginia, *Advertised Budget Plan, Fiscal 1991, Overview*, 55.

8　Glendale, Arizona, *1989/90 Budget and Financial Plan*, 414.

9　Girard Miller, "GFOA's Program of Awards for Distinguished Budget Presentation," *Governmental Finance* (September 1984): 33.

10　Robert B. Albritton and Ellen M. Dran, "Balanced Budgets and State Surpluses: The Politics of Budgeting in Illinois," *Public Administration Review* (March/April 1987): 144.

11　Governmental Accounting Standards Board, *Measurement Focus and Basis of Accounting —Governmental Funds*, Proposed Statement of the GASB (Stamford, CT: GASB, 1987), 10.

12　San Luis Obispo, California, *1989–1991 Financial Plan & Approved 1989–1990 Budget*, 1 July 1989, B-4.

13　Jon David Vasche and Brad Williams, "Optimal Governmental Budgeting Contingency Reserve Funds," *Public Budgeting & Finance* (Spring 1987): 74.

14　Ibid., 75.

15　Ibid., 77.

16　Michael Wolkoff, "An Evaluation of Municipal Rainy Day Funds," *Public Budgeting & Finance* (Summer 1987): 56.

17　Montgomery County, Maryland, *County Executive's Recommended FY 91 Budget*, 2–2.

18　Fort Collins, Colorado, *1990 Adopted Budget, Budget Overview*, vol. 1, November 1989, C-15.

19　Robert L. Bland, *A Revenue Guide for Local Government* (Washington, DC: International City Management Association, 1989), 113.

20　Dayton, Ohio, *1990 Program Strategies*, 35.

21　San Luis Obispo, California, *1989–1991 Financial Plan*, B-7.

3 Budget preparation and adoption

Budget preparation and adoption

This chapter provides an overview of the major steps in budget preparation and adoption, highlighting the role of the budget office in developing and updating revenue estimates, soliciting departmental budget requests, and combining revenue projections and budget requests into a proposal that achieves preliminary balance and satisfies legal constraints.

Budget preparation and adoption is a complex process that requires communication and cooperation among a number of different parties, including the chief executive, the budget office, department heads, the governing body, and the public. The chapter examines a number of approaches to improving the process: ensuring that participants' roles and responsibilities are clear, creating and following agreed-upon procedures, and developing incentives for active public participation.

The role of the budget office

The primary function of the budget office is to assist the chief executive in preparing the budget proposal for legislative consideration. If the council or board, rather than the mayor or manager, has primary responsibility for the budget, then a comptroller or finance director will normally collect requests from the departments—and, after ensuring that requests balance with revenues, pass the proposed budget to the council or board.

In carrying out their responsibilities, budget offices used to routinely refuse departmental requests. In recent years, however, this role has come to be regarded as wasteful and ineffective. In its new (and still evolving) role, the budget office has taken on more of an educational function—helping departments rather than opposing them; explaining budget constraints to the manager, mayor, and council; and presenting the budget to the public, the media, and the financial community. The new role also places more emphasis on fiscal conservatism—being careful with public money and getting your money's worth—than on control of spending.

Location and functions

In the early days of public budgeting in the United States, the comptroller was responsible for putting together the budget, sometimes borrowing a clerk from another office to help compile budget figures. As the demands of the task grew, this temporary position became the budget office. Gradually, two distinct organizational arrangements for the budget office developed. In one pattern, the budget office is housed in the office of the chief executive, and the budget director reports directly to the executive. In the second pattern, the functions of accounting, purchasing, payroll, and personnel are combined with budgeting and handled by a separate finance department.

Writing in the 1920s, Arthur Buck, a prominent early budget reformer, described the implications of these arrangements: a budget director housed in the executive's office prepared the budget but had little role in budget implementation.[1] When the budget office was located within a finance department, the budget director's role was much broader: he provided the chief executive with financial advice on all budgetary matters and ran the local government's financial affairs—including revenue collection, purchasing, financial record keeping, and budget implementation.

In addition, with the budget office located within a finance department, the finance director buffered the budget office from the political and policy concerns of the chief executive, enabling the budget office to play a more technical role and to have less direct involvement in public policy. This effect is still evident in budget offices today. In Boston, for example, the budget office is located in the Administrative Services Department, which functions much like a finance department. The department heads, including the head of Administrative Services, are political supporters of the mayor and come and go with new administrations. The head of Administrative Services deals directly with the mayor, interpreting the mayor's priorities for the budget office. In this setting, it suits the more politically inclined appointees to rely on the trained professionals in the budget office for what one official called "good numbers"; in other words, the head of Administrative Services helps maintain the expertise and neutrality of the budget office by shielding it from direct mayoral influence.

When the budget office reports directly to an elected official such as a mayor, the budget director may be a political appointee and may not be professionally trained in budgeting or accounting. In that case, the budget director must be particularly sensitive to the electoral needs of the chief executive. A change in the chief executive is likely to result in a change in the budget director as well. In a council-manager jurisdiction, if the budget office reports directly to the manager, the manager can serve as a buffer against political demands. The budget office must nevertheless be sensitive to the manager's goals and views on budgeting.

Although many of the functions of the budget office are the same, regardless of organizational location, the form of government may give rise to subtle differences in the way budget office responsibilities are carried out. In Rochester, New York, for example, a mayor-council city, the budget director reports directly to the mayor. A former budget director noted that at election time, citizens care less about the cost of repairing each pothole and more about the number of potholes filled. Such sensitivity to reelection issues is likely to be more marked in a mayor-council jurisdiction than in a community with a history of council-manager government.

The role of the budget office depends not only on its location and on the form of government, but also to some extent on staff size. In a small local government, a budget office that performs no finance functions may consist of one person; if the budget office includes some finance functions, there may be an assistant to the budget director and several clerks. In larger governments, the budget office typically employs a much larger staff with graduate degrees in public administration, and staff may have opportunities to specialize—in revenue projection, grants and intergovernmental revenues, or capital budgeting, for example. Larger governments may also have budget analysts to help provide objective assessments of departmental needs and capabilities—advising departments on budget issues, reviewing their requests for the forthcoming budget period, and recommending changes in departmental requests. A particular budget analyst may have responsibility for several departments and specialize in grants or capital budgeting. At a later stage in the process the analysts may double check all the numbers and participate in the assembly and production of the budget proposal.

The changing role

Regardless of its location or size, the budget office has traditionally collected spending requests from departments and, with the advice of the chief executive, trimmed the requests to meet expected revenue levels. This pattern leads to a conflict between the budget office and the departments: because of the expanding demand for public services, the departments always ask for more funding; because of revenue constraints, the budget office often refuses. One budget officer described the relationship as follows: "There may ultimately be some 'yesses,' but it starts with 'no' to get the discussion going."

In many local governments, the budget office's routine denial of requests led department heads to devise strategies to ensure that they had the resources they needed to manage properly. From the departments' perspective, the budget office micromanaged their operations, and the challenge was to outmaneuver the budget office. The task of the budget office, in turn, was to catch the departments at their game. According to a longtime city hall employee, until Tampa, Florida, opted for target-based budgeting, the system in place encouraged bureaucratic gamesmanship:

The fire chief would close a fire station in a wealthy neighborhood, knowing it would be restored during the year. Recreation would close a recreation center, or transit would eliminate ten buses. There was no more justification than that, just ten buses. They would negotiate, and take a cut of five instead.

Department heads' efforts to evade the budget office's scrutiny often led to a pattern of surveillance and suspicion on the part of the budget office. Moreover, without adequate information, budget offices were unable to make sensible, detailed cuts in departments' proposals and resorted to thoughtless, across-the-board cuts in departmental spending requests. Alternatively, budget analysts scrutinized each line item, opening themselves to accusations of micromanagement.

In some cases, the adversarial role of the budget office became so ingrained that expenditures that should have been approved were denied. The disaster in Chicago, when water from the Chicago River sank into the tunnels below the city and into the basements of downtown buildings, was the result of routine refusals on the part of the budget office. The leak in the tunnels had been called to the city's attention, and the department in charge had petitioned the budget office for a contract to fix the leak. The job went out to bid, but the budget office rejected the bid as too high. The job was rebid, and again the bid was rejected as too high. Before the job could be bid a third time, a public works nightmare had occurred.

In order to recast their role, many budget offices now use a form of target-based budgeting, under which the budget office assigns maximum funding levels to each department. As long as department heads keep their budget requests for the forthcoming year within the targets, they can choose what to include in their requests, with minimal interference from the budget office. Target-based budgeting enables the budget office to limit total budget requests to expected revenue levels, while allowing department heads the discretion to identify those items that are most urgent.

Tampa changed to a target-based budget in 1978. According to the former budget director, the older system encouraged budget requests that were "30 to 40 percent too high," and his job "was to find what to cut." While Tampa's former budgeting system involved across-the-board cuts, the former system in Phoenix, Arizona, involved detailed, line-item evaluations. In the late 1960s and early 1970s, the budget office "dealt with the entire departmental budget, deciding this tool versus that tool."

In recent years, the relationship between the budget office and departments has gradually become less contentious, with considerably less strategizing. In some cases, a clearer division of labor has lessened antagonism. Under target-based budgeting, for example, the budget office determines the total for each department's budget request, and departments have more autonomy within those totals. Neither is allowed to interfere with the other's legitimate decision making. According to a budget analyst in Dayton, Ohio, city government is "a pretty centralized place," but the introduction of target-based budgeting represented "a kind of decentralization"—a way of giving departments flexibility. According to a former budget department staffer in Tampa, target-based budgeting eliminated accusations from department heads that the budget office was "arbitrary," giving the budget office

an objectivity people can live with. Now, we can say here are the facts, here is what your money is. They stopped seeing us as the enemy. I got tired of being the enemy. The big change was to get out of the adversarial relationship. There was more teamwork.

In short, in many jurisdictions the budget office no longer functions primarily as the bottleneck in the budget preparation phase. The new role is more complicated, more supportive, and generally less contentious.

The modern budget office

Even though the budget office has assumed a more supportive role, its main tasks remain the same: estimating revenues, assembling budget requests into a proposal, and ensuring that total requests do not exceed estimated revenues. In carrying out these tasks, the budget office typically assumes a number of roles: it educates participants about the budget process, adjudicates among participants both within and outside the local government, manages the computing facilities, represents the values of accuracy and fiscal conservatism, and provides public accountability.

The budget office must first serve the role of educator—taking the lead in disseminating financial policy and ensuring that all the participants in budget deliberations know what is possible and permissible. The budget office must not only prepare accurate revenue estimates but also convince other participants in the process that these numbers are accurate, defensible, and represent the outside limits for expenditures. If council members try to spend fund balances because they think of them as available resources, the budget office needs to educate the council on the meaning of the fund balance and to identify the portion that is truly available for allocation. If council members want to transfer money out of utility funds to balance other funds, the budget office (or the chief executive) needs to educate the council about the laws governing such transfers and the obligations to investors holding utility bonds. The budget office is responsible for educating the council about the budget format and how to use it and for educating departments about budget request forms and how to submit them. And it is responsible for educating the financial community about the soundness of the local economy and the local government's commitment to professional financial management practices.

Because they have primary responsibility for educating other participants, budget analysts must have effective communication skills. The budget office cannot operate if it fails to persuade departments to fill out financial reports; and if it cannot persuade the council that tax revenues are likely to drop and that the jurisdiction should slow down the spending rate, year-end deficits may result. In other words, the budget office must not only have command of the numbers but also be able to convince others of its conclusions.

In addition to playing the role of educator, the budget office must often adjudicate among participants in budget preparation. According to a former budget director from Rochester, New York, the budget office "finds out the real priorities from the departments' request forms" and decides which reductions to recommend, limiting the issues that are sent "upstairs"—that is, to the mayor's office. Sometimes, however,

the department heads want trade-offs, and want to battle with the mayor. In cases where the department takes the matter to the mayor, the budget office wins in about 98 percent of the cases.

The preparation process in Dayton provides an example of how the budget office can help adjudicate requests from outside city hall. As a budget office staff member explained, in the course of the planning process the budget office gathers about ten thousand suggestions from the entire community, then winnows them down into a set of about seventy general goals and objectives—for example, "increase the control of drugs, increase negotiation with other governmental units to improve sanitation, facilitate good relations between ethnic groups."

Because the budget office often plays the role of adjudicator, it helps define the relative worth of programs or requests. For example, by explaining what is equal to what in the budget, the budget director may help frame the trade-offs the chief executive has to make. If the chief executive needs a specific sum, the budget office may say, "You can get it here, or here, or here," pointing to different programs. The budget director can also make clear the immediate consequences of cuts and additions. One budget director described how this is done.

The mayor makes the trade-offs. I phrase them—"Hold the line on the police department or lose the tree trimming"—and he chooses which way he wants to go. With newly refined budget measures, he can choose not only between programs but also between levels of programs. I can tell him that if he expands the immunization program to include a hundred more children, he will have to give up or delay planting 20 new trees on the parkway.

Another function that often accrues to the budget office is management of computing facilities. The budget office depends heavily on historical data: tax receipts by month from prior years, bond issuance and repayment history, interest rates on different types of investments, and records of past budgets and spending are essential to putting together a budget proposal. As a result, the budget office may become the keeper of the computer, developing a close relationship with accounting and the management information systems department and helping to structure the financial information system. The budget office typically becomes the strongest voice in government for updating computing capabilities.

The credibility of the budget office and its ability to persuade others to take action or to refrain from overspending depend critically on the accuracy of its numbers. During budget preparation, budget staff check and recheck totals for accuracy and consistency throughout the budget document. The budget office becomes an advocate for accuracy, both in estimates and in actual figures included in year-end financial reports. If the council wants to round up revenue estimates, the budget office must argue for its own, more precise estimates. When Tampa's budget director was asked whether he had ever underestimated the utility tax to compensate for the difficulty of predicting this revenue source accurately, he sounded offended.

We don't underestimate utility taxes. We attempt to project accurately, based on what we know. We don't say we expect $12 million and use the figure of $11 million. I want to get a good number. I use the contingency fund and the fund balance and constant review to compensate for overages and underages. I give people a hard time if their estimates are way off.

The budget office is also a voice for the values of fiscal conservatism—taking extreme care with public money and avoiding imprudent risks. This extra caution shows not only in the budget office's spending and revenue recommendations but in the financial management policies that it recommends. Thus, the budget office may argue for somewhat larger fund balances or for a larger **contingency account** as a precaution against growing dependence on an unstable revenue source like the sales tax. The budget office is often expected to play this role, to argue for this point of view.

Among the many roles of the budget office, perhaps the most important is to provide public accountability. The budget office, through the budget document, explains to citizens how their money is spent. That information must be accurate and understandable: given the large amount of information that goes into a budget, it is easy to overwhelm citizens with confusing and intimidating technical detail. In recent years, with the guidance of the Government Finance Officers Association, budget directors have placed greater emphasis on preparing user-friendly documents. In the face of citizen rejection of tax referenda and support for tax limitations, it is essential to explain clearly how public money is being spent.

Budget preparation

Budget preparation involves several stages: (1) preparing and updating revenue projections; (2) developing budget guidelines; (3) requesting estimates from the departments; (4) reviewing departmental estimates for accuracy; and (5) conducting **executive budget hearings** to decide what to recommend for funding.

Revenue projections

Because the amount that will be available frames the request and approval process, estimating the amount of revenue available for the budget year is the first step in budget preparation. Under target-based budgeting, revenue projections help set the targets for departmental requests; in other forms of budgeting, the projections determine the maximum allowable spending if balance is to be achieved. Typically, a revenue forecast is prepared for each major revenue source, such as property and sales taxes and utility services. For smaller revenue sources such as regulatory fees, a revenue forecast is prepared for the combined totals, often on the basis of historical trends in the amounts received.

Methods of projecting revenues   Four types of techniques are used to project revenues: informed judgment, deterministic techniques, time series techniques, and econometric models.[2] There is an ongoing debate about which method provides the most accurate forecast; in practice, however, most budget offices combine several methodologies, depending on the type of revenue source.

Regardless of other methodologies used, **informed judgment**, or a **professional guess**, is essential to preparing defensible estimates. Even the most elaborate statistical projections require the critical eye of an experienced budget director. Professional judgment comes with experience and careful observation. In Illinois, for example, experienced budget directors have learned that the state's estimate of sales tax growth for the coming year is often overly optimistic. Budget directors and chief executives who may have been caught short in the past also learn to watch carefully for changes in state laws that affect revenue sources—for example, tax limitations, redefinitions of the tax base, changes in the remittance schedule for tax liabilities, authorization of new revenue sources, or changes in the formulas for the distribution of state aid.

Officials learn to distinguish between money they might receive during the year and money they probably will receive—and budget accordingly. For example, local officials know that if the state is usually late in paying its bills, it may try to improve its cash flow by delaying payment of shared revenues to local governments.

The second family of revenue projection techniques—**deterministic**, or **formula based**—relies on a simple mathematical formula. Many local revenues are projected on the basis of such formulas. To calculate the property tax, which is generally the most important source of general revenue for local governments, forecasters multiply the property tax rate by the **assessed value** of all taxable property (the tax base): this equals the levy (the amount of revenue due to the government from this source). This estimate is not necessarily perfect: collection rates may fall, or estimates of assessed valuation may be off. The forecaster takes these possibilities into consideration and adjusts the revenue estimate accordingly.

State aid to school districts is formula driven; state allocation of other shared funds may also be based on formulas. In Illinois, the portion of the state income tax that goes to local governments is computed on the basis of a formula, as is the portion of the gasoline sales tax returned to local governments for road projects. To determine their local government's pro rata share of state revenues, local officials typically determine the total pool of funds available for distribution, then plug their own numbers into the formula. Such estimates are normally close enough for budget preparation purposes. Sometimes the state provides a figure to estimate revenues per capita, in which case the budget office multiplies the state figure by the jurisdiction's population.

The third family of forecasting techniques, **time series analysis**, is based on trends from prior years' data. For some revenue sources, especially those that are not particularly elastic with respect to economic growth (i.e., yield does not change much in response to expansion or contraction of the economy), trend analysis provides a useful and accurate estimate. For example, because growth in fines, fees, licenses, and excise taxes is usually steady from year to year and depends roughly on population size, a simple trend analysis may provide reliable estimates. If revenue from regulatory licenses has been increasing at a steady rate of 4 percent a year, the best estimate for how much they will grow next year is probably 4 percent.

An improved approach to revenue forecasting   Chesterfield County, Virginia (pop. 220,000), has developed a simple, low-cost means of improving its revenue forecasting. In essence, twice a year Chesterfield County invites local business leaders and economic experts to informal meetings with county officials and listens to what they have to say.

County officials call this the Revenue Forum, which they began in 1991. They discovered that the local business leaders and experts in local business activity were more attuned to what the local economy would be like in the near term than were sophisticated national and regional models. County forecasters used information gleaned from the informal forums to adjust their own forecasts and reaped a bushel of benefits. Like most local revenue forecasting, the work done in Chesterfield County was a mixture of techniques that nonetheless was error prone.

Forecasters learned that even small mistakes had multimillion-dollar effects that could hamper crucial county services. They used

Judgmental methods, the use of in-house experts to make judgment calls

Trend analysis, the prediction of the future based on recent trends

Deterministic and econometric models, ones that plug in a variety of variables using what can be very expensive hardware and software.

County forecasters discovered that these were either too "in-house," too married to the past, or too tied to national—as opposed to local—developments. That is when they thought of bringing in local experts who were more attuned to local trends.

Some of the types of local experts asked to contribute to the Revenue

Forums have been the chief economist of the Federal Reserve Bank of Richmond (Chesterfield County is directly south of Richmond), the chief economist of the state's department of motor vehicles, a real estate analyst of a real estate investment firm, the president of a local car dealership, the president of a tax preparation company, the director of a real estate research center at a state university, and the senior vice president of a local bank.

The county staff organizes the Revenue Forums, which are held twice a year, usually over lunchtime, and last about two hours. At the opening of a forum, county forecasters give a summary of their projections. The meeting is then thrown open to the invited outsiders. No one is required to make a formal presentation, but speakers are welcome to show slides or overheads. The main point is to get them to open up about their own areas of expertise and how they see trends in those fields. Consequently, there is a free and candid flow of information.

In the first two years of the forums, the county reaped significant dividends for its $200 investment (for lunch) for each meeting. In one, the county learned enough to make corrections to avoid a $13 million shortfall; in another, it made adjustments that resulted in tax revenues exceeding budget by $2 million— at a time when nearby localities were suffering shortfalls.

Other benefits: elected officials have more confidence in staff projections; the business community is more involved in and has more confidence in the government budgeting process; and the press coverage is favorable.

Source: Adapted from "An Improved Approach to Revenue Forecasting," *What's Working in State & Local Government* (formerly *Financing Local Government* 7, no. 22 [15 May 1995]: 7–8), published by Government Information Services (703/528-1000).

For revenue sources that have more volatile yields but that still grow at a reasonably constant rate, a common approach is to project the yield for the coming year by averaging the yield for several recent years. An estimate based on "running averages" assumes that next year's yield is unlikely to reach either the peaks or the troughs of previous years. This approach minimizes the possibility of badly over- or underestimating revenues.

For highly volatile revenue sources, time series models do not provide accurate forecasts because past history may not be representative of what will happen in the coming year. More sophisticated time series methodologies, such as autoregressive moving averages, mathematically replicate the underlying pattern of change over time and use that pattern to predict future revenue. Suppose, for example, that there had been a long period of growth in sales taxes followed by a dip, then a leveling out, then a resumption of growth. Time series analysis—in its more sophisticated as well as in its simpler forms—assumes that the pattern will repeat itself in roughly the same time frame. For revenues that vary cyclically, such techniques are useful.

However, sometimes a pattern may not repeat itself in exactly the same way. A major annexation and growth in new businesses, followed by a recession and the closing of several retail outlets, may never recur. In addition, even recurring economic patterns—such as recessions—may not be predictable enough for revenue projection. For example, the time from the beginning of one recession to the beginning of the next usually varies between three and seven years. Moreover, the local economic profile and tax base may change, which means that the impact of recessions on revenues may vary from one time period to the next.

Because of some of the shortcomings of time series analysis, many experts recommend **econometric**, or **causal**, **modeling** instead. Econometric models assume that the yield from a particular revenue source, such as the general sales tax, is affected by a number of factors such as per capita income, inflation, and population change. If the approach worked perfectly, these indicators (independent variables) would predict what the sales and income tax yield will be during, say, the next eighteen months. Of course, econometric modeling does not work perfectly, but a statistical model can be helpful in showing how tax revenues respond to the local or regional economy.

The larger and more complicated the local economy and the more complicated the revenue sources, the more useful such models are. In a mid-sized city, it is relatively easy to determine whether revenues are growing because of an annexation or because of a new industrial park. In a massive economy with multiple tax sources, lagged effects, and constant in- and outmigration, such details can get swallowed up. To help determine what affects the economy's growth and how the rate of economic growth affects various revenue sources, officials may need to make a model of their economy; New Orleans used a model like this for many years.

Modeling can be done at many levels of sophistication, from the simplest correlations to the most complex input-output matrixes. At the simplest levels, the forecaster may simply want to know how a rise in building permits or a decline in the unemployment rate (indicators of economic growth) in the current year correlates with—or predicts—sales or income tax yields in the following year. A close correlation means that such indicators can be used to predict how revenues will behave in the coming year. In more complicated models, economists make a statistical map of the local economy and show how changes in the economy affect local revenues. This approach can be effective, but it requires a lot of work and continuous updating; it may also be incomprehensible to noneconomists.

An in-between approach is to purchase a service that provides annual updates of the regional economy and then work out the linkages between variables in the regional economy (such as unemployment rates or personal income) and the local one. For example, do recessions hit your community later than they hit the region, but last longer? Or are recessions milder in your community than in the surrounding region because of a large proportion of businesses that do well during recessions?

Issues in revenue projection   No matter what combination of techniques forecasters apply, some types of revenue are difficult to project, and virtually any type of revenue is difficult to project for the long term. In the case of highly volatile revenue sources, the forecaster will have to rely extensively on informed judgment and careful monitoring of the economic environment. Although it may be tempting to underestimate such revenues, underestimation creates its own difficulties. More and more local governments are undertaking multiyear projections, which can be valuable in averting future problems, but these projections must be made cautiously and with a full understanding of the assumptions on which they rest.

While econometric modeling can help budget forecasters understand the relationship between revenue levels and changes in the economy, its usefulness declines when it is applied to highly volatile revenue sources such as utility taxes. If the local government levies an excise tax on utility charges, revenue yield is obviously affected by any rate change, but it can be affected by a number of other variables as well. For example, if the costs of building a nuclear power plant are above estimate, the cost of electricity may rise, but state regulation may limit the increase that can be passed on to consumers through higher rates. How can anyone predict this? In Illinois, the state deregulated the purchase of natural gas so that large users could make out-of-state purchases. Because of the way that state statutes allowed local governments to tax natural gas, local governments experienced a completely unexpected and unpredictable revenue loss on all out-of-state purchases. A long, hot summer may increase water and electricity usage—and revenues from these utilities; a power outage may increase revenues from telephone use; and a fire in a main telephone transfer station may reduce city revenues from a telephone service utility tax.

When dealing with truly hard-to-predict revenues, a forecaster must use a variety of techniques concurrently. An experienced forecaster looks for announced rate increases and monitors state regulatory agencies that control utility prices. To verify that the government is receiving the revenue to which it is entitled, budget office staff may also need to use the agreements that the locality has (hopefully) negotiated to examine the books of utility companies.

Although underestimation of revenues by the budget office provides a safety margin and is better than overestimation, it should be used cautiously; it is not cost free or policy neutral. The best strategy is accuracy: estimates should be within 1 to 2 percent of actual receipts. Estimates may not be that accurate every year with every revenue source, but this is a realistic goal and an appropriate performance indicator for budget forecasts. Because governments are more likely to aim for accuracy in projections if sufficient reserves exist for unexpected revenue shortfalls, the budget office should push for the creation of rainy day or contingency funds.

One problem with routine underestimates of revenue yields is that they create a general mistrust of the budget office, encouraging political leaders to adjust the numbers upward, often without adequate justification. Second, low estimates may cause unnecessary reductions in departmental staffing or delay capital purchases. Third, low revenue estimates may ultimately create a pool of unallocated revenue that can be spent at the discretion of the manager, mayor, or council during the fiscal year; thus, low estimates may hold down budgeted expenditures without limiting actual expenditures. Expenditures from this revenue pool are more often made in response to political demands than in accordance with technical budgeting considerations; moreover, this type of spending undermines accountability and efficiency because it tends to occur with little publicity or competition among requests.[3]

Revenue projections are essential to preparing a credible budget proposal. Although all local governments prepare revenue projections for at least the forthcoming year, an increasing number prepare multiyear projections that include annual revenue and expenditure estimates for up to five years into the future. One advantage of multiyear projections is that an early, relatively small corrective action can avert a relatively large problem several years down the road. If spending cuts must be made, the longer the lead time, the less drastic the reductions. A second advantage is that multiyear revenue projections can give sufficient lead time for implementing a tax increase or averting an ill-timed revenue reduction. They also give a jurisdiction the flexibility to reduce staff through hiring freezes and attrition rather than through expensive and disruptive reductions in force or other radical measures.

While their potential usefulness is unquestionable, long-term revenue projections have several problems. First, everything else being equal, the longer the period covered by the projection, the lower its accuracy. Inevitably, the longer the forecast period, the more unexpected events intervene—recessions, inflation, regulation or deregulation, changes in state statutes, natural disasters, the relocation of a major employer. Budget preparers should not rely too heavily on projections for the "out-years"—the years after the budget year. Projections more than three years into the future may be so far off as to mislead public policy choices.

A second difficulty with long-range revenue projections concerns credibility. Such projections depend on a variety of underlying assumptions, all of which must be clearly identified, valid, and defensible. (Clearly identifying the assumptions underlying a long-term forecast has the added benefit of alerting elected officials to important budgetary contingencies.) For example, if the half-percent sales tax increase is implemented in March, then the first year's revenue will be $3 million. If inflation remains at 3 percent and there are no new major shopping centers or strip malls, then the sales taxes will increase 6 percent per year. However, if any of these assumptions proves wrong, the credibility of the forecast will be called into question.

Finally, even accurate long-term projections may raise credibility issues. If a local government heeds the warnings of the long-range forecast and takes action to avert the problem, then the problem never occurs. When the budget office next predicts a serious problem, public officials may be skeptical. The very success of long-range forecasting can thus cause a loss of credibility.

Developing budget guidelines

Once revenue projections are in place, the chief executive, in consultation with policy makers, develops budget guidelines for departments to use in preparing their requests. It is at this point that members of the legislative body have an opportunity to provide guidance on spending priorities for the next year.

The budget director or the chief executive explains to elected officials and department heads how the revenue estimates were derived. The budget office, in consultation with the chief executive, may also develop an overall target for expenditures, as well as specific targets for departmental requests.

The budget guidelines are essentially policy statements that provide departments with a sense of the budgetary environment for the forthcoming year: for example, there will be no increase in the property tax rate; to hold down tipping fees for solid waste, we will continue to encourage recycling; more resources will be allocated to economic development; we will continue to support the police department's efforts to control drugs and gangs; we will staff and equip a new fire station coming on line in the budget year. In mayor-council communities, such priorities may come from the mayor; in council-manager jurisdictions, the manager may meet with the council to explore their priorities for the budget proposal.

Other policy decisions that may be addressed at this point include whether to borrow for capital projects (and if so, how much) or whether to lease instead; what the appropriate balance between capital and operating budgets for this year should be; and whether the annual fund balance should be drawn down or increased during the year. In some years, other policy issues may surface, such as how to deal with a decline in intergovernmental revenues, how to allocate resources for road repair, or how much to allocate to neighborhood revitalization or downtown redevelopment. Sometimes the budget office makes recommendations; it may point out, for example, that since interest rates have dropped, it may be the right time to refund outstanding debt obligations and achieve savings in debt service expenditures. The budget office may be called upon to provide estimates of the cost of alternatives: How much will this project cost if we borrow? How much will it cost to lease police vehicles as opposed to purchasing them? On the basis of such information, the chief executive may recommend particular options and build them into the budget proposal.

In some cases, this policy-making phase includes soliciting guidance on goals from the public. The chief executive may meet informally with various groups in the community—the chamber of commerce, the League of Women Voters, neighborhood associations—or convene a town meeting and focus groups to discuss priorities. To help frame the budget proposal, cities such as Dayton, Ohio, regularly collect advice on priorities from neighborhoods; other cities, such as St. Louis, arrange occasional planning sessions with broad segments of the public.

Requesting proposals from departments

To assist departments with the preparation of their requests, the budget office typically prepares a budget manual. Before the budget manual can be prepared, however, the budget office must decide what information it needs from departments. Budget offices tend to ask for far more information than is ever used and to be more quick to request additional information than to drop obsolete or marginally useful forms. This occurs, in part, because from the budget office's perspective, asking for additional information is cost free. The added cost for researching and responding to a request for more detail on capital purchases, for example, is borne at the department level. Unless they are convinced that the additional information will strengthen their case with the chief executive or the governing body, department heads are understandably reluctant to accept this added burden. As a rule, budget offices should carefully scrutinize their forms for obsolescence and redundancy. To help ensure that the manual is clear and that the amount of information requested is reasonable, one approach is to ask budget directors from other units of government to review the manual.

The budget manual Budget manuals are fundamentally similar, but there is some variation in what gets included. At a minimum, a manual contains blank forms and instructions on how to complete them, and examples of completed forms. Typically, it also includes a list of definitions and a **chart of accounts**. Other features that routinely appear in budget manuals include a calendar of the budget preparation schedule, specifying who does what and when. Some manuals include the guidelines for that year, usually in the form of a memo from the chief executive. Many manuals provide a description of the budget process, including the responsibilities of key actors, when they meet, the scope of the issues they will discuss, and the criteria used to judge requests. Some budget manuals include a personnel classification for reference. Others include detailed information on the costs of various supplies and materials routinely purchased by departments.

The contents of the budget manual reflect the comprehensiveness of the budget: some local governments include the **capital budget** process and the grants application and approval process with the operating budget as part of a **unified budget** process, while others separate one or all of these components into distinct processes with their own calendars. Boston, which was under court order to complete a number of large capital projects, established a separate office for the capital budget. That office prepares its own budget manual. The community hearings required under the Community Development Block Grant (CDBG) program are typically conducted separately from public hearings associated with the operating or capital budgets. In San Antonio, Texas, the community development office prepares its own brochure on the budget process for the

---

Common elements of budget preparation manuals

Budget preparation calendar, including due dates for budget forms

A list of forms to be filled out, including budget summaries, supporting data, and estimates of revenues to be generated

Examples of forms to be filled out

A list of definitions (e.g., the number of hours for the calculation of a full-time position)

Instructions for filling out each form

Assumptions, such as inflation rates by type of expenditure

A chart of accounts

CDBG, with a budget calendar in English and Spanish, an explanation of the program, and detailed suggestions on how citizens can participate.

The most important sources of variation in budget manuals are the budget format and the departments' level of involvement. A performance budget, for example, involves a very different set of instructions from a line-item budget; instructions for a target-based budget differ widely from those that would be used with a more traditional, bottom-up process.

Local governments that use a program or performance budget include in the budget manual the forms for enumerating the objectives for the forthcoming year. In the case of performance budgeting, the objectives and **performance measures** are often included in the budget document. Performance budgeting represents a kind of service agreement between the chief executive and council on the one hand and the departments on the other: departments are responsible for achieving the agreed-upon quantity and quality objectives with the money granted.

Dayton's objectives submission form uses four columns. The first asks which, if any, of four community goals the department's objectives are designed to forward. The second calls for a list of objectives. The third column asks for measurable performance criteria. The fourth column asks for a comparison between the number of units promised for the coming budget and the number achieved in the current budget (see Figure 3–1). Thus, the performance criterion may be number of potholes filled; the number last year may have been 5,500 and the number promised this year 5,700. "Units" refers to whatever measures the program uses—percentage approval rates, days to completion of a task, or some more complicated ratio.

In a local government that uses target-based budgeting, the budget manual will explain what is to be excluded from the target budget. In Dallas, for example, capital budget requests are not included in the operating budget targets.

A manual for target-based budgeting may also specify how departmentally generated revenue should be treated. For example, sometimes departments generate **salary savings**, reductions in expenditures that oc-

Figure 3–1 Performance objectives form, Dayton, Ohio.

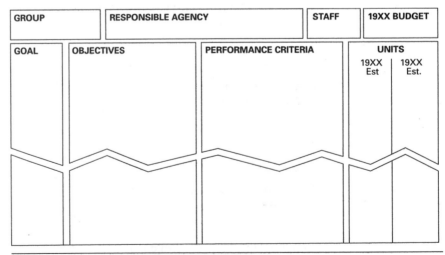

OBJECTIVES SUBMISSION FORM

GROUP	RESPONSIBLE AGENCY	STAFF	19XX BUDGET

GOAL	OBJECTIVES	PERFORMANCE CRITERIA	UNITS
			19XX Est. / 19XX Est.

Source: City of Dayton, Ohio, *Budget Procedures Manual*, August 1981, sec. 3, p. B-3.

cur when personnel changes leave positions unfilled for part of a year. Some local governments estimate salary savings for each department and exclude them from their budget targets. Others allow departments to keep salary savings but place limits on their use—requiring, for example, that these savings be applied to a temporary intern's position.

In a target-based budgeting system, the targets are sometimes too low to permit all necessary and urgent expenditures. Separate forms are usually used to request funding for new items and for old items that do not fit within the department's target but that are still needed. These items are then ranked against requests from all other departments and funded to the limits of available revenue. In Dallas, the budget office incorporates the unfunded list into its longer-term planning for operating expenditures; the long-term consequences of the currently proposed budget—including cuts—are thus more clear, and the city has several years to accommodate unfunded expenditures.

Budget forms   Budget forms are designed to serve several purposes. If the governmental unit does not use target-based budgeting, and if the total of departmental requests exceeds estimated available revenue, the budget office may need enough detail on the request forms to determine what to cut, so that the proposal put before the council is balanced. This information needs to be in a uniform format to ensure that requests make sense when they are totaled; a uniform format also enables the budget office to make comparisons across departments. In target-based budgets, the forms are used to check departmental requests against the targets; they also document the impact of cuts departments have made to meet their targets.

Typically, budget request forms require a summary sheet and supplemental attachments showing the derivation of the numbers in the summary sheet. But different local governments require different levels of detail and request the detail in different locations. Dayton, for example, requires departments (or major divisions within departments) to complete an annual budget request summary that is broken into four main categories: personnel, contracts and materials, capital equipment, and debt service (see Figure 3–2). The first column shows the current year's budgeted amount for each item, the second shows the budget request for the coming year, and the third shows the percent change. A space is left for comments by the office of management and budget (OMB). Requests for program expansion use the same summary form but are presented on a separate page that is clearly marked "Request for Expansion." A detailed list of capital purchases requires estimates of the value and number of the items being purchased and their net cost rather than any comparison with the preceding year. Departmental travel, which is just a line item under contracts and materials, requires a separate, detailed justification. This form lists each trip, with separate columns for the cost, the purpose of the travel, the destination, and the name of the traveler; another column distinguishes travel as part of the job from travel for education or career development, and another column is used to indicate the priority the department places on the trip.

Dallas's summary sheet for each department combines information in an easily readable form (see Figure 3–3): it includes the budget request and three years of comparative data, a mission statement, expenditures by program, worker-years by program, department revenues by program, and departmental totals for each of these categories.

Chicago requires an executive summary sheet for each department, which includes the budget summary, the department or bureau mission,

Figure 3–2 Budget request summary form, Dayton, Ohio.

FUND CODE _____	FUND NAME _____	SERVICE LEVEL

☐ Existing
☐ Reduction
☐ Expansion

ORG. CODE _____   ORG. NAME _____

OBJECT OF EXPENDITURE	1989 BUDGET	1990 REQUEST	% CHANGE	OMB ONLY
TOTAL PERSONNEL COSTS				
2200 Travel				
2301 Waste Disposal				
2302 Communications				
2303 Rents & Leases				
2304 Professional Services				
2305 Maintenance of Equipment				
2306 Maintenance of Facilities				
2307 Insurance & Bonding Service				
2308 Advertising				
2309 Printing & Reproduction				
2310 Election Expense				
2311 Miscellaneous				
2312 Property Taxes				
2313 Non-Departmental Transfers				
2314 Public Service Contracts				
2319 Indirect Cost				
2321 Electric & Power				
2322 Gas				
2323 Steam				
2324 Water				
2401 Supplies & Materials				
2402 Inventory				
2403 Gasoline & Diesel Fuel				
TOTAL CONTRACTS & MATERIALS				
2502 Furniture & Assets				
2506 Motorized Equipment				
TOTAL CAPITAL EQUIPMENT				
2601 Retirement of Debt - Bonds				
2602 Retirement of Debt - Notes				
2611 Interest - Bonds				
2612 Interest - Notes				
TOTAL DEBT SERVICE				
GRAND TOTAL BUDGET				

Submitted By: Approved By:

_____ _____   _____ _____
Division Head   Date   Department Head   Date

Source: City of Dayton, Ohio, budget preparation packet distributed to department heads, 1990.

the status of previous year's initiatives, and proposed program initiatives for the upcoming year. In the budget summary section, only a handful of highly aggregated items are tallied: personnel, nonpersonnel, reimbursements, total number of positions, and grant funds (excluding CDBG). Each of these aggregated items includes a comparison of the current appropriation with the proposed amount; a third column shows the percentage of change.

Chicago requires departments to submit 17 different forms, in quadruplicate, plus 4 more forms to justify personnel changes. Dallas requires 12 operating budget forms, 3 personnel forms, and an additional 7 forms for capital budget requests. Dayton requires 5 operating budget

Figure 3–3 Departmental summary form, Dallas, Texas.

Court services

The Department of Court Services supports the Municipal Court adjudication of Class C misdemeanor cases through clerical, managerial, and law enforcement operations.

Expenditures by program	1989–90 actual	1990–91 budget	1990–91 estimate	1990–92 proposed
Fiscal services	3,036,104	3,098,121	3,098,121	3,098,121
Case management	3,347,775	3,069,123	3,069,123	3,069,123
Total	6,383,879	6,167,244	6,167,244	6,167,244

Worker years by program	1989–90 actual	1990–91 budget	1990–91 estimate	1991–92 proposed
Fiscal services	98.1	95.4	95.4	95.4
Case management	114.5	110.4	110.4	110.4
Total	212.6	205.8	205.8	205.8

Department revenues	1989–90 actual	1990–91 budget	1990–91 estimate	1991–92 proposed
Traffic	13,793,498	10,968,334	10,968,334	10,968,334
Nontraffic	2,673,315	2,228,372	2,228,372	2,228,372
Driver improvement school	399,997	354,981	354,981	354,981
Warrant service fee	723,601	386,281	386,281	386,281
Total	17,590,411	13,937,968	13,937,968	13,937,968

Source: City of Dallas, Texas, *Budget Instructions Manual, 1992*, 25.

forms: the annual budget request summary, contracts and materials detail, capital equipment requests, revenue estimate forms, and departmental travel program summaries. In addition, Dayton's budget office requires 2 forms in which departments state their objectives for the year and 4 additional forms for the capital budget. By contrast, a suburb like St. Charles, Illinois, with a population of 25,000, has only 4 budget forms. Where there are many forms, the budget submission process can be complicated and frustrating for department heads.

Assistance for departments   The budget manual generally provides fairly detailed directions on how to complete the budget forms. The manual ordinarily includes specific instructions (e.g., "Fill in the name of the program in the upper–right-hand corner, and be sure to put page numbers on every page") and also specifies the assumptions department heads should use in making their requests (e.g., "Assume a 4 percent rate of inflation unless the budget office tells you otherwise"; "As the travel proposal for next year, use this year's budgeted amount for travel, not the estimated actual").

Filling out the request forms is nevertheless a fairly complicated process, and most budget offices provide training to assist department heads. Chicago requires two days of training—which is perhaps not surprising, given the number of forms and their complexity. Other cities require a one-day workshop or provide one day of training at the option of the department head. In addition to training, some local governments provide a contact person to answer questions—usually a budget analyst who serves as liaison with that department. The most effective approach—a clear, step-by-step manual (with suitable examples), combined with one-on-one problem solving—focuses the budget office's attention on those departments that need the most help.

To help the departments, some budget offices provide basic information with each department's budget packet—for example, a list of full-time personnel, their current salaries, and any step increases that are due. The budget office may list full-time staff and expect departments to provide information on part-time positions, or it may ask only for changes to a list the budget office already has. These approaches greatly simplify the budget preparation process for departments and tend to make their requests more accurate.

In recent years, some budget offices have further simplified the process by having departments submit requests on computer. Computerized budget forms are distributed to departments on diskette or made available on a network. The budget manual gives instructions for completing each screen. Computerized programs automatically total columns for the budget preparer and alert the preparer to errors before the final request is transmitted to the budget office.

Reviewing departmental requests

In smaller local governments, budget requests may be due from all departments on the same day, but in larger jurisdictions, requests are typically returned to the budget office at staggered intervals. This arrangement distributes the budget office's workload and allows larger departments with more complicated submissions additional time to prepare the documentation.

The budget office first checks the requests for mistakes and for compliance with the guidelines. For example, the budget office may check to see that a department's request includes all mandated costs and reflects the full costs of projects or new staff. It is particularly important to verify that the budget proposal includes items specifically requested by the chief executive or the council.

Under target-based budgeting, departments give the budget office two lists: one of continuing programs funded within the target, and a second of prioritized requests that cannot be funded within the target. The budget office scrutinizes both lists to verify that all required spending—for telecommunications or motor fuel, for example—is included in the base, and that none of the items on the unfunded list should be part of the continuing base appropriation. Departments are typically asked to describe the consequences of not funding each item on the unfunded list. The budget office must examine these explanations to make sure that they make sense and are not exaggerated.

The budget office, often in conjunction with a committee appointed by the chief executive, then prepares an integrated list of unfunded priorities on the basis of a number of criteria, including the council's priorities, the chief executive's goals, information from citizen surveys, estimated impacts on service levels, potential gains to efficiency, and fairness to each department and program. If a department received a substantial new project or piece of equipment one year, the feeling may be that it is now another department's turn, if revenue growth permits.

In local governments that do not use target-based budgeting, departmental requests may be unrealistically high. Some department heads or program managers assume that if they ask for the moon, they will get more than if they had submitted a modest request. Using an across-the-board figure to cut all requests favors those who ask for large increases and penalizes those who ask only for what they need. Instead, the budget office should compare each request with the previous year's allocation and determine whether the requested increase results from mandated expenses, increased workload, innovations that will reduce unit costs, or just aggressive budgeting. Departments that are inflating their requests in hopes of gaining a larger budget share should have their requests pared proportionately. The budget office should also examine proposals for items that have low political priority or appear to be wasteful. Proposals that relate most clearly to the council's priorities should receive funding if at all possible.

Where budget offices are staffed by budget analysts who scrutinize requests from particular departments, each analyst becomes familiar with a unit's budget and its history of prior requests, typically making field visits throughout the year to observe the unit's activities and quality of performance. The analyst becomes a critical resource, advising the budget director on the merits of the unit's spending requests. Budget examiners may ask for further explanation of an item or may be able to analyze a request on the basis of information from prior years. If this information seems inadequate, executive budget hearings provide a second chance for departments to justify their requests—explaining how costs were estimated, what the perceived need is, and what community goals and objectives will be served.

Executive budget hearings

After an initial review by the budget office, the next phase in budget preparation is executive budget hearings, which may be organized in several ways. Department heads may meet one-on-one with the budget director or with the chief executive, explaining the request and answering questions. Alternatively, the chief executive may form a committee to review departmental requests and the budget office's recommendations. The mayor or manager usually chairs the committee; other members may include the deputy or assistant managers and the finance and budget directors (if these positions are separate). Department heads are sometimes included on this committee; the advantage of this arrangement is that it gives department heads an opportunity to see requests made by other units in the context of overall revenue limits. On the other hand, department heads tend to be easy on each other, in the expectation that the kindness will be returned. Executive budget hearings are treated as managerial staff meetings and are normally closed to the public.

In the executive hearings, the department head or program manager offers support for the budget request or for specific items in the request, citing prior accomplishments, the heaviness of the workload, or problems with current equipment. The presentation is often focused on making a vivid case for an expenditure or expansion. Questions may deal with underlying assumptions, such as an anticipated increase in labor costs. Sometimes questions arise about alternative strategies to accomplish the goal or meet the need, but the questions are often just requests for elaboration. What is this project? Do you have blueprints for the building? Where did the cost estimates come from? Do they represent a full year of expenditures? What will be the costs of the proposal in year two or year three?

The chief executive may explore the consequences of not funding the proposal or of delaying it for a year. The discussion at this stage may be exploratory, with the manager or mayor looking through budget requests to find padding and identify requests linked to departmental and communitywide performance goals and objectives. The chief executive may also be trying to read critically the department's answers to certain questions (e.g., What will the consequences be of not funding this item?). If the budget office has effectively screened departmental requests, only the more controversial items will be passed to the manager or mayor for resolution.

Budget review and approval

After the executive hearings, the budget office prepares the budget proposal that will go to the council for consideration. (Chapter 8 describes some of the considerations that go into designing the budget document and preparing it for presentation to the governing body and the public.)

The budget office is normally responsible for the physical layout and production of the budget, which means that decisions such as page size, paper color, binding, cover design, and the location and type of graphics are all part of budget preparation. The document should be user-friendly: given the graphics capabilities of microcomputers, photocopying computer printouts of budget proposals or charts and graphs is no longer sufficient. Before the budget goes to the printer, the budget office staff may spend many anxious hours searching for typos, checking for accuracy and consistency, and ensuring that all totals and percentages are correct and properly labeled.

After the budget is printed, it is formally delivered to the council, often in a three-ringed notebook so that pages can be substituted as changes are made. Council members examine the proposal and pass or reject it— or, to the extent allowed by law, modify the proposal. Local elected officials usually hold formal hearings on the budget proposal. **Legislative budget hearings** are of two types, although they may be combined. In the first type, the manager, with technical support from department heads, presents the proposed budget to the council or board in a series of budget work sessions, during which members of the governing body have an opportunity to question the manager and department heads on spending recommendations.

The second type of legislative budget hearing is a formal public hearing, which may deal solely with proposed revenue increases or may be on the budget proposal as a whole, including proposed tax increases as well as expenditures. A public hearing is a courtroom-like procedure with a formal transcription of the proceedings.

Legislative review

Local legislative bodies typically begin their formal deliberations on the budget by holding work sessions (with the manager, if there is one). Legislative work sessions to analyze the budget proposal are especially important in communities that do not have an executive budget and executive budget hearings. In many small cities, villages, and counties that retain an older pattern of legislative dominance over budget preparation, the departments prepare budget proposals that are then presented either to a commission or to a committee of the local governing body, which reviews the proposals and makes decisions on them.

In legislatively dominated budget processes, parts of the budget proposal may be reviewed separately by a substantive committee of the governing body with oversight responsibility for that section of the budget: a police committee may examine the budget proposal for the police department, or a public works committee may examine the proposal for the public works department. The whole proposal is also reviewed by the finance committee. The substantive committee is generally supportive of expenditures; the finance committee, which is responsible for budgetary balance, is usually more inclined to reduce expenditures to match available revenues.

Committees with jurisdiction over a portion of the budget may hold meetings with the appropriate department heads. However, unless the chief executive or the chair of the finance committee is present to represent the larger need for balance, such meetings can deteriorate if the legislative committee, oblivious of the total effect on spending, adds projects to the budget proposal.

An example from a small community illustrates the need for clarity, appropriate procedures, and some sort of direction in the conduct of legislative work sessions. The work session in this case was a preliminary joint meeting of the finance and public works committees with the director of public works. The mayor and the finance officer were both present, but the finance committee chair was not.

The basic procedure was for the director of public works to go through his budget proposal, subunit by subunit—and almost line by line—and answer council members' questions. Council members, however, were less interested in the lines and more interested in projects—things they could visualize—and in whether costs were recoverable (and hence need not show up in the budget). Although the mayor could have substituted for the finance committee chair and kept the discussion flowing, he failed to do so. The hearing proceeded at cross purposes: no one took notes; often, decisions were not reached—and, according to their own reports, committee members often did not know later what decisions had been made. Moreover, the meeting occurred before the determination of revenue estimates. To say that the order of decision making was confused understates the case.

Whether work sessions are with the full council or with council committees, staff must report on the most current revenue estimates to ensure that the sessions are effective. Without at least some budget guidance, each department head may create a wish list that overwhelms council members. In the case described, the council had told the public works director that he should pare down his proposal before they saw it—and that they would then try to pass it. He drew up his wish list instead. The council then insisted that he pare down his requests for the next session, vaguely threatening to cut each line by 10 percent if necessary.

One factor contributing to the confusion in the work session was that the public works director had omitted many major items from his proposal—some by accident, some intentionally. The finance officer should have gone over the budget request before the meeting to verify that all items were included. There were two additional problems—one circumstantial, the other structural. First, the chair of the finance committee happened to be absent from the meeting; his presence might have provided some of the order and direction that the meeting lacked. Second, budget deliberations were structured so that personnel costs were not addressed during departmental work sessions but considered in a separate series of sessions devoted to personnel only. Thus, the departmental totals that the committee was considering *excluded* personnel.

In the community cited in the example, because the council members did not know the sum of departmental requests until the end of the first round of hearings, they felt free to add their own requests to those of the department. Although this approach may facilitate the council committees' involvement in the development of budget requests (because each committee may add to departmental budget requests, without constraint), the disadvantage is an overwhelmingly large volume of budget requests that the council has no rational way to reduce. In the example, council members added their own requests to the budget request. Before the work sessions begin, the chief executive or finance director should review with the council the totals of the requests across departments and determine what needs to be done to balance the budget if it is not yet at that point.

In the example, several points of confusion concerning what should be included in the budget ran throughout the workshop. For instance, because he did not want the council to forget about it, the public works director kept a project in the budget that had not been funded in prior years. In addition, the council seemed to believe that if a project was to be self-funded—even if that meant that the city had to lay out funds in the current budget with the expectation of being paid back sometime in the indefinite future—the project could be excluded from the budget.

The proceedings would have run more smoothly if criteria had been laid out in advance specifying what should appear in the budget and how reimbursables should be treated. In short, budget and finance policies, such as those described in Chapter 2, should have been reviewed and updated in advance of the budget workshops. Someone needs to take responsibility for reminding council of the legal constraints on their deliberations and of prior policy decisions that they are working under—including what funds, if any, should be excluded from the budget. A mayor or manager can take this responsibility, as can the chair of the governing body or of the finance committee.

In the example, the council committee and the department head knew each other well. In this small, intimate group, feelings were more important than facts. At one point in the hearings, a committee member told the public works director "not to bite her head off." A little more formality in the proceedings may have helped keep emotions at a lower pitch, and clearer ground rules would have reduced the level of conflict. The council members' reaction to the emotion the budget process generated was to take the easy way out: in one case, they agreed to take money from an unused line in the water department budget—without telling the director of the water department because he might get upset if he knew. In another case, council members argued that they would cut line items across the board because it "doesn't look like much." By cutting each item in the budget by the same percentage, the council avoided contentious policy choices.

Budget work sessions tend to run more smoothly when there is a professional manager to recommend what should be in the budget, ensure that council members do not have to resolve technical issues themselves, and call attention to legal and policy constraints at the beginning of the budget process. The manager also ensures that by the time the council sees the proposal, it is already balanced, so that policy makers are not overwhelmed by requests that exceed revenues. Local governments that do not have a manager must find a substitute for one. One possibility is for the budget director or comptroller to collect and review budget requests in advance and tentatively balance the requests: this is how budgeting was done in cities before executive budgeting reforms gave more budget power to the mayor and, later, the manager.

When there is a manager, the department heads' opportunity to make a presentation comes during the executive budget hearings before the finance or budget director and the manager. The presentation to the council should be made by the manager—although a department head whose portion of the budget is being presented by the manager should be available to answer questions. Presentations by department heads directly to the council encourage the kind of personal relationships that result in emotional decision making. Equally important, direct presentations undermine the council's view of the manager as the individual in charge of the executive agencies, opening the door to end runs around the manager by members of council.

If they do not already exist, the finance director, in cooperation with the finance committee, should work out a set of policies to guide budget deliberations. One of the policies should specify the level of formality— requiring, for example, a transcription of the meeting with a summary of issues decided and those awaiting action. Another policy should describe the steps in decision making, specifying that the revenue estimates should precede budget workshops. Even in small jurisdictions with a limited professional staff, budget workshops between board members and department heads need not be as chaotic as in the example.

Public budget hearings

Any citizen can make a statement before the council, although the ease of doing so varies. Some local governments require citizens to sign up in advance and do not tell them when they will speak, forcing them to attend the full session—often during work hours. Others ask citizens to sign up just before the meeting begins, then provide an opportunity to speak at the beginning of the meeting, usually in the evening.

When public hearings are legally required but citizens do not attend, the hearings may become a formality. The mayor may say, "The hearing is now in session. Will citizens come forward to speak?" No one comes forward. The mayor closes the hearing and proceeds to the next item on the agenda.

Local government managers and budget officers often complain about citizens' lack of interest in budget hearings, although citizens do sometimes participate in tax hearings—especially in states such as Florida and Utah, where property owners receive individualized notice of the impact on their liability of a proposed change in the tax rate. Local officials' experiences with hearings tend to be negative, which reinforces the tendency to treat such hearings as mere formalities. Because many local officials have lost sight of what hearings are supposed to accomplish, they take few steps to ensure that the hearings are successful.

Moreover, the council's role, which is to review and approve the executive budget proposal, sometimes becomes confused with the role of citizens in a way that interferes with the goals of a public hearing. For example, if the only citizens who attend public hearings are the angry ones, the council may spend its time defending prior choices rather than listening to citizens or learning from staff. Legislative examination of the budget is more effective if it is not concurrent with a public hearing; council members can then ask the questions that puzzle them or explore issues in depth.

In 1927, budget reformer Wylie Kilpatrick argued that elections alone did not give the public sufficient control over government. Kilpatrick felt that budget hearings should be used to consult citizens about what they wanted from government.

The public budget hearing now used does not do this. The public hearing is a conspicuous failure; it assumes a spontaneous welling up of interest from the public; it is generally perfunctory. The hearing presumes that the voter can recreate for himself out of haphazard information a balanced picture of local finance. He cannot. His interest is special. It relates to the special services of import to him personally. It is rarely spontaneous. It is roused by particular subjects and a definite responsibility.[4]

Kilpatrick argued that to motivate citizen participation, budgets must address specific interests. Citizens want to know how the budget affects them: higher attendance at tax hearings than at budget hearings confirms this view.

Unfortunately, most local government budgets are written so as to obscure individual interests—perhaps to avoid stimulating more demands or to avoid creating an impression of inequity. The fear of controversy has resulted in a numbingly boring document. Equally numbing are the oral presentations that often accompany the unveiling of the printed document. Rather than get involved in local government and develop a feeling of ownership in the services provided, citizens either turn away from government altogether or support ill-considered, across-the-board tax limits. Instead of damping down controversy and putting the public to sleep (except at tax time, when anger is likely to erupt), budgeters may need to learn to spark interest in the budget and to handle any controversy that results.

Budget and even tax hearings have tended not only to be formalistic and dull, but also to be intimidating, often unintentionally. Staff and elected officials can easily forget how difficult it may be for an ordinary citizen to speak in front of the council, reporters, staff, and neighbors; it is also easy for staff and council members to lapse into a discussion of the intricacies of the budget, further intimidating citizens who lack an insider's knowledge of the budget. The overall impression may be that citizens' opinions are not welcome because policy makers have already made up their minds.

A few excerpts from a hearing on a tax proposal illustrate how easy it is for citizens to leave a hearing feeling that their opinions are not wanted.

The hearing took place in 1990. The mayor had set up the agenda so that the first item would be a presentation by the city manager explaining why expenditures were up and why new revenues were needed; this would be followed by comments from the council and then from the public.

The structure of the hearing had an intimidating effect. Forcing the audience to listen to council members' views before they expressed their own deprived citizens of an opportunity to simply express their opinions: any disagreement with the council would appear to be a challenge. Moreover, the arrangement undermined any sense that the citizens could actually affect the outcome; council members seemed to have already made up their minds. At the close of the manager's presentation, for example, one of the elected officials commended him for a clear and excellent report. Any citizen who might have criticized the manager's report would have had to think twice: the audience had just been told that it was "an excellent report." The rest of the meeting only intensified the adversarial aura of the proceedings.

The first public witness was a well-known, strongly critical citizen activist. After objecting briefly to the proposed tax, the citizen told the meeting that she wanted to defend herself and her husband.

The mayor said we are new here and can't comment. We have donated thousands of hours of volunteer time and dollars, we are renovating our Victorian home, we studied [the community's] history, we created five jobs. The mayor is sending a message to newcomers, "You'd better not say anything." That is not democracy.

The mayor, in turn, defended himself.

What I told your husband was about the landfill contract. You came one-and-a-half years ago; we have dealt with it over the last twelve years. You need an answer on the proposed restaurant tax. You have a right to ask questions. You didn't take it the way I meant it. These issues are years accumulating. We have done one heck of a job, providing quality and quantity of services. We have experienced mandated loss of revenues. I have been at this for years. If my comments were taken in the sense that you shouldn't be allowed to speak, that wasn't my intention.

First, by arguing back, the mayor gave the impression that the council would refute or debate key points made by citizens, which has a chilling effect on all but the most practiced debaters. Moreover, although he was attempting to refute the witness's argument, the mayor in effect confirmed it: the implication of his words was that only those who had struggled with the issues for years—that is, longtimers at city hall—were in a position to speak. Second, council members may have felt annoyed by some of the witness's opinions, but their responses created an environment in which some comments were clearly off-limits; later comments from witnesses referred to this prohibition. In case the council's intolerance for criticism was unclear, one of the council members made an emotional speech confirming it.

Quoting out of context the city manager, the mayor, and me—it's not appreciated. To ask whether we are good enough. Let them sit up here. We don't like the decisions we have to make. I don't like to hear derogatory comments about the staff—these people work eight, ten, twelve hours a day. They would like to eat and stay home with their families. I don't like comments about staff. Those things don't help us make decisions. I will listen to people, but not to be put down. We don't appreciate it.

To cap things off, when one public witness asked why automobile sales received more favorable tax treatment than restaurants, a council member shot back, "I guess they have a stronger lobby than you do." What made this comment especially egregious was that, as one of the council members had pointed out, the tax on restaurants was considered more acceptable than other taxes because it fell more heavily on students than on permanent residents, not because of the restaurant lobby. The comment about the lobby is the sort that breeds cynicism and a sense of powerlessness among citizens.

This tax hearing was an example of local officials and citizens operating at cross-purposes. Council members had called the hearing not because they wanted to hear citizens' opinions but because they were required to do so by law; they then used the opportunity to defend themselves rather than to solicit citizens' views. Moreover, the council set various limits on what citizens could legitimately say: citizens could not be critical of staff and had to know the history of various issues before they could comment. Finally, the meeting was structured as if council members had already made up their minds. Given that the council's views were presented before citizens had had a chance to say anything, it would have been difficult for any citizen to believe that his or her opinions could influence council decisions. The citizens who attended were interested parties who would be affected by the new tax laws: they came expecting to influence the outcome and left feeling that the council was hostile to them.

Requiring public hearings on tax increases remains popular as a means of controlling the overall tax burden and ensuring that government does not grow beyond politically acceptable levels. However, if the tax hearing is held after local officials have winnowed through proposals and arrived at one they think least likely to upset a majority of voters, the council will probably act defensively when citizens voice discontent.

A better approach would be to involve citizens earlier in the budget process by inviting them to a hearing at which several taxing alternatives, all of which are under consideration, would be presented. An added benefit of this arrangement is that as citizens listen to each other's concerns, they may learn more about the overall burdens and consequences of taxation and realize that they are not being singled out. The council may ultimately choose to distribute the burden or to eliminate some groups from consideration for additional taxation. In either case, citizens are likely to feel more satisfied with the outcome of the hearing and more effective in shaping local government policy.

If council members have not made a final decision, they are less likely to try to defend the government's performance or the executive's proposal; they are free to listen and to learn about objections to various proposals, as well as to judge the level of support. In short, public hearings are more effective if they occur earlier in the budget process, when there is still flexibility to choose among alternatives and before policy makers are locked into defending their preferences.

Citizens come to tax hearings because they can see how their interests are affected; if they could see how the budget proposal affects services that they want—and if they thought that their participation might affect the outcome, citizens would come to budget hearings as well. Research on hearings associated with general revenue sharing indicates that when cities held hearings voluntarily, resource allocations were actually changed, but when cities were forced by law to hold hearings, nothing changed. It was almost as if local officials said, "Okay, we'll hold the hearings, but we don't have to listen." Over time, citizens lost interest in revenue sharing hearings.[5] Evidently, citizens became convinced—correctly—that they had no effect on the outcomes of decision making. Why should they participate? Failure to create incentives for participation in tax and budget hearings risks seriously alienating voters, which fuels general anger at government and increases the likelihood that tax and bond referenda will be rejected.

Approval

Whether the governing body has a large or small say in the formulation of the budget and whether it can add spending proposals or only cut the executive's proposed budget, elected officials normally must approve the budget before it goes into effect.

Council members reviewing the budget may approve it as a whole or break the budget into parts and vote on each separately; the decision is usually strategic. If there is little controversy over the budget, then it may be approved as a whole. If parts of the budget remain controversial even after hearings and after proposals have been modified to meet council members' expectations, some policy makers may show their dissatisfaction by refusing to approve the entire budget unless their concerns are addressed.

The budget is considered for approval at either a regular or special public meeting. Inquiries and decision making have generally preceded this session, but council members may use this occasion to take symbolic stands and to provide sound bites for the press. Provided that the statements designed for public consumption are made at the end of the decision-making process, rather than when citizen opinion is being sought, it should be possible to allow council members to express their views without jeopardizing the passage of the budget: explaining votes to the public is not an unimportant part of the public budgeting process.

After the budget is legislatively approved, the mayor often has the power to **veto** parts or all of it. A **line-item veto** permits the mayor to eliminate individual line items; less frequently the mayor has the right to unilaterally reduce line items. In keeping with the system of checks and balances at the state and federal levels, the council then has the option of overriding the mayor's actions. Mayoral veto power is usually used circumspectly, but it is used on occasion. Also, the budget may be formally amended after both the mayor and council have approved it, and the budget may be reprinted to show the amendments. If a collective bargaining agreement is reached after the budget has been approved, a **budget amendment** may be necessary to reflect the results of the new labor contract. If revenues fall below expectations or grow beyond projections during the year, local charters or state statutes may allow for a formal budget amendment. Changes sometimes accumulate without formal amendment, in which case the council usually passes a year-end budget amendment to reflect what actually transpired. Formally amending the budget during the year has the advantage of bringing requested changes back to the council for discussion and public airing. On the other hand, making too many budget amendments conveys the impression that the chief executive and the governing body have done a poor job of estimating revenues and planning expenditures. Many communities limit formal budget amendments to one or two major changes and make smaller changes informally, passing them retroactively at the end of the year.

Summary

Although the precise roles and responsibilities of the budget office may vary somewhat, depending on its location within the organizational structure and the size and form of the local government, the budget office generally undertakes revenue projections, assists in the development of budget guidelines, collects and reviews departmental requests, and participates in executive budget hearings. The budget office is also typically responsible for preparing the budget proposal for consideration by council.

Legislative review of the proposal often occurs at council work sessions involving department heads, the budget office, and the chief executive. The budget will also be presented at public hearings. Both council work sessions and public hearings can often be improved. In the case of work sessions, a set of policies to guide budget deliberations can be of considerable help. Increasing citizen participation in budget and tax hearings requires a number of steps: first, clearly stating the issues that affect citizens; second, including citizens before decisions are complete, to reduce elected officials' defensiveness and to increase their opportunity to listen and learn; third, making clear in the budget and in press releases when citizens' opinions have influenced decision making. Citizens need to know that they were effective in shaping the outcome of the budget.

A successful budget process depends, in part, on the participants' fulfilling their roles: first, the chief executive and the budget office must present a balanced budget proposal and educate the governing body about legal and financial constraints; second, elected officials and the public must present their opinions to staff; third, staff must incorporate these policy statements into the budget. The result should be a balanced budget that responds to the preferences of the council and the community. Although citizens' and council members' requests should not be allowed to upset budgetary balance, balance should not be achieved at the expense of closing the budget process to citizens and elected officials. Over time, such a solution is much too costly in terms of public support.

1   Arthur E. Buck, *Public Budgeting* (New York: Harper, 1929), 442–43.

2   For a good discussion of these techniques and an extensive bibliography, see Howard Frank, *Budgetary Forecasting in Local Government: New Tools and Techniques* (Westport, CT: Quorum Press, 1993).

3   See Irene S. Rubin, "Estimated and Actual Urban Revenues: Exploring the Gap," *Public Budgeting and Finance* 7 (winter 1987): 83–94; John Forrester and Daniel Mullins, "Rebudgeting: The Serial Nature of Municipal Budgetary Processes," *Public Administration Review* 52 (September/October 1992): 467–73;

Thomas Lauth, "Midyear Appropriations in Georgia: Allocating the 'Surplus,'" *International Journal of Public Administration* 11, no. 5 (1988): 531–50.

4   Wylie Kilpatrick, *State Administrative Review of Local Budget Making: An Examination of State Supervision of Local Taxes and Bonds in Indiana and Iowa* (New York: Public Administration Service, 1927), 36.

5   Richard L. Cole and David A. Caputo, "Citizen Participation Mechanism: A Case Study of the General Revenue Sharing Program," *American Political Science Review* 78 (June 1984): 404–16.

4 Budgeting as policy making

Budgeting as policy making

Policy and budgeting cannot be separated: all budgets reflect decisions about a variety of policy issues such as whom to tax and how much, what new programs to fund, and what programs to reduce or terminate.

The policies made in the course of the budget process can be developed openly and deliberately, or they can be made with little purposeful attention or systematic exchange of information and ideas. Making policy decisions openly may increase the level of conflict: policies that are neither examined nor discussed cannot be challenged. Although those who benefit from current policies may prefer that they remain unexamined, there are disadvantages to ignoring policy issues in order to maintain the status quo.

First, failure to scrutinize policy issues denies managers an opportunity to consider new options or to evaluate new technical information. Should streets be blacktopped or paved with concrete? What are the relative costs of the two methods? Are concrete roads built now as durable as those built in the past? New techniques and construction materials may affect decisions about how streets should be paved, and calculations made forty years ago may no longer apply.

Second, without explicit consideration of a policy, it is impossible to sort major conflicts into smaller, more resolvable pieces or to reframe problems so that they are less contentious. For example, major urban renewal projects sometimes create tensions between downtown and outlying neighborhoods. One way to reframe the problem is to redraw the boundaries of decision making: Dayton, Ohio, for example, created wedge-shaped capital improvements zones; each wedge contains a portion of the inner city and a portion of the outlying area.

Third, suppressing discussion keeps in place the policies of prior elected or appointed officials. This deprives citizens, interest groups, and recently elected or appointed officials of the opportunity to make an impact; moreover, those who made unsuccessful efforts to gain elected or appointed office are similarly denied a forum in which to air their views. If local government is perceived as a closed system that excludes citizens, interest groups, newly elected or appointed officials, and office seekers alike, participation is discouraged; the result is dangerously undemocratic.

Fourth, if policies are not periodically reexamined, staff can feel left out of policy making. The cost of alienating local government staff is the loss of their creativity and extra effort. For example, if those who represent a valid, innovative outlook (e.g., in the fire service, an emphasis on prevention rather than suppression) cannot make themselves heard, they may put their energy elsewhere—and the local government may lose a major resource for improving productivity and service effectiveness.

The cost of alienating citizens is even steeper. Residents who view local government as unaccountable and uncontrollable are more inclined to vote for rigid tax and spending limitations, hamstringing local officials. When citizens cannot see how their participation influences public decisions, they often cease to participate; many have done just that. Moreover, citizens who continue to be active are often those with narrow interests or strong ideological agendas; for public officials to deprive themselves of access to a broad spectrum of public opinion does not make governing any easier.

The costs of failing to make explicit, deliberate decisions are powerful arguments for opening up policy making in the budget process. Although the resulting level of conflict may be higher, controversy can be controlled and constructively channeled to yield a lively, involving, and productive process.

This chapter examines a number of policy decisions that are made in the course of budget deliberations—decisions about taxation, revenue transfers, allocation, and the budget document. The chapter also provides guidelines for involving various participants in the budget process and for handling the controversy that may arise when policy making is "opened up."

Policy issues in budget deliberations

At least four sets of policy decisions are made during budget deliberations: (1) decisions on taxation; (2) decisions on the transferability of revenue from one purpose to another; (3) decisions on allocations; and (4) decisions on budget presentation. The next four sections examine these issues in detail.

Taxation

Every public budget reflects decisions about taxation—what taxes to levy, at what rates, and what exemptions to grant and to whom. When elected officials are asked to consider new or increased taxes, they often do a rough sort of policy analysis: they analyze the political acceptability of increases in different taxes and ask staff (1) how much revenue will be generated by different taxing alternatives and (2) how likely consumers are to relocate or to purchase goods elsewhere to avoid higher tax burdens.

Policy decisions about revenues are often made or expressed explicitly at the beginning of the budget process. The council may give guidance such as "Freeze the property tax rate this year," or "Try to increase service charges." There may also be an implicit policy of looking for taxing options that will place some of the burden on nonresidents; for example, a hotel/motel tax falls largely on tourists.

Some policy making on taxes is triggered by external events that force a jurisdiction to decide how to replace lost revenues. For example, a community may experience a sharp decline in intergovernmental grants; or, as long-distance phone rates decrease, a tax on long-distance phone calls may produce less revenue. Statewide caps on particular revenue sources can require a local government to reexamine its dependence on particular taxes. If a community has become dependent on an **income elastic** source of revenue (one that increases or decreases as the economy grows or shrinks), such as a general sales tax, it may find itself in trouble when revenue growth slows significantly at the end of an expansionary period. Many revenue declines are linked to trends that can be monitored; the finance department can give early warning that certain revenue sources are shrinking and that new policies are needed.

In the taxation area, some of the policy decisions that may require discussion during budget deliberations include the following:

1. Whether to increase, maintain, or reduce the level of specific revenue sources
2. Whether to target nonresidents through hotel/motel taxes, general sales taxes, or gambling taxes
3. What balance of income-elastic and inelastic revenues to aim for
4. Whether to reduce unpopular taxes, such as property taxes, in favor of more popular taxes, such as sales taxes
5. Where there is local discretion to alter the tax base, how **regressive** (relatively more burdensome on lower-income households) to make sales taxes
6. How much effort to put into obtaining intergovernmental grants, especially when such grants include matching or maintenance-of-effort requirements
7. How much to depend on fees for service and how to make such fees affordable, if necessary.

Revenue transfers

Within legal limits (and sometimes outside them), local governments often make transfers for policy purposes—for example, to keep property taxes down; to subsidize the costs of services such as water, electricity, mass transit, or airports; and to balance the budget without increasing taxes or cutting services. On the one hand, the ability to transfer revenue increases budgetary flexibility; on the other hand, excessive transfers seriously alter priorities in the budget and may obscure chronic deficits, delaying corrective action. In addition, such transfers may shift the burden of taxation from one group to another, sometimes with odd consequences. This section examines the constraints, disadvantages, and purposes of transfers between funds.

Earmarking   A set of legal constraints known as **earmarking** sometimes preempts policy decisions on transfers. Any dollar of revenue may come with strictures about how it may be spent. Many state and federal grants, for example, are earmarked for particular types of projects, denying local governments authority to shift grant funds from one purpose to another.

Because of the confusion that can result from excessive transfers between funds, many states have made transfers illegal. In some states, such as Illinois, the property tax levy is divided by law into a series of levies for non–home-rule communities. If these small cities raise a levy for recreation, the revenue is earmarked for recreation only; similarly, the levy for police protection can be spent only for that service. Such extreme earmarking is designed to keep taxes down, by preventing money that is not needed for one function from being transferred elsewhere. The result, however, is a budgetary straitjacket: a jurisdiction that has more money than it needs in one fund and less than it needs in another is unable to legally transfer the surplus to cover the deficit.

Very narrowly defined levies can lead to some odd effects. For example, in non–home-rule communities in Illinois, police protection funds and police pension funds are separate, with revenue earmarked for each one. However, the revenue to be levied for police protection is capped by law, while the revenue that can be levied for police pensions is not. This difference encourages local governments to limit police salaries (from the police protection fund) and offer larger pensions (from the police pension fund) to compensate. Since salaries are more visible to the public than pensions, the structure creates a bias toward less visible expenditures in police compensation. The lack of a cap on pensions also means that financial management practices in this area may receive less scrutiny. Local governments may estimate pension costs and set the levy to cover them, without asking whether the costs are as low as they can be.

While the level of earmarking often seems beyond the control of local governments, there are a number of areas of potentially greater choice. For example, by structuring their budgets so that the general fund is larger and more inclusive and other funds are smaller and fewer, home-rule jurisdictions in Illinois can maximize managerial discretion over how revenue is spent.

Constraints on enterprise fund transfers   Enterprise funds are set up for programs such as utility services, which operate like businesses, bring in revenue from the sale of goods or services, and generally cover their operating and capital costs. Because transfers involving enterprise funds raise a number of policy issues, they should not be made without due consideration of potential consequences.

First, enterprise fund transfers may be limited by state and local laws. In addition, **bond covenants** or bond enabling ordinances often make such transfers illegal. When adding to or renovating a municipal or county enterprise, local governments sell revenue bonds to pay for the improvements, then repay the loan with revenue earned from the enterprise. To make investors feel secure about purchasing the bonds, the bond covenant may require net income from the project to be significantly larger than the amount of debt service; the covenant may also stipulate that surplus revenue from the enterprise is unavailable for transfer. Failure to observe such restrictions leads to bondholders' lawsuits. When local governments issue such bonds, the governing body or board must approve the sale, and the **bond ordinance**, or law approving the sale, specifies how revenues may be spent.

Apart from legal constraints, however, there are a number of other reasons to limit transfers into and out of enterprise funds. First, by obscuring actual costs and revenues, transfers make it difficult to determine rates for publicly provided services. The simplest way to set rates is to charge exactly what the service costs to produce, assuming no transfers in or out. Setting the price at the cost of production has two advantages: (1) it helps ensure budgetary balance in the enterprise fund and (2) it protects against the temptation to transfer money out of the enterprise fund to balance other funds—without dealing with the underlying problems that created the deficits in those funds. Any rate changes should reflect changes in production costs.

A second reason to be wary of enterprise fund transfers is that they can mislead citizens, auditors, and representatives of higher levels of government. Citizens may not realize, for example, that they are paying for police, fire, and public works through their water bills—which is what occurs if the water fund is transferring surplus revenue to the general fund. Jurisdictions that transfer money out of enterprise funds to subsidize the general fund are adding an invisible—and hence uninterpretable—tax to the service being sold. Multiple transfers can also be used to mislead auditors and granting agencies: if, for example, money is transferred out of one account into another for a legally acceptable purpose, then transferred out of the second account for a purpose that would not have been permitted if the transfer had come from the first account. If the transfer had been made directly, it would have been illegal; made indirectly, it leaves a less visible trail for auditors.

Third, if revenue is transferred out of an enterprise fund to the general fund, the result may be that citizens pay for police and fire services in proportion to their use of electricity, water, tennis courts, or golf courses. Some cities, for example, sell electricity and transfer some of the "profits" from electricity sales to the general fund. As a consequence, households with electric ranges pay more for police and fire protection than those with gas stoves, because households with gas stoves are likely to use less electricity. Paying for services in this manner has obvious implications for the distribution of the burden for financing local services.

Finally, a number of other problems arise when transfers are made from the general fund to an enterprise fund; such transfers constitute subsidies from general taxpayers to the customers of the enterprise. Even when there are good public policy reasons for a subsidy, it can be difficult to determine an appropriate level for the subsidy. Moreover, because they create the impression that deficits will be covered, subsidies to enterprises may encourage poor management.

Uses of enterprise fund transfers Despite the many reasons to separate enterprise revenues from other local government money, transfers between enterprise funds and other funds are fairly common. One source of the appeal of enterprise fund transfers is the public's preference for user fees over taxes. Because citizens feel that they can control their level of usage—and hence control the level of their fees—it is often easier politically to raise revenues by increasing water or sewer fees than by increasing tax rates. The more virulent the antitax sentiment, the more likely a community is to use enterprise revenues to subsidize general-fund activities. For example, one common practice involves the purchase and resale of electricity. Some cities buy electricity from a private utility company at wholesale prices and resell it to residents at near-retail prices. The profit transferred to the general fund is used to hold down property taxes or expand services. In Florida, cities with weak tax bases use the profits of electric utilities to obtain revenues from tax-exempt institutions, homeowners, and nonresidents.[1] Selling services to keep taxes down is a policy choice.

One appeal of transfers *from* the general fund *into* a public enterprise is to keep prices below market levels. For example, the history of power production in Los Angeles indicates that representatives of the business community wanted the city to produce power and sell it to them cheaply—that is, the business community wanted a subsidy from the general taxpayers.[2] In other situations, the governing body has been the source of political pressure to set lower rates for low-income households or to extend credit and maintain service when customers were unable to pay their utility bills.[3]

A local government that uses transfers into or out of enterprise funds should do so with great care. Setting limits on the transferred amounts allows flexibility but protects against some of the more serious consequences of excessive transfers. Such limits maintain the integrity of the initial budget; avoid repeated bailouts—which encourage mismanagement; and help ensure that pricing policies makes sense.

Local governments use a variety of methods to decide how much money is appropriate to transfer. For example, many jurisdictions that transfer money from enterprise funds into the general fund use the argument that such payments are in lieu of taxes. That is, if a private company were delivering the service, it would have to pay taxes to the local government. Since the local government is providing the service itself, it can pay itself the equivalent of what the private company would have paid in taxes. Assuming that this argument is legal under state law, it is one justifiable basis for determining how much to transfer—and hence, how to set rates.

Another way to set a limit on funds that can be transferred is to argue that a publicly provided service is entitled to a return on capital investment comparable to what an investor would obtain in the private sector. Assuming that the local government correctly determines the comparable return on investment for private industry, this can provide an appropriate rationale for transfers.

While water departments and electric utilities often earn profits—and hence may be viewed as sources of money for other purposes—other enterprises often lose money. Large regional airports usually earn revenues in excess of expenditures (the public sector's version of a profit) but the vast majority of small municipal airports regularly lose money. Mass-transit operations, even large regional authorities, normally operate at a loss, and the deficits may be made up through transfers from the general fund. However, unless such transfers have a clear rationale and justifiable limits that are stated in advance and adhered to, continual bailouts may encourage or obscure poor management.

In summary, a number of policy decisions are associated with interfund transfers. One issue is the trade-off between flexibility and accountability. Generally speaking, the more transfers and the more flexibility, the less comprehensible and less accountable the budget. When the issue is transfers between enterprise and other funds, a host of additional policy issues emerge. Who is being subsidized by the transfers, at whose expense, and for what purpose? Is there a public policy purpose, or is the goal simply to cover the deficit of one fund with the surplus of another? Are transfers obscuring managerial or pricing problems? Moreover, do citizens understand what is being done, and would they approve if they did?

Allocation

The allocation of resources to various projects and programs raises a number of policy issues: For example, will services and capital projects be distributed on the basis of need or geography? Where technical standards conflict with neighborhood demands, which will prevail? Should funding for downtown redevelopment be increased or decreased?

If a county has five commissioners, all elected at large, there may be little, if any, pressure for geographical distribution of projects or services. In many local governments, however, at least some members of the governing body are elected from districts. In one council-manager city in which the council was elected by district, a quarrel erupted because one area of the city had received less funding for street repairs than other areas. It turned out that in that part of the city there were many concrete streets, which last longer and require less maintenance than blacktopped streets. The public works department had based its maintenance schedule on need, with the result that a disproportionate amount of money went to areas with blacktopped streets. The council members from districts that had more concrete streets objected to the allocations, arguing that street repair budgets should be roughly proportional to district size—and that if concrete streets made that impossible, then all streets should be blacktopped.

There are many instances in which technical standards may conflict with neighborhood demands or with distribution of funds by election district. Although department heads and program managers may feel that technical requirements should be the sole basis for allocation decisions, this may not always be the case. Technical requirements for traffic signals consider the number of cars coming through an intersection, the speed of the traffic flow, and the history of accidents at the intersection. For the neighborhood, the loss of one child's life may be so devastating and the perceived threat to children so urgent that technical considerations are immaterial. The residents' desire to use government to solve a pressing problem is reasonable; not to respond in such a sensitive situation would risk turning these residents against local government officials. Demand for stop signs, streetlights, or additional police officers can reach an absurd level in some neighborhoods, but technical criteria are not always the sole values on which to base decisions. Where there is sufficient flexibility under state law, the budget process should allow for compromise between technical needs and political responsiveness. The challenge for mayors and managers lies in finding and implementing the right balance between efficiency and political responsiveness.

By allocating funds to one program or another, the budget emphasizes preventive, suppressive, or restorative strategies. How much is spent on preventing versus suppressing crime, or preventing versus suppressing fire? How much is spent on new construction versus the restoration of existing buildings? What are the costs of jailing drug users, compared to the costs of rehabilitating them? Most local governments would benefit from a more explicit discussion of the most cost-effective balance among allocation strategies. One can easily argue, for example, that public health services have been allowed to deteriorate too far, and that a more active program of community nursing, with its preventive orientation, could deliver health care much more cost-effectively. Similarly, one could argue that fire prevention is more cost-effective than fire suppression.

Another set of policy issues inherent in allocation decisions is the balance between current and future needs. This policy choice is inherent in all budget deliberations. For example, every budget reflects a balance between taxes and borrowing: crudely speaking, taxes are a burden on today's taxpayers, whereas borrowing shifts the burden to tomorrow's taxpayers. Many projects can be financed either from current (or retained) revenues or from bond issue proceeds. Similarly, budgets reflect choices to spend today's tax revenues on routine maintenance or to delay upkeep and shift to tomorrow's taxpayer the greater costs of rehabilitating public facilities.

Allocations also reflect choices between present and future burdens by placing varying emphasis on salaries and pensions. Salaries show up immediately as increased operating costs, whereas underfunded pensions defer compensation to the future. Local governments may not have full autonomy over the allocation of funds between salaries and pensions, particularly if the state government mandates salary or pension levels, but they often have some leeway in emphasizing present or future costs. For example, local governments sometimes underfund pensions, borrowing from the future to fund the present. The level of underfunding should be monitored yearly and addressed immediately if it becomes problematic.

The allocation process also routinely addresses the balance between capital and labor. Should a local government buy new garbage trucks that can be operated by the driver alone? Will they be more efficient? What will the impact be on current employees? Will they be transferred or laid off? In many communities, unemployment is a serious problem, and jobs created at city hall are particularly valuable politically and socially. While it might seem more efficient to buy machines and reduce staffing levels, such a decision may encounter considerable resistance. If it takes three people to do the job of one machine, at approximately the same cost, which is preferable, the three people or the one machine? For reasons similar to those that may govern the balance between capital and labor, some local governments have a policy of privatizing only if the contractor can accommodate current employees.

The most obvious policy made through the allocation process is the decision to increase or decrease funding for programs or services. When the Mainstreet Association asks for a $70,000 grant, or when a local homeless shelter or day care center asks for financial support, local officials have to decide how to respond. Sometimes officials step forward with support even when interest groups do not make direct petitions. One city, to maximize a state contribution to economic development, drew the boundary of a tax increment financing district for a sales tax around the entire commercial area, which had the effect of earmarking for the commercial district all increases in sales tax receipts collected in that area. Normally, the city's share of the sales tax increase would have been general revenue, available to be spent anywhere in the city or on any project. Because of the new earmarking, street and stormwater projects throughout the city were put on hold while budget makers identified projects for the commercial district. All this happened despite the fact that the commercial district had shown little interest in developing its own list of projects.

When budget makers decide to grant, reduce, or deny budget requests, they choose not only among alternative strategies for solving problems (e.g., drug suppression vs. gang outreach), but also among departments and services. What should receive the highest priority this year: economic development, which means extending water service to empty lots to make them more attractive to developers; or fighting drugs, which means assigning undercover agents to a countywide team? Which is more important, sidewalk repair or building maintenance?

In answering such questions, managers have to make yet another important policy choice. Should they try to solve problems, or should they take symbolic actions that create a sense that problems are being addressed? An example of a symbolic action in budgeting is the creation of a list of capital projects that satisfies policy makers, citizens, or department heads but is never funded. One city, for example, put the same flood control projects in the budget year after year. Drug squads in suburban police departments may also be more for window dressing than for problem solving. Every budget includes a mix of symbolic and practical solutions, and symbolic solutions are not necessarily wrong or deceptive. Making people feel safer may be as important as reducing the actual crime rate; creating the impression that the business climate is favorable may be as important as expensive economic development incentives.

The budget document

After at least tentative allocation decisions have been made, the mayor or manager, in consultation with the budget office, prepares a budget document that displays the revenue and spending decisions. How the budget document is laid out has a number of policy implications.

One of the major policy decisions made at this point in the budget process is how accessible the budget should be to citizens. Budget documents vary in their degree of user friendliness. They may be written in plain English, with narrative descriptions of programs and goals, or they may resemble a computer printout, overwhelming users with rows and columns of unfathomable numbers. Is there a budget summary to explain this year's key issues and the approaches that staff recommend? Are there summary tables that describe trends and offer comparisons with other governments, to create a sense of context for budget decisions? Is the budget unified and comprehensive, so that different sources of revenue, including grants and various types of loans, all show up? Does the budget focus on demonstrating legal compliance or on addressing citizens' priorities?

A second policy choice concerns budget format: line-item, program, performance, zero-base, or target-based budgeting. Zero-base and target-based budgeting reflect a desire to control spending; program budgeting emphasizes the possibility of trade-offs between programs; performance budgeting emphasizes outputs and improved efficiency in delivering various services. Historically, line-item budgeting emphasized spending control, but it also offers a way to trim or add to the budget without making explicit policy trade-offs.

In theory, the problem of integrating policy making with budgeting was resolved by PPBS—**planning, programming, budgeting systems**, a set of budget reforms introduced at the federal level in the 1960s by Robert McNamara, then Secretary of Defense. Under PPBS, the budget process began with the specification of community goals: program funding was then linked to the accomplishment of those goals. Government services were organized into programs, each with a set of activities (work elements) that had a common set of goals. PPBS required staff to analyze the effects of programs in the light of community needs, to determine whether the programs were actually solving community problems.

Although PPBS aroused a great deal of interest, the extensive analysis required to implement it became a formidable hurdle for many local governments. Moreover, its emphasis on identifying community needs and addressing them through collective (i.e., government) action was difficult to sustain when local governments fell on hard times financially. In the 1970s, when a deep recession was accompanied by increasingly severe tax limitations, identifying community needs and addressing them through collective effort were incompatible with the political climate, and the focus of budgeting shifted to cutting spending and identifying priorities among existing programs.

In recent years, as tax limitations and general skepticism toward government have increased the emphasis on efficiency, effectiveness, and accountability, some of the ideas from PPBS—such as goal setting, a program structure, and policy analysis—have begun to sift back into budget practice. In 1992, for example, when Milwaukee, Wisconsin, adopted its first strategic plan, Mayor John Norquist explained in the preface that the plan's purpose was "to identify and analyze key problems so that specific strategies and actions can be implemented to solve them."[4]

Unlike the earlier versions of PPBS, however, newer versions are more explicitly attentive to limiting spending and assigning priorities to needs. In Milwaukee's 1994 budget, Mayor Norquist stated in his transmittal letter that the budget reflected the goals that the city had set and the goals that it had achieved. The next sentence, however, noted that "in 1994 we will hold city spending in check and we will reduce the city tax rate." More recent versions of PPBS also recognize more explicitly the need for public participation and approval as a means of giving the budget greater legitimacy. As a result, the focus has shifted from technical planning and efficiency to demonstrating the accomplishment of goals, which have been determined in consultation with citizens and elected officials.

The choice of line-item, program, performance, zero-base, or target-based budgeting influences what information is put in the budget document and the role of community goals in making budget choices. Apart from format, however, every budget document is an exercise in selective revelation. Some pieces of information are emphasized and others obscured or omitted. For example, some budgets list planned transfers between funds, but most do not. Some list all revenue sources—including, where appropriate, the use of fund balances; many do not. Sometimes enterprise funds and auxiliary services are included in the budget in some detail; sometimes they are simply sketched in, with little useful detail; frequently, they are omitted completely. The definition of programs may obscure some policy decisions. For example, few local governments describe in detail what they spend for economic development, especially abatements or other **tax expenditures** (tax breaks), so the true cost of economic development goes unreported and unscrutinized by budget makers.

In many cases, stating policy choices more explicitly would improve the quality of decision making and increase the level of democratic participation. While explicit and open policy making has a number of important advantages, it also creates problems. Fortunately, the major problems can be anticipated: one is deciding who should participate in budgetary policy making and then ensuring that all the appropriate participants have a role in the process; the second problem is the increased level of conflict that arises when policy making is opened up.

Defining roles in the budget process

Early in the budget preparation process, policy makers should help set priorities among goals and inform management of their preferences on a variety of allocation issues. Figure 4–1 is a sample questionnaire used by several Texas cities to help establish the council's spending preferences for the coming year.

Council members may not always be willing to set policy or interested in doing so, but they should be given the opportunity. The appointed staff should make it easy for the mayor and council to guide policy making. Staff should help frame the policy issues and, where appropriate, make recommendations as to the preferred policy alternative. Such recommendations make it less difficult for the council to make decisions. More politically divisive issues are best left to the council or board, with staff providing objective analyses of the merits of each alternative. The budget office may frame some issues, especially those dealing with finance or budget format, and make recommendations in those areas. The budget office should undertake some policy analysis, too, such as determining how much revenue will be generated by various changes in tax rates or whether leasing is more economical than purchasing.

Citizens

The public should play a substantial role throughout the budget-making process. It is especially important, however, to involve citizens when community goals are being developed and to seek their opinions on key policy decisions related to taxation and expenditures. With few exceptions, how-

Please complete both Sections A and B according to the instructions on the cover page.

1/26/96

SECTION A									SECTION B
Service area	No opinion	Eliminate current effort	Substantially reduce current effort	Reduce current effort	Continue current effort	Increase current effort	Substantially increase current effort	Initiate new effort	Priority of response 1–7 (1=low; 7=high)
Public safety–type services									
Police patrol	0	1	2	3	4	5	6	7	
Crime investigation	0	1	2	3	4	5	6	7	
Drug abuse/enforcement programs	0	1	2	3	4	5	6	7	
Community-oriented policing (COPS)	0	1	2	3	4	5	6	7	
Parking/traffic enforcement	0	1	2	3	4	5	6	7	
Fire prevention	0	1	2	3	4	5	6	7	
Emergency medical (ambulance)	0	1	2	3	4	5	6	7	
Fire suppression	0	1	2	3	4	5	6	7	
Emergency preparedness (management)	0	1	2	3	4	5	6	7	
Environmental health (inspections, etc.)	0	1	2	3	4	5	6	7	
Animal control	0	1	2	3	4	5	6	7	
Municipal court	0	1	2	3	4	5	6	7	
Juvenile justice system	0	1	2	3	4	5	6	7	
Auto theft prevention programs	0	1	2	3	4	5	6	7	
Child-oriented safety programs	0	1	2	3	4	5	6	7	
Public works–type services									
Street maintenance/repair	0	1	2	3	4	5	6	7	
Street construction/rebuilding	0	1	2	3	4	5	6	7	
Street sweeping	0	1	2	3	4	5	6	7	
Traffic signalization/engineering	0	1	2	3	4	5	6	7	
Airport development	0	1	2	3	4	5	6	7	
Community development–type services									
Public transportation (SPAN, etc.)	0	1	2	3	4	5	6	7	
Neighborhood services (NICE, etc.)	0	1	2	3	4	5	6	7	
Downtown redevelopment (Main St., etc.)	0	1	2	3	4	5	6	7	
Low- & moderate-income housing	0	1	2	3	4	5	6	7	
Long-range comprehensive planning	0	1	2	3	4	5	6	7	
Development review process	0	1	2	3	4	5	6	7	

Figure 4–1   Excerpt from council priorities questionnaire, Denton, Texas.

Source: Memorandum from Jon Fortune, chief finance officer, to city council members, Denton, Texas, January 1996.

ever, public involvement in local budget making is superficial and undertaken only to satisfy legal requirements.

Public officials do not want to raise expectations that they cannot satisfy. Thus, many local governments resist greater public involvement because they fear that citizens' expectations for spending or for tax reductions will be unrealistic; they may also fear that the costs of responding to the public's wish list will be unbearable to the community as a whole or to wealthier taxpayers. A second reason for resisting involving the public in budgeting is that different portions of the community want different or even contradictory programs, which leaves public officials in the difficult position of not knowing how much of what to deliver to whom. A third argument raised by local officials is that citizens are simply not interested in participating—and that trying to involve them is time consuming and frustrating. Although there is some basis for these concerns, all of them can be addressed in ways that will allow budget makers to benefit from citizen participation.

Strategic planning and focus groups, neighborhood councils, citizen budget commissions, and capital budget committees are all ways of involving the public in the budget process before final approval. Once the budget is final, the chief executive can make press presentations and take the budget proposal on the road, presenting it to meetings of civic groups, service clubs, and neighborhood and homeowners associations. Some federal grants, such as the Community Development Block Grant, require community participation in the review and selection of projects; these requirements provide a further opportunity for citizen involvement in budgetary policy making.

Strategic planning sessions and focus groups   Because it takes time to form the appropriate groups and to stimulate public participation, it may be best to conduct strategic planning sessions and focus groups apart from the annual budget cycle. If the initial choice of groups to participate is limited, and if little effort is made to interest the public, the results are likely to be disappointing. Since the goal is to get a wide range of opinion about the community's priorities, it is better to err on the side of inclusiveness.

In one strategic planning format, designed to formulate community goals, the local government designates a facilitator to organize planning sessions. Ideally, such sessions should include representatives from all socioeconomic strata, from small businesses and larger ones, from the downtown and from neighborhoods; if there are defined racial or ethnic groups in the community, these should be represented as well. This structure forces participants to listen to each other's arguments and facilitates the development of common goals.

In an alternative strategic planning format, designed to provide information for decision making, the local government holds town meetings on particular topics and invites citizens to testify, to identify local problems, and to recommend solutions. In some neighborhoods, empty buildings may be the most urgent problem—and in others, poor street lighting or lack of parking.

The information obtained through focus groups is similar to that provided by strategic planning sessions, but the structure of focus groups is similar to that of a group interview. In a focus group, people gather from a neighborhood or from across the city, county, or district, and a moderator encourages them to describe the most urgent problems they see facing the community and the actions they think should be taken. In this format, ideas emerge as people respond to one another's suggestions.

Focus groups are less formal than hearings—and, ideally, they allow issues to be discussed in greater depth.

The strategic planning process arouses public expectations that the local government will act on the recommendations formulated by citizens. Thus, it is necessary not only to develop a plan of action but to keep citizens apprised of progress on the plan. Implementing citizens' recommendations involves three steps: restating them as goals, winnowing them down to a manageable number, and translating them into realistic objectives for departments. The final list of goals and objectives should be printed in the budget document for citizens to see. Performance measures can also be important here, to show that progress is occurring year by year.

Staff must take care with the selection and wording of goals, to ensure that they do not appear to favor particular interest groups or neighborhoods. Goals such as "downtown redevelopment" or "neighborhood revitalization" sound harmless enough, but they may create the impression that the accomplishment of one goal comes at the expense of another. Preferable phrasing may be "increasing the number of jobs, preserving the city's architectural heritage, and improving the condition of streets." It is easy to envision how everyone in the community would benefit from the achievement of such goals, whether the improvements are in the downtown area or in surrounding neighborhoods.

Some of the goals citizens recommend may be more easily accomplished by the private sector or by public-private partnerships. If possible, the budget should include performance measures for these goals, too. Such a report is likely to give citizens a clearer sense of the destiny of their proposals and also make clear who has responsibility for various goals.

Neighborhood councils   Dayton, Ohio, makes extensive use of neighborhood councils to involve citizens in the budget. Neighborhood councils are boards elected in each district of the city to formulate and winnow proposals for capital budgeting projects in that district. The city sets aside a certain amount of money for these projects, and unless department heads demonstrate that the proposed projects are not technically feasible or that there are better ways to achieve the same goals, the budget office follows the citizens' priorities.

The Dayton system has a number of attractive features. First, in training sessions conducted by city officials, members of the neighborhood councils learn how the budget is prepared and the trade-offs involved in preparing it. The training helps allay staff concerns about government by amateurs as well as their fears about unrealistic requests. Second, the boards are elected from districts that are shaped like pie wedges: each wedge contains a portion of an inner-city neighborhood and a portion of a more affluent area. Representatives from each portion of the district must propose and discuss their priorities, and hence learn about each other's neighborhoods and needs. If district representatives cannot agree on priorities, they lose the funding set aside by the city. Another pot of money is set aside to fund projects if two or more sectors can agree on a single proposal. Thus, not only is there a strong incentive to come to agreement, but the neighborhood councils learn to represent a range of interests and needs: cooperation, not insularity, is rewarded.

Citizen advisory boards   Some local governments use advisory boards to help formulate and advise on the operating budget or on capital projects. In Phoenix, Arizona, for example, city departments prepare capital needs studies for review by citizen councils, which examine the studies and recommend which proposals should be taken to the voters. The city council makes the final decision. The citizen councils also review the preliminary capital improvements plan, to ensure that it is in keeping with their intent.

Citizen advisory boards can review the operating budget as well as the capital budget. In one approach to the use of such boards, citizens are appointed to examine the local government manager's budget proposal before final review and adoption by the council. The board has no decision-making power, but board members can ask staff questions and make recommendations to the manager.

Sometimes citizens' questions remind the chief executive that the budget needs to be accessible to outsiders as well as to those who have worked with the programs for decades. Where does the money for the tax increment financing district come from? Where does it appear in the budget? Why was money transferred from the airport fund to the general fund? Why can't all these different economic development funds be merged? Why did the tax rate for pensions go up so sharply for firefighters and stay relatively stable for police officers? Items in the budget may look odd to citizens. What they look for may not be there, or at least not in the place they expect. Until such issues are brought up by citizen advisory boards, the chief executive and the budget office may not realize that the operating or capital budget is uninterpretable to citizens: by making the budget more comprehensible for all users, citizen review boards can perform a valuable service.

Because of their particular expertise, members of citizen review boards may also question things in the budget that council members had not noticed or that had not been of concern. For example, a professor of finance might question the use of reverse repurchase agreements (in which banks lend money to local governments), or various kinds of derivatives, as cash management tools. The chief financial officer of a local company may question the handling of pensions. If citizens expect to see the same kind of reporting from all recipients of local government grants, they may be bewildered by extensive reporting requirements that apply to nonprofit social service agencies but not to the downtown business association. Citizen review boards may also express dismay that particular expenditures are never listed in the budget but are routinely approved later in the fiscal year and paid for out of fund balances. (These are all real examples.)

In one community, the council had been trying to expand the airport in order to qualify for larger federal grants. The chair of a finance advisory board questioned the size of the city's subsidy to the airport, noting that as the airport grew in size, so did the **operating deficit** funded by general revenues. The chair suggested that rather than allow the subsidy to rise each year, the city should have a budget policy on the maximum size of the subsidy. The local government manager agreed that the board chair's recommendation made sense for the general fund.

In addition to challenging assumptions or raising issues that council members had not considered, citizen review boards may ask questions that council members had been reluctant to raise because of the risk of antagonizing important constituencies. Sometimes issues raised by citizen review boards change the way the budget is prepared; at other times, however, the board itself antagonizes important constituencies. The head of the review board may then be asked to resign, or the entire board may be dissolved.

Because meetings of citizen advisory boards often attract the press, the issues aired at the meetings are at least partially reported to the broader public. Even if it also provokes controversy, any procedure that offers the press an opportunity to observe detailed consideration of budget issues, that enhances reporters' understanding of the issues, and that sparks public interest ultimately promotes broader support for the final budget choices. The major problem with public participation has not been too high a level of controversy but a yawning lack of interest and understanding.

Although advisory boards do involve citizens and the meetings occasionally attract the press, the appointed boards involve too few citizens and are generally too unrepresentative to serve as the primary vehicle for eliciting citizens' responses to the budget. Nevertheless, advisory boards can be a useful mechanism when combined with other approaches to citizen participation.

Community Development Block Grant hearings   Some federal grants require public participation in decision making, thus providing another means of bringing the public into budgetary policy making. The most prominent of these grants is the Community Development Block Grant (CDBG). Because the requirement for citizen involvement in CDBG decision making is rather loosely defined, practice varies widely. Some cities have made their CDBG allocations without soliciting or using public recommendations, then held a hearing to comply with the law. Others have taken the requirement for public involvement more seriously, and, particularly where council members have strong neighborhood ties, have tried to develop meaningful mechanisms to elicit citizens' views.

In a 1993 book on federal policy making, Michael Rich recounts the history of public participation in the CDBG policy-making process in Chicago. When the grants began, Mayor Richard Daley (Daley the elder—years after his father's death, Daley's son became mayor of Chicago) set up a citizen participation mechanism that amounted to public hearings in various parts of the city. A conflict developed between neighborhood groups and citywide groups (e.g., the League of Women Voters, Business and Professional People for the Public Interest). The citywide groups wanted scattered-site lower-income housing, while many of the neighborhood groups wanted lower-income housing to be concentrated in the poorer neighborhoods, where need was most acute. After an acrimonious public split, the groups met and developed a compromise position that was eventually adopted by the city.

In succeeding years, the role of citizens was increased: a citizen advisory board was created, staff were assigned to the board, and the role of neighborhoods on the advisory board was strengthened. Initially, the advisory board was divided into subcommittees that could address separate issues; thus, the board had no way to address overall policy. Also, the neighborhood members were initially picked by city staff or by council members, rather than by the neighborhood groups themselves. Both these problems were eventually resolved in favor of the neighborhood groups. During the administration of Mayor Harold Washington, the city held a public forum before the start of the CDBG decision-making process to invite citizens "to present their views on community priorities, the scope of the city's CDBG program, and the direction it should take."[5] The attendance the first year of the forum was over 500; the second year it was over 800. Mayor Washington's ability to implement the policy directives he solicited from the public was limited somewhat by council opposition and by a traditional view of CDBGs as funding for projects distributed to city wards. The mayor persevered, however, and often at least partially succeeded in implementing publicly requested changes.

Some cities have used the federal requirement for citizen participation in CDBG as the basis for a more general community-based organizing effort. Organizing the neighborhoods allows city staff to talk to neighborhood representatives and hear their concerns and ideas; staff generally welcome such communication and find it unthreatening. Interestingly, even the business community tends to welcome more active participation of community and neighborhood groups in economic development activities. In Burlington, Vermont, for example, one downtown business leader observed that when neighborhood groups were excluded from decision making, they were likely to protest proposals put forth by businesses and to block them at unpredictable times. Once neighborhood groups were made players in the process, deliberations became more predictable. One way of describing the shift would be to say that the situation had become less confrontational.[6]

CDBG's requirement for public participation offers an excellent opportunity to include the public in budgetary decision making. The cases of Chicago and Burlington suggest several possible sources of opposition to including the public as a genuine—as opposed to symbolic—budgetary participant: sometimes community groups disagree among themselves about what should be done; those who have traditionally benefited from economic development dollars may protest increased neighborhood influence over priorities; elected officials who have traditionally used grant revenues as resources to build political support may fear a reduction in the number of projects given to their supporters; and city staff may fear a loss of professional control.

These cases also suggest potential solutions. The citizen groups can resolve their differences among themselves and present a common policy to the city; mayors and council members may find that community groups represent a newly defined constituency; and city staff may find it beneficial to open the channels of communication to community-based councils and advisory groups. The inclusion of formerly excluded groups can, over the long term, make decision making less rather than more rancorous, softening opposition from those who feared the participation of new groups in decision making.

Presenting the budget to citizens   In some communities, after the budget proposal has been made final, the chief executive and the budget director present the budget to citizens by holding press conferences and making presentations to civic organizations and neighborhood groups. The mayor or manager may present the budget proposal with a bit of drama, slides, or even a film.

In Tampa, Florida, the city solicits citizens' views before formulating the budget and widely circulates the budget proposal after it has been assembled. The budget office makes regular budget presentations to a core group made up of chamber of commerce and press representatives, but also responds to requests from neighborhood and civic groups. The presentation itself has become more elaborate over time, moving from slides and overheads to more sophisticated audiovisual productions. As the budget director explained, the audiovisual aspect became increasingly important: "The slide shows got more sophisticated. The graphics got better and the production got better. You want to get the word out to as many folks as you can."

Phoenix takes a different approach when taking its budget proposal to the community. Council members have forums in their districts throughout the year. When the proposed budget is ready, council members solicit citizens' responses to the proposals at these forums, then prepare a list of changes they will propose on the basis of these hearings. In the view of the budget director, the budget forums are successful. "Maybe between twenty and two hundred people show up at a forum. It's small, but it's positive citizen input."

Budgets that communicate Once local officials accept the need for greater public involvement in budgetary decision making, they often must rethink how the budget document can more effectively communicate policy decisions.

Research confirms that budget format matters when spending and taxing choices are being communicated to citizens. A 1988 survey revealed that most cities use multiple methods to communicate with the public: 96 percent of those surveyed used some form of public hearings; 58 percent used budget summaries and other explanatory materials; and approximately 25 percent used advisory groups or committees prior to budget completion, presentations before interested groups, and special analyses for the media.[7] Most important, cities that had a program or performance budget were more likely to report successful integration of citizens into the budget process, and larger cities that used at least some output measures were more likely to report successful citizen participation.

As the budget director in Tampa noted, improved communication with the public had become urgent. The city needed to convince citizens that they could influence budget choices, then solicit timely recommendations, and later report on how citizens' views were integrated into the budget. The budget director went on to note that the city had created a partnership between the community and the local government; that partnership led to changes in the budget format.

The governing body

Budget staff sometimes complain about the difficulty of getting policy guidance from council members who would prefer to avoid controversy and sidestep thorny problems. Because policy makers often refuse to make policy decisions—even when explicitly asked to do so by staff— local governments have evolved a number of approaches to soliciting council members' opinions. At a discussion on the capital budget, for example, one city manager complained that the council had failed to assign priorities to a list of projects drawn up by the departments. The manager speculated that there were unresolved policy issues underlying the choice of projects, such as how much to spend on streets versus drainage, how much to spend on system maintenance versus expansion, and how much to depend on special service areas. (Special service areas are like special assessments and are paid for by a narrow group of beneficiaries.) After some reflection, the manager decided that the way to get council members to make policy in the area of capital budgeting was "to draw up a five-year plan with assumptions in it, and ask the council to react to it, what they liked and what they did not like."

Elected officials usually have an overall sense of what they want to achieve and where they want the community to go. Thus, one of the easiest ways to encourage council members to disclose their policy preferences is to ask them to formulate goals for the community, without necessarily ranking them. The goals can then appear in the budget, with yearly progress reports.

The budget office in Phoenix works closely with the mayor and council, consulting at least monthly before the budget is presented to the council for adoption. Council members are asked to assign explicit priorities to cuts. According to the deputy city manager for public safety, issues are taken to the council for rating:

Each department prepares a 10 percent cut list and creates a priority list of what they will add back, in order. The 10 percent the police department identified is about $14.7 million. Of that, [the manager's office] will implement $1.9 million in cuts, which we can do without significant service impacts. Then we will take additional issues to the council. There will be about forty issues citywide, and the council will rate them using a six-point scale. We get council ratings almost every year—unless the council isn't interested. We've gotten ratings about ten out of twelve years.

A number of local governments solicit legislative recommendations on a form that gives policy makers the option of increasing, decreasing, or holding constant the level of funding for services. Requesting that council set priorities has several advantages: first, some policy makers have no sense of staffing limitations and will continue to demand new projects all year long, expecting everything to be done. For staff, knowing which projects have higher priority can be a great help. Second, if council members are compelled to recognize that adding new tasks may slow the completion of tasks assigned earlier, they may use more discretion in assigning projects.

Another approach to identifying legislative priorities is to arrange a retreat staffed by a professional facilitator. Facilitators are skilled at eliciting opinions in a nonthreatening environment. At a retreat, council members may feel less need to posture for voters and the media, and individual preferences can be recorded without having to be defended. A retreat may reveal, for example, whether the entire council thinks that economic development is the first priority, or whether some members feel that, at the moment, it is more important to alleviate the tax burdens on elderly citizens or to improve the storm drainage system. Retreats can uncover depth of feeling and breadth of support for particular issues; they are also an opportunity to build consensus among policy makers on the most pressing issues facing the community.

Yet another approach to determining council members' policy preferences is to review meeting transcripts for explicit policy statements. Council and board members often make policy statements during meetings, and if departments take these statements seriously and use them to shape budgets and guide performance, council members will be encouraged to consider the implications of their policies and to state their policies clearly. Even council members who are reluctant to formulate policy because of a fear of controversy are likely to be pleased when they see the policy implications of their public statements implemented by staff.

Not every policy statement made by an elected official is practicable; the local government manager may have to select those that are most feasible from among the stated policies. One way for the manager to reduce ambiguity is to distill these policy pronouncements, put them together as proposed public policies, point out where contradictions appear, and recommend solutions for any apparent contradictions. Sometimes just seeing the policy implications of a decision may cause council members to reconsider. The local government manager might say, for example, "The council just approved assigning a city vehicle to the assistant fire chief. Should all department heads and assistant department heads get similar benefits? The cost to the city would be about X dollars. The advantages are such and such; the disadvantages are such and such. I recommend doing it (or not doing it) because. . . ."

To summarize, the chief executive should solicit policy recommendations from elected officials on a variety of budgetary issues. The techniques for doing so may vary with the type of recommendation being sought. Generally, it is easier to obtain goal statements from elected officials and to elicit their opinions about whether funding for particular programs should be expanded, contracted, or left unchanged. Policy guidance for future decision making—for example, how to handle trade-offs between salaries and pensions—is usually more difficult to obtain. If such policies can be formulated in the abstract, they may be easier for elected officials to make on technical grounds—that is, without having to attend to the political specifics of a given case. That does not preclude policy makers from changing their position when confronted with the specific implications of a choice. It does mean, however, that policies can be established that council members would have to take active steps to change, risking a level of confrontation that they would normally avoid.

The assignment of priorities is probably the most difficult policy choice for elected officials to make, because priorities identify winners and losers and are likely to provoke the most immediate controversy. Nevertheless, elected officials in some communities regularly identify priorities for staff. The more closely staff communicate with elected officials on the policies included in the budget, the more likely the budget is to pass without major controversy.

The chief executive

In some cases, the staff and the chief executive may want policy makers to do more than simply rank policy alternatives. The chief executive may, for example, frame specific policy choices and then ask the council for guidance. Staff may also prepare policy analyses: For example, is it better to have one officer in a squad car or two? How should patrol zones be configured? Generally, when asking council members to approve a policy, staff should provide several alternatives. This approach focuses the council's attention on the key issues, making the trade-offs in the budget proposal easier to understand.

The alternatives may vary widely in scope. One year, a local government manager told the council that thirteen new staff positions were needed and that an increase in the tax rate would be required to pay for them. The council had to decide whether to fund thirteen new positions—and, if not, which ones to eliminate; it also had to decide which of several tax alternatives to recommend. In another year, the manager asked council members whether they wanted to add two secretaries or to put the money in a contingency fund for emergencies—a much narrower set of choices with fewer implications.

In 1989, the city manager of DeKalb, Illinois, introduced the budget to the council with the following statement:

We want to discuss policy through the budget process. We can look at the policy question without specific projects in front of us. Water is the one utility we can control—that and stormwater. It is the only one that is properly funded. Do we want to use it to plan development? We can be aggressive and put in mains where we want development, and assume that that will be a more desirable location for developers. Or we can be proactive for other reasons, such as looping the water mains. Or should we be reactive to projects that walk in the door? And if so, should they be funded with water fund money, instead of venture capital money?

To make it easier for the council to consider policy issues, the manager abstracted the policy issues from specific projects. Then he framed the issues, introducing them in terms of the limited tools the city had to encourage economic development. A manager framing policy choices in this way will not always get definitive policy direction from the council, but he or she will air the issues and get some sense of the council's preferences.

Sometimes the council sets priorities, then fails to implement them. One year, the council in DeKalb decided that flood control projects were the highest priority. The manager put funding for flood control in the budget, but the council was unable to agree on specific projects and the money was not spent. The manager persisted, noting that important policy questions needed to be resolved by council.

There are key policy issues; the staff doesn't want to go ahead without council guidance. On stormwater, should the concentration be on neighborhoods that flood in the rain? And if so, should the priority be on cost-benefit calculations: How many houses can be served with a project how small in dollars? Or should the criterion be willingness to share the cost with the city? Do small projects make any sense at all, when a project in one location may make the situation worse in another location, or make development more difficult?

Note how the manager has framed the policy issues: once he has answers to these questions, he and the staff can select projects and recommend them to the council.

The budget office

The role of the budget office in policy making depends on two factors: (1) whether the office is separate from or combined with the finance department and (2) whether the chief executive expects the budget office to have a policy role. At the least, it is appropriate for the budget office to call attention to policy issues looming in the budget, such as future imbalances between revenues and expenditures. Budget offices typically map longer-term trends in revenues and expenditures and use the results to alert management to impending problems. Also within the purview of a budget office are recommendations for policies on revenues; purchasing and leasing; bonding; funding for new programs; reducing or eliminating existing programs; and economic development initiatives.

The budget office may also undertake policy analyses—for example, evaluating social service needs, estimating future electricity usage, or determining the costs and savings associated with new, energy-efficient equipment. It is also relatively common for budget offices to make recommendations concerning computer hardware and to conduct cost-benefit analyses of capital purchases. How much analysis the budget office undertakes depends on the staff's expertise, its reputation for objectivity, available staff time, and the managers' and the elected officials' level of interest in such reports. Such analyses sometimes become political liabilities if elected officials dislike the recommendations. This problem may limit the scope of policy issues the budget office feels free to address.

Handling controversy

By their nature, budgets generate conflict: after all, they allocate resources in situations in which demand exceeds available funding. Local officials have often handled this unavoidably competitive aspect by deemphasizing the policy making accomplished through the budget process. An **incremental budgeting** process and format, for example, obscure policy trade-offs. An increase of $100 for office supplies says nothing about whether the police can catch more burglars; a decrease of $1,000 in travel says nothing about whether the engineering program will be able to sample the quality of road construction at fewer sites. Historical shares determine how funds will be allocated: increases in revenue from one year to the next are allocated roughly in proportion to existing departmental shares of the budget. If the police department in prior years received 25 percent of the total budget, then it would receive 25 percent of the new revenue available this year. Because departments and programs are not really in competition with each other, there is little conflict over the budget; however, there is also little public interest in the process. The budget simply does not speak to the public, and the budget process rarely involves citizens in other than a pro forma way.

The wave of tax and expenditure limitations that swept the country in the 1970s underscored the need for governments to regain public trust by making budgeting more open and responsive to citizens and elected officials. One result, however, is a potential increase in the level of conflict in budgeting. Public officials may have to learn how to keep such conflict constructive and within acceptable bounds.

Conflict on the council

Asking for policy guidance from the council can increase the level of conflict, as the following exchange demonstrates. The issue is the allocation of funds for street repairs.

City manager: The division is 65 percent of the street department's budget for repairs on asphalt and 35 percent on concrete streets. If you want to change the percentages, fine; otherwise, we will use that proportion.

Council member M: The present balance gives me problems. . . .

Council member H: We need a bond issue on the streets to rebuild some of the streets. . . .

Council member R: If we eliminate the formula, what happens to my concrete streets? You can't fix 'em for nothing. You have to have a certain percent. They're fifty to sixty years old, and nothing has been done to maintain them. The people in my district pay taxes, too. What am I supposed to say to my people?

Council member M: But what am I supposed to say? These blacktopped roads aren't built like your concrete streets.

City manager: There is another pot of money; you could use the pot to bond and reconstruct. We left $475,000 unallocated to give you flexibility.

Council member B: I think maintaining what we have is sound, like painting a house. But maintenance alone won't do it. Reconstruction is needed. I don't want to get us to "my versus your streets." . . . There is a dilemma, but it should not be "my ward versus your ward."

Council member R: It's not "my ward versus your ward," it's the ends of town. The third and fourth wards of council member H and me are the old ends of town. The roads have provided sixty, sixty-five, seventy years of service with nothing done.

Council member B: How will the money be spread out?

Council member R: I don't know, but you can't tell people they'll have to wait. It's down to stone. . . .

Mayor: How about a bond issue?

Technically, the city needed to spend disproportionate amounts of money to repair the short-lived blacktopped streets: decay on blacktopped streets greatly accelerates when the streets are between ten and fifteen years old, whereas the rate of deterioration for concrete streets is constant over forty or fifty years. However, the allocation of funds on the basis of need was transformed into a conflict over "my ward versus your ward." The exchange became so heated at some points that one council member almost began to cry and another threatened to leave the meeting. The final compromise was the bond issue proposed by the mayor, which allowed the city to borrow enough money in the short term to repair both the concrete and blacktopped streets.

Several principles of conflict management can be helpful in such a situation.[8] First, it is a good idea to ensure that essential information needed for decision making is presented early and objectively. In this instance, some facts emerged only in the course of the discussion—when, for example, the mayor asked the public works director for the relative rates of deterioration of blacktopped and concrete streets. Other information never came out at all—the proportion of concrete streets in older districts, the number of concrete streets in need of repair, the distribution of capital dollars between older and newer districts, and the variations in overall capital spending from district to district.

Second, the intensity of conflict can sometimes be defused if issues are framed in a way that shows recognition of the concerns of each side. In this case, it may have been helpful to acknowledge both the number of blacktopped roads that would require expensive rebuilding and the number of broken and unrepaired concrete streets. Clarifying competing interests, then proposing alternatives that address the various interests at stake can smooth the way for decision making. In the example, the problem could perhaps have been redefined in terms of an overall goal, such as smoother roads. The discussion might then have been redirected so that concern was focused not on dollar allocations but on the goal of achieving more uniform quality in road surfaces in different councilmanic districts.

In summary, focusing budget deliberations on policy issues will probably increase the level of conflict—but it may also make the deliberation process less boring and provide clearer guidance for staff. It is essential, however, that the chief executive be prepared to deal with the resulting conflict; fortunately, most conflict can be handled in a constructive way.

Conflict with the public

If the local government solicits public opinion without preparing for the possibility of conflict, the results may be counterproductive. It is easy to envision a group of angry citizens making inflammatory speeches at a hearing, not listening to each other, and putting public officials on the defensive. It is also easy to imagine that if the budget is open to the public, citizens will make conflicting or unaffordable demands. The result will be more distrust of government, not less.

In the case of particularly volatile issues, it may be tempting to make "nondecisions"—to form policies without public discussion. The fear is that if some issues are openly discussed, they will create a level of social and political cleavage that will either derail existing policies or set the stage for political conflict. The challenge is to raise policy issues in a forum that allows genuine public discussion without disruptive controversy. Some level of controversy not only is more interesting to the public, but also improves decision making: different points of view are aired, and citizens who may have made unsuccessful bids for office have a reason to continue to participate in government. Rather than being divisive, a well-modulated debate can even help create or reinforce a sense of community.

Handling overt conflict   Suppose a local government is required by law to hold a hearing on a proposed tax increase, and the public shows up en masse and angry. Each speaker has prepared a statement, complete with inflammatory prose. Speakers are accompanied by groups of supporters who laugh, boo, and cheer at the appropriate moments. The jurisdiction holds the hearing because it must; staff try to keep order, and particularly boisterous individuals may be ejected from the room, to the accompaniment of camera flashes. At the very least, this is not a constructive approach to a difficult situation; at worst, it reinforces a variety of negative images of city hall.

The role of the local government is to invite the participants, provide space and ground rules, and listen to the discussion. Restructuring the meeting may prevent it from deteriorating and may also create an environment in which council and staff have an opportunity to discover the public's true feelings about a proposal. The Samoan Circle and other techniques for handling potentially confrontational meetings have been used widely and successfully in public settings (see sidebar). Such approaches need not be followed exactly but can be altered to fit the situation. The point is that restructuring the situation can transform potentially stormy meetings into constructive exchanges.

Curbing excessive demand   Local governments are sometimes reluctant to solicit citizens' opinions early in the budget process for fear that the public will make demands that cannot be satisfied. One way to reduce the risk of unreasonable demands is to solicit citizens' views on issues other than what they want from government. For example, staff can ask for suggestions on how particular proposals should be worded. When asked whether they want a particular tax, citizens almost always say no; but if citizens are asked to consider how a particular proposal should be worded, what it should include and exclude, and why, budget makers may get more useful and subtle advice. Citizens may say, for example, that levying taxes in a particular manner is especially burdensome, or that the level of taxation is less immediately disturbing to them than its unpredictability. Citizens' concerns may be entirely reasonable and relatively easy to satisfy; for example, even though the additional billings have higher administrative costs, water consumers may prefer smaller, more frequent bills to larger, less frequent ones. It is far better in such circumstances to solicit and follow citizens' advice; moreover, if public officials take citizens' advice, they should go out of their way to inform citizens that their advice was followed.

A second approach is to ask citizens directly what they want from government, but to set an upper limit within which they must keep their requests. Citizens then have to negotiate among themselves to determine which projects are more important, which should be done first, or which can be pared back to allow other projects to be undertaken. A related technique is to ask citizens what services they would like to have expanded even if doing so required a tax increase. Such questions force citizens to identify less important requests and give staff an idea of what the community really wants.

A third approach is to ask a citizen's advisory committee for a list of recommended projects, then to go down the list, accomplishing one after another over a number of years. Each year, as community needs change and programs are implemented or phased out, the committee will update the list. In other words, the dimension of time is built into the request process. The local government might need to set some guidelines—for example, projects that facilitate clean water will be viewed more favor-

The Samoan circle The goal of the Samoan Circle is not to resolve conflict but to elicit thoughtful opinions that do not alienate others. Participants in a Samoan Circle learn to listen to each other's opinions, which may strengthen their sense of community.

To conduct a Samoan Circle, a round table is set up in the center of a room, with chairs for four citizens; other participants sit in a circular pattern around the table. Anyone can speak, but to do so, a participant must come up to the table and sit down; he or she is then free to talk to the other people at the table. Participants can interrupt, change the subject, applaud, cheer, or jeer if they wish, but only when they are seated at the table. When a speaker has finished, he or she leaves the table—unless someone at the table wants to engage the speaker in additional discussion. Citizens can speak as often as they like, as long as they return to the table to express their thoughts.

This format has several advantages. First, although the audience is listening, speakers must talk to each other: they are not talking either to their supporters or to elected officials. The incentive to grandstand is reduced because the audience is not supposed to cheer or jeer—only those at the table may speak. Second, the rules are minimal, but they are generally self-enforcing. Because they benefit directly from following the rules, citizens themselves have a reason to enforce order. Taking turns does not depend on parliamentary rules; no one is shut out; and participants don't have to be clever to be heard. Because staff are less likely to be called on to impose order, scenarios involving protesters being asked to moderate their behavior or leave the room are less likely to occur. Finally, since citizens can express a variety of opinions in a forum designed to support a free exchange of views, staff and elected officials can listen and learn rather than feel that they have to defend their views.

Source: Lorenz W. Aggens, "The Samoan Circle: A Group Process for Discussing Controversial Subjects," in *Resolving Conflict: Strategies for Local Government*, ed. Margaret S. Herrman (Washington, DC: ICMA, 1994), 108–114. Used with permission of Lorenz W. Aggens, INVOLVE: Lorenz Aggens and Associates, 1915 Highland Avenue, Wilmette, IL 60091.

ably, and projects that benefit fewer people will be viewed less favorably. The key is to make sure citizens understand and agree to the time frame, then to build trust by implementing the list of projects. If citizens perceive that the projects they recommend are usually shunted aside for higher-priority projects recommended by staff, they are likely to lose interest or to organize for collective action.

A fourth approach is to ensure that the citizens who are making requests understand the constraints the local government faces. Dayton, for example, trains the citizens who are chosen as neighborhood leaders to ensure that they understand the limits of the city budget. After such training, citizens are less likely to make proposals that are wildly out of line with the local government's resources.

Avoiding unnecessary conflict To attract public participation, local officials have to state budget issues clearly and explain the policy implications of budget choices. Clarifying policy issues enough to attract citizen participation, however, may exacerbate social and political conflict. Ideally, policy issues should be framed so that they are interesting and meaningful but do not provoke undue conflict.

Whenever possible, avoid asking yes or no questions. If the mayor asks the public whether the city should build a stadium, for example, some residents will favor the idea and some will be opposed to it. Whatever the city decides, those whose opinions did not prevail will be offended. Moreover, yes or no questions tend to push people to take extreme positions that they may not have taken on their own.

Unless a local government is taking a formal vote and abiding by the majority outcome (in which case the minority expects to lose), it is better to ask such questions as, "What is it you like most and least about the stadium proposal?" Officials should look for areas of potential compromise. Neighbors of a sports facility, for example, may be opposed to having fans park on their streets and lawns but may favor a new facility that includes adequate parking.

Asking citizens for more detailed information about their likes and dislikes may also make explicit the costs and benefits of a project. Neighborhood residents, for example, may see a potential cost if the stadium attracts "hooligans" who cut off shrubs and break off car antennas. Owners of local restaurants, however, may see a benefit in a new, captive market.

Asking citizens to help set priorities can lead to conflict if the priorities of one group clash with those of another. One way to handle this problem is to ask representatives of the various groups to work together to devise a consolidated list of recommendations. Thus, each committee represents a microcosm of the community and must achieve its own compromises: being compelled to examine the needs of others and present one's own preferences at the same time often builds a sense of community. A professional facilitator can help to ensure this result. Because priority setting does not usually involve dollar amounts, a lot of the potential controversy is drained from the discussion, and budget makers are less likely to receive radically divergent opposing proposals.

Planning goals can be stated either in oppositional terms—"More projects for the downtown versus more for the neighborhoods"—or in terms that cut across the lines dividing geographic areas or interest groups— for example, "Police foot patrols and citizen crime watches will be established to help make people feel more secure and bring the police and citizens into a more cooperative relationship." Phrasing goals in cross-cutting terms is less likely to arouse conflict.

Controversy and budget format

Budget formats can reduce or intensify the level of conflict over the budget. Line-item budgets obscure trade-offs, allowing every department to maintain a "fair share." Newer budget formats, including program and performance budgeting and zero-base and target-based budgets, have made trade-offs clearer.

Although, for example, a **program budget** format makes the budget more comprehensible to council members and to the public, it also reveals that if police patrols are increased, something else will have to be reduced, such as tree services or street repair. If the budget reports performance data, it may be clear precisely how much of one service is being traded for another: enabling 5 percent more residents to say that they feel safe may require a 30 percent decrease in opportunities for kids to play league softball during the summer. Although program and performance budgets allow decision makers and the public much greater awareness of trade-offs and make for livelier reading, they may also generate more conflict.

Theoretically, in zero-base budgeting, every item in the budget competes with every other item, which has led some analysts to predict an unmanageable level of conflict. In practice, however, even in zero-base budgeting, most departments are never seriously considered for elimination, although a periodic **sunset review** may give policy makers the opportunity to redirect an agency's purpose and funding level. More commonly, only a portion of the budget is seriously scrutinized by the council. The rest may be examined by department heads, each of whom considers his or her own programs. In other words, the level of potential conflict is controlled by limiting the scope of the items that will be examined and compared.

Target-based budgeting is one way to allow open discussion of trade-offs while keeping the level of conflict between departments and the budget office within acceptable bounds. Trade-offs can be built into target-based budgeting in three ways: first, the targets themselves may reflect trade-offs, if an executive-level decision has been made to give one department a proportionately larger target than another department; second, department heads are free to make trade-offs among existing programs and between new proposals and existing programs; third, the chief executive, the budget office, and whoever else helps assign priorities to unfunded requests can make trade-offs between departments.

Under target-based budgeting, the actual level of trade-offs in any one year may be limited, both within and between departments, to hold down the level of controversy. To keep a general balance and to maintain the peace, there is a tendency to give more to one department or program one year and more to another the next. More permanent trade-offs are likely to be made with the targets themselves; budget offices report, for example, that when reductions in spending are required, they routinely cut some departments more deeply to compensate for cutting police and fire less deeply.

In target-based budgeting, the desire to reduce the level of controversy may eliminate policy-based trade-offs completely. However, there are other ways to contain the level of controversy, including the use of time ("My turn this year, your turn next year"); limiting the scope of trade-offs to 5 or 10 percent of the budget; and decentralizing some trade-offs to the departmental level.

Conflict that results from trade-offs that are made clear by the budget format may not be all that harmful if the discussion occurs in the open, in good faith, and does not necessarily cause divisions along social or economic lines. Ideally, trade-offs can be discussed in terms of community well-being, with participants calling on supporting technical information as necessary. Comparing the urgency of two needs may be difficult, but is unlikely in itself to provoke splits along ideological, racial, ethnic, economic, or territorial lines. Trade-offs become potentially inflammatory, however, if the services being cut are identified with a particular interest group, racial or ethnic group, economic group, or geographic area.

How the local government defines programs in a program budget can also influence the level and nature of conflict over trade-offs. For example, if a county has housing in the budget, and housing is defined as being for lower-income households or for a particular racial group, then trade-offs that involve housing are likely to be seen in economic or racial terms. If programs are defined as "for" downtown or "for" neighborhoods, a loss in one program or a gain in another will exacerbate economic and geographic divisions in the community. Defining programs so that a broader group of beneficiaries identifies with each program may help reduce conflict. An economic development program that creates local jobs by encouraging commercial and industrial development, for example, may appeal across economic and geographic boundaries.

Not only should local governments avoid characterizing programs in ways that exacerbate rifts in the community, but they should also avoid false dichotomies in general, because they tend to exaggerate antagonisms. Many dichotomies are too simple, dividing programs or services into two large and seemingly opposite entities, when in reality there are more than two entities and they are not opposites in any meaningful sense. A case in point is the distinction commonly made between basic and social services: this distinction intensifies conflict by implying that streets and water services are important (basic), whereas social services, such as special transportation for elderly residents or day care for children, are less so. Particularly when such distinctions reflect ideology—that is, are meant to persuade—rather than being based on genuine technical differences, they may exacerbate conflict.

Summary

Local officials who ignore the policy dimensions of budgeting may make poor policy choices by default—for example, by allowing outdated policies to remain in effect. Moreover, by trying to insulate the budget from policy making, public officials may prevent citizens from exercising their right to influence public decisions. Government at all levels is under enormous pressure to open up the decision-making process, to improve the quality of decisions, and to improve accountability. One way to address such concerns is to ensure that budgetary policy making is open and deliberate, that the roles and responsibilities of the participants are well defined, and that any conflict that arises is handled constructively.

Central to the policy process is the budget document itself. The format, presentation, and even the wording of the document all influence the level of participation and interest on the part of both citizens and the governing body. Although a budget document that explicitly reveals trade-offs may initially increase the level of conflict over the budget, a well-designed budget process can mitigate conflict, while ensuring that the making of policy—rather than the obscuring of policy—is primary.

1 Ruth Hoogland DeHoog and Bert Swanson, "Tax and Spending Effects of Municipal Enterprises: The Case of Florida Electric Utilities," *Public Budgeting and Finance* (spring 1988): 48–57.

2 Nelson VanValen, *Power Politics: The Struggle for Municipal Ownership of Electric Utilities in Los Angeles, 1905–1937* (Ph.D. diss., Claremont Graduate School, 1964).

3 Carolyn Teich Adams, *The Politics of Capital Investment: The Case of Philadelphia* (Albany, NY: SUNY Press, 1988).

4 *Strategic Plan, City of Milwaukee: Issues and Actions* (Milwaukee, WI: Department of Administration, Office of Strategic Planning, 1992), ii.

5 Michael J. Rich, *Federal Policy Making and the Poor: National Goal, Local Choices, and Distributional Outcomes* (Princeton, NJ: Princeton Univ. Press, 1993), 188.

6 Pierre Clavel, *The Progressive City: Planning and Participation, 1969–1984* (New Brunswick, NJ: Rutgers Univ. Press, 1986), 177.

7 Daniel O'Toole and James Marshall, "Citizen Participation through the Budget," *The Bureaucrat* (summer 1988): 51–55.

8 Roger M. Schwarz, "Ground Rules for Effective Groups," in *Resolving Conflict: Strategies for Local Government*, ed. Margaret S. Herrman (Washington, DC: ICMA, 1994), 95–107.

5 The budget as a management tool

Management applications of line-item budgets

Management applications of program and performance budgets
Productivity
Linking performance measures with allocations
Decentralization and control

Implementing performance budgeting
Creating performance measures
Linking performance measures to the budget
Reporting
Integrating performance measurement

Summary

The budget as a management tool

Local governments often use budgets to improve management: budgets help officials identify impending problems, improve productivity, maintain service quality, and achieve performance targets. Increasingly, however, budgets are being used not only to improve internal management but also to increase accountability to citizens and to the elected officials who represent them. Local officials wrestling with revenue constraints need information about which programs are working and which are not; given an appropriate format, the budget is a logical place to house such information. Thus, the budget is becoming a means of monitoring what the voters are getting for their tax dollars.

Interest in government performance has begun to move from what goes into government programs to what comes out. Citizens and government officials are concerned not only about the amount of spending but about whether government programs are achieving intended results at a reasonable cost.[1]

Management applications of line-item budgets

Although line-item budgets are simple in comparison to program or performance budgets, they still have a number of potential uses as management tools if managers know which line items to watch and how to use the information. By examining trends in line items, managers can track expenditure patterns and ratios, obtain warning of emerging problems, control insurance costs, and monitor policy implementation. For example, if the wages category is broken into regular wages, overtime, part time, and temporary, a manager can look at the data over time and determine whether the use of either part-time or temporary staff would reduce overtime expenditures. In the past, when expenditures for part-time or temporary staff increased, did overtime costs rise more slowly or decrease? Did an increase in part-time or temporary staff reduce overtime in one department but not in another? Improving the balance between overtime hours and part-time or temporary hours is one way to provide more services for fewer dollars.

Monitoring trends in line items also provides early warning of potential problems. For example, using figures in the personal services lines, a manager can determine the ratio of overtime to regular wages and prepare a spreadsheet of these figures for the past decade. Is the ratio increasing, and if so, when did the trend start? If analysts can determine approximately when a trend began, they may be able to pinpoint the cause, such as a change in court rules for police witnesses or in policies for calling police back to testify after their shifts are over. Once the cause is known, managers may be able to work out a solution. For example, in one local government in which court testimony was driving up overtime costs, officers who were scheduled to testify were assigned to patrol the zone near the courthouse until the bailiff signaled that it was time to testify. Because officers did not have to wait around the courthouse doing nothing, overtime was substantially reduced.

Local officials often use line items to monitor the cost of insurance. One approach involves mapping the dollar costs of different kinds of insurance over time and calculating various ratios, such as the ratio of health and life insurance costs to regular wages or the ratio of liability insurance to the number of employees in each department. Such analyses help identify costs that may be growing too quickly. Depending on the result of the analysis, managerial solutions might include creating a self-insurance fund, joining an insurance pool, establishing a risk management office, or buying membership in a local health club to help reduce health insurance and workers' compensation costs. Even a line-item budget can pinpoint departments that are generating disproportionate workers' compensation costs.

Another use of line items is to monitor policy implementation: for example, a local government may decide that **capital outlays** will be no less than 40 percent of total outlays or that debt interest will not exceed 15 percent of operating expenditures.

Line items have their limits in providing managerial information, however, particularly if they are not used in conjunction with a program or performance format. For example, unless the budget is organized by program and provides information on the output quantity and quality for each program, questions about productivity cannot be addressed through the budget. Line items can tell a chief executive whether the community is spending as much on capital improvements as official policy dictates, but line items offer no information on whether capital programs are achieving their goals.

Management applications of program and performance budgets

Instead of dividing expenditures along departmental lines, a program budget classifies expenditures into groups of activities that are designed to achieve a common purpose. A police department, for example, may house several different programs, including a stolen property recovery program, a crime suppression program, and a drug education program. A performance budget provides information on how well public sector activities are being carried out—in terms of quality as well as quantity. Thus, a performance budget would address costs per unit (e.g., cost per pothole filled) and would also ask (1) whether services are being provided at an agreed-upon level of quality and (2) whether programs are achieving their goals. Although it is possible to use elements of performance budgeting without breaking administrative units into programs, performance measures are more meaningful and useful when combined with a program format.

Although program and performance budgets can be difficult to design and implement, the advantages of doing so are considerable. One benefit is the ability to monitor and improve productivity. Another benefit is the possibility of linking performance to budget allocations. A third advantage is improved accountability. Managers can be held accountable for a given level of outputs and outcomes (as opposed to being held accountable for the consumption of inputs), allowing for more decentralized decision making and more creative management.

Productivity

Public pressures to increase governmental **productivity**—to provide more services of equal or better quality for less money—undergird many twentieth-century reform initiatives. Since productivity is a ratio of inputs to outputs, unless both inputs and outputs are measured over time, managers cannot determine whether productivity has increased or decreased.

Measuring program or project inputs requires careful delineation of the boundaries of the program or project and accurate attribution of costs. How many staff hours were spent on the project? Which truck was used? (Different trucks may have different operating costs per hour.) How much material was used, and how much did it cost? What is the project supervisor's salary, and how much time did the supervisor spend on the project? Governments that do not keep sufficiently detailed records will have difficulty attributing costs to specific activities.

Defining programs and attributing costs to them can help call attention to programs with low or declining productivity. For example, a local government may scatter expenditures associated with an economic development program throughout the budget, obscuring actual costs. If an economic development effort brings fifty-five new jobs to the community, it may be viewed as a success, but this result may have been preceded by fifteen failed projects that used mammoth amounts of time and substantial public subsidies. If the costs of all these failed projects were totaled and divided by the fifty-five new jobs, the cost per job created may be so large that the entire program would be targeted for restructuring or elimination.

Measuring output requires attention to quality as well as to quantity. If policy makers and managers do not measure service quality, the temptation may be to "improve productivity" by increasing workloads or reducing funding, while assuming (or pretending) that quality will remain the same. In one recent example, a state drastically increased the number of cases assigned to each probation officer, preventing the officers from doing any useful follow-up. Although the cost per person served decreased—making the program look more productive—the quality of service declined substantially: the state was paying less, but it was also getting less.

Productivity programs are often geared to make employees work harder, longer, or smarter, but they can also be used to protect quality. For example, if elected officials press police to increase the number of arrests (quantity) and the number of complaints of police incivility (quality) increases as a result, productivity may actually decrease. With adequate measures of quality, managers would be able to detect such perverse consequences and intervene.

Although some measures of quality are conceptually complicated or have many components, others are relatively straightforward. For example, how long did the pothole patches last, and how long should they have lasted, given the weather conditions at the time the patches were made? More complex issues arise in connection with other types of services, such as rehabilitation programs or economic development efforts. In the first case, one measure of quality might be how many clients returned to productive lives within how many weeks or months. In the area of economic development, common measures of basic output include the number of jobs created and the number of participants graduating from job training programs. Adding the issue of quality to such measures brings up a host of additional questions: Are the jobs created by economic development projects low-paying, service-sector jobs? Are they jobs with little security, without medical insurance, and with little possibility of promotion? What are appropriate criteria to measure the quality of the job training given to unemployed workers?

Sometimes quality measures can be combined with cost-per-unit ratios—allowing managers to create, for example, an index of cost per conviction or to track costs per lane-mile when snow is cleared within two hours after the end of a storm. If, however, the quality indicator is citizen complaints (fewer complaints equal higher-quality service), a precise measure that combines quality of output and cost per unit may be elusive.

Where such measures can be sensibly constructed, the average cost per unit of output of a given quality provides some basic information about productivity. To accurately determine costs that can be compared across time or with expenditures in other communities, however, more information may be needed. For example, factors such as wind speed, icing conditions, and time of onset may help explain higher or lower costs for plowing after a particular storm.

One simple framework for tracking productivity uses two types of measures, one for quantity and one for quality. Thus, quantity indicators for a police department may include the number of calls responded to and the number of reports written; quality indicators may include the proportion of calls that result in arrests or in tickets being issued, the proportion of arrests that lead to convictions, the proportion of stolen merchandise recovered, and the proportion of citizens who say that police are doing a good job. Similarly, a clerk's office may track the number of meeting minutes prepared and circulated (quantity) as well as the number of days between the meeting and the release of the minutes and the number of mistakes in each report (quality).

In short, a genuine productivity improvement program must be based on a performance budget that divides government activities into programs, assigns costs by program, and defines and measures quantity and quality of program outputs. On the basis of this information, program managers and department heads can examine the ratio of inputs to outputs over time and devise strategies to improve productivity.

Linking performance measures with allocations

Some local governments link performance to budget allocations by awarding larger allocations to managers who have achieved or surpassed performance targets. The theory behind this approach is that other departments will try to emulate the budgetary success of the better managers—and that overall productivity may improve. In addition to creating benefits for those who meet or exceed targets, many elected officials try to reduce funding for those who fail to meet targets.

Although such links are a potential incentive for productivity improvement, they raise complex management issues and must therefore be handled with caution. When elected officials use funding reductions to punish poor performance, the result may be a reduction in productivity. For example, if the additional material or personnel that the department has requested would actually improve productivity, denying the request does not penalize poor management but instead aggravates a productivity problem. Second, if program managers are punished for failing to reach targets, they may simply lower their targets—reducing, or even reversing, productivity gains. Thus, although failure to achieve a performance target may signal the need for reduced funding, it may also signal the need for more funds.

To ensure that performance measurement leads to improved productivity rather than to defensive target-setting, performance budgeting requires program managers to submit quarterly or monthly performance reports describing their progress toward objectives and explaining where and why programs are falling behind. Obstacles to the timely achievement of goals need to be identified and addressed: by examining these reports, the chief executive can determine whether more equipment or staff is likely to solve a backlog problem or whether more supervision or a different incentive system is necessary. The results of this review can be fed into the budget process as concrete advice about allocations of equipment and staff time.

It is important to note, however, that performance reports are likely to be useful only if department heads and program managers feel that the information will be used to help them, not to hurt them. Recognition of good performance is more likely to yield improvement than is punishment of poor performance. In fact, punishing program managers for failing to meet objectives simply increases the likelihood that poor performance will go unreported. The goal should not be to punish, but to identify and assist poor performers.

Decentralization and control

The third potential advantage of performance budgeting is that it can increase accountability, permitting greater decentralization of decision making. Under performance budgeting, program managers promise a given level of service at a given quality for a given number of dollars and are held accountable for both the level of service and the level of quality. Once the chief executive is satisfied that programs are operating reasonably efficiently and that allocations are being used wisely, line-item controls may be relaxed. Overspending on one line has to be made up somewhere else, and a program manager who has targets to reach is not likely to intentionally overspend on labor or machinery. Program managers will allocate funds efficiently to complete the job they promised to do. Ideally, failure to achieve performance targets shows up quickly in monthly or quarterly performance reports.

One advantage of decentralization is that it reduces or eliminates micromanagement—the practice of higher-level managers making detailed operating decisions about programs they do not understand with consequences they cannot predict. A second advantage is that lower-level managers granted more budgetary flexibility are likely to be more innovative in devising strategies to achieve targets.

Such decentralization works only if the department heads and program managers are reasonably skilled. If they are not, their shortcomings will be immediately apparent, and higher-level managers can take the necessary actions to train, assist, or replace them.

Although the managerial advantages of program and performance budgeting are significant, they are not always realized. It can be difficult to design and implement an effective program and performance budget and integrate it into an organization's decision-making framework. The following section outlines some potential problems and solutions in the implementation of performance budgeting.[2]

Implementing performance budgeting

There are four stages of performance budget implementation: creating performance measures; linking performance measures to budget allocations; reporting performance accomplishments; and institutionalizing the process. The four sections that follow consider the obstacles that characterize each stage.

Creating performance measures

Although local governments can choose from a number of lists of performance measures, it takes time to tailor appropriate measures, to develop systems to gather the necessary data, and to persuade program managers and department heads to participate.[3]

Initial design   Two years of intense effort are typically required to devise appropriate performance measures. Although rushing the design phase may result in poor or *pro forma* measures and generate skepticism about the process, it is not unusual for policy makers to instruct staff to develop and implement the system as quickly as possible.

Pressure for swift implementation may be particularly likely to occur in mayor-council communities, where performance budgeting is sometimes adopted for political reasons and is therefore of value to elected officials only if adoption occurs rapidly. In Boston, for example, most of the new budget system was completed within a year. Departments were instructed to come up with a number of measures, regardless of how good they were; the expectation was that the measures would be discussed and refined over time. Even the budget director was concerned about the speed of the initial phase—in her view, until good measures were arrived at, program managers and department heads were unlikely to buy into the process.

Because measures of quantity—such as demand and workload—can be devised more quickly and easily than measures of quality, local governments in the early phases of performance measurement programs tend to develop and implement quantity measures first. In some local governments, performance measures never extend beyond simple quantitative indicators. As a consequence, department heads and program managers may feel that the measures being used do not adequately capture the quality of the work being performed. Moreover, inadequate measures can create perverse incentives, encouraging departments to emphasize activities that are measured (and rewarded) and to deemphasize other, more important work that is not measured. If quality continues to be unmeasured, officials may be tempted to try to increase productivity by reducing inputs, further alienating program staff.

One strategy for dealing with an overly brief design phase is to begin with a few measures that capture the essential activities of a unit, rather than to rely on a multitude of measures that have little utility to decision makers. One or two good measures of *quality* for each program may convince departments that the budget office is serious about measuring quality and that it will encourage the development of additional measures of quality as the process continues. Introducing useful measures early in the development phase will encourage staff to have confidence in the system.

A second problem that often occurs during the design phase is that program managers and department heads may have difficulty understanding what it is they are trying to measure. One budget director noted, for example, that when he asked the departments for measures of demand, workload, outputs, and outcomes, he got the same measure four times. Such a response may reflect a desire not to be evaluated on anything other than effort—but it may also reflect a genuine confusion about what is to be measured.

If the community does not have a long tradition of program budgeting, identifying the programs whose performance is to be measured can be a real obstacle. A second problem is determining what aspect of a program is to be measured. As noted earlier, one common way to organize performance measures is to divide the measures into quantity and quality of work done; a second approach is to devise measures of demand, workload, outputs, outcomes, and impacts (see Figure 5–1). A third approach focuses on productivity (cost per unit produced of a given quality). Sometimes local governments use a combination of all three approaches.

Measures of quantity and quality focus on how much of a task is done and how well. To return to an example used earlier, the clerk's office prepares the minutes for four council meetings a month (quantity), issuing the minutes within two days of each meeting (timeliness—an aspect of quality) and with a maximum of one mistake per typed page (accuracy—another aspect of quality). For an antiburglary program, the quantity of output might be measured by the number of arrests, and the quality of the arrests might be determined by the proportion of arrests leading to convictions or by the number of complaints of excessive force.

A performance measurement system that monitors demand, workload, outputs, outcomes, and impacts tracks various steps in work processes and results. Demand indicators might include, for example, the number of calls or requests for service, and workload indicators the number of activities, reports, or projects undertaken. The number of services or products successfully delivered is a typical output measure, and the degree to which program goals are achieved is a typical outcome measure. Impacts are the broader results of outcomes: for example, a reduction in the crime rate—an outcome—may contribute to impacts that include a greater feeling of safety in neighborhoods, lower residential turnover, and higher sales prices on property. (Program managers rarely monitor impacts; this is more likely to be the responsibility of the chief executive's office or the planning department.)

Productivity measures usually rely on ratios of cost (input) to output, such as the cost per job created through an economic development program, controlling for the quality of the job.

To help department heads and program managers design measures,

Figure 5–1 Sample performance measures, police department theft investigation and recovery program.

Type of measure	Example
Demand	Number of reported thefts, past five years Number of calls for burglary in progress, past five years Dollar value of material reported stolen
Workload	Number of burglary and theft calls responded to Number of burglaries and thefts investigated Number of hours per investigation Number of reports written Number of court appearances in theft or burglary cases
Output	Number of arrests for burglary and theft Number of convictions for burglary and theft Dollar value of recovered goods Percentage of reported dollar value of stolen goods recovered
Outcome	Decrease in reported burglary and theft Increase in proportion of residents and merchants reporting that they feel safe Decrease in number of citizens taking out gun permits Reduction in insurance costs for residents
Impact	Higher assessed valuations Higher sales tax base (more businesses in the area) Lower turnover rate in homes and apartments, lower vacancy rates More stable middle class

the chief executive should make clear at the outset the focus of the measures and how they will be used. Program staff may well be able to distinguish demand from workload if they realize that increases in demand—reflected in higher workloads—may be an effective argument against reductions in budget allocations or in favor of increases in staff.

In summary, if measures must be designed quickly, it may be helpful to start with a limited number or to designate a few programs as pilots to demonstrate the merits of performance budgeting. A small program that is working well can encourage other programs to participate, whereas a larger program that is working poorly is likely to discourage participation and foster the perception that performance budgeting is more for appearance than for the improvement of budget allocations or program management. To help department heads and program managers understand what they should measure, the chief executive and the budget office need to define and explain the focus of measurement and the intended use of the measures.

Data collection If a local government decides to include performance measures in the budget, it is often necessary to begin collecting new types of data or to alter the presentation of data already being collected. For example, although departments may have been keeping records, those records may not address the identified performance measures. Other similar problems include records that are not kept on a fiscal year basis, records that are not sufficiently detailed to allow personnel or equipment costs to be attributed to specific programs, and inconsistent records (e.g., records kept for larger but not for smaller units and programs).

Thus, one of the first problems encountered during the design stage is the lack of sufficient historical data. The burden of preparing and keeping such records falls on department heads, who may already feel that they lack sufficient resources to get essential work done. Moreover, for fear they will be subject to funding reductions, department heads may resist assigning costs to programs, preferring to make some programs look free or inexpensive. (Program and performance budgeting make it much more difficult to manipulate costs.)

Because both record keeping and departmental cooperation are essential to the success of any performance measurement effort, local governments have developed a number of approaches to these problems. One strategy is to make trade-offs, allowing a department to drop selected current reporting requirements in exchange for adding those required by performance budgeting. The budget director in Dayton, Ohio, used this approach, hiring experts to go through departmental file cabinets to help eliminate paperwork. The departments were pleased with the results: "Unnecessary copies were eliminated. They liked that. They could give up ten things to do one."

A second approach to data collection is to construct performance measures using available data wherever possible. Portland, Oregon, for example, judged that new measures could be developed easily because departments already kept usable data. The cost of data collection for Portland's performance measurement program was, in fact, quite moderate and declined dramatically over a two-year implementation period. "Time spent annually by service departments collecting SEA [service efforts and accomplishments] data has varied from five hours in one department to twenty hours in another."[4]

A third strategy is to allow departments to choose between being evaluated (1) on the basis of readily available data and (2) on the basis of data that are more work to gather and monitor but that give a more accurate picture of performance.

Finally, computerizing the budget request process can help reduce paperwork. Under this approach, the budget office provides much of the basic data, and the departments adjust the information only to reflect proposed changes.

Departmental resistance   Department heads may resist performance measurement not only because of the time and cost involved in collecting data, but also because they fear that they will be held responsible for outcomes they cannot control. For example, the extent of fire damage can be affected by a number of factors, including wind conditions, the density and age of buildings, the materials used, and the amount of time that elapsed before the fire was reported; the performance of the fire department is only one factor contributing to the outcome. Given the range of factors beyond their control, fire chiefs may be reluctant to be held accountable for dollar losses due to fire. For similar reasons, many departments never buy into the performance budgeting model. When asked for performance measures, they provide workload and demand measures, ignoring the call for outcome measures.

To help departments accept performance budgeting, the chief executive and the budget office should give departments substantial control over performance measures, provided that they follow certain guidelines about the focus of measurement, such as measuring (1) quantity and quality of outputs or (2) demand, workload, outputs, and outcomes. If department heads can design measures that help them manage, they are more likely to see the utility of the system. If they can choose measures that reflect the work done, rather than employ measures over which they have little control, they are also more likely to accept the system.

Additional strategies for bringing department heads and program managers on board include incentives (e.g., more freedom in budget implementation), additional help when unexpected problems prevent the accomplishment of objectives, and increased budget support when appropriate.

Most important, however, in winning over department heads and program managers is persuading them that performance budgeting will not be used against them. Many department heads and program managers fear that the evaluations will be based on cronyism or program popularity rather than hard work. Staff may feel particularly uneasy about measuring quality, because they perceive such measures as having a vague, indefinite quality that leaves room for favoritism and manipulation.

Although department staff may complain about having to develop concrete, measurable indicators and keep verifiable records, the fact that other departments are called upon to do the same thing helps reduce the perception of favoritism or manipulation in system implementation. When departments that work harder or smarter gain benefits, they realize that the system is not stacked against them. Instead, they learn to use the system to identify their needs and to communicate those needs more effectively to budget makers.

Linking performance measures to the budget

The second phase in implementing performance budgeting links reported accomplishments to budget allocations. As noted earlier, elected officials may be eager to reduce allocations to programs that perform poorly; budget offices, too, have a tendency to use poor performance reports to justify funding reductions. In response, department heads may simply set minimal goals or include only favorable information in their performance reports.

A link between budgeting and performance that is both more respectful of departments and more responsive to their needs requires (1) monthly or quarterly performance reports, (2) a careful assessment of barriers to meeting objectives, and (3) thoughtful analysis of the implications of the report for budget allocations.

Underlying the entire system, however, are credible reports from the departments. According to local governments that have performance measurement systems in place, performance reports are not necessarily assumed to be truthful or useful. While some finance directors inquire only about questionable or missing information, others systematically audit the data underlying the performance reports. When departmental reports are clear and well documented, the chief executive gets a continuing record of objectives achieved, problems encountered, and solutions devised and implemented. This information provides a basis for deciding whether more money is needed or whether it would be wasted.

To ensure that the original numbers have not been fudged and that reporting is regular rather than sporadic, departments must monitor data collection internally. The more detailed the data and the more monitoring required, the greater the cost to departments. If some departments reduce the staff hours committed to record keeping, the credibility of their reporting declines, and the ability to compare performance across departments deteriorates proportionately.

The performance measurement and reporting system can feed into the budget indirectly through a management by objectives system, which links the merit-based salary increases of senior managerial staff to the achievement of goals stated in the performance budget. Unfortunately, this system creates strong incentives to set minimal goals—"like coming to work in the morning," as one local government staff member noted. To allow department heads to learn to set goals without the pressure of having them linked to salary increases, performance measures and goals in St. Louis, Missouri, were developed separately from the personnel evaluation system. As one staff member noted, this was a lengthy process; staff had to identify measures

to capture whether we were doing a good job. For example, in the jail, we used the number and severity of inmate incidents—not something vague, like "Does rehabilitation occur?"—but more tangible.

The same staff member noted that the intention was, over time, to link the performance measurement and personnel evaluation systems.

In an organization where performance measures are fully connected to the budget, performance objectives are negotiated with each department head, and budget allocations are based on the cost for achieving the agreed-upon service levels. Monthly or quarterly reports on performance measures reflect the accomplishment of objectives on which the budget is based. Performance measures may also be integrated into the personnel system. Performance measures are tracked, variations from the promised plan are explained, and their budgetary implications are evaluated by the chief executive or his or her staff.

A performance budget creates a kind of contract between elected officials and the departments: so much service of such a quality for so many dollars. The performance measures help generate information about how much service levels cost, and impact measures suggest the effects on the community of decreases in program spending. This information helps defend departments against council members who want to increase levels of service without increasing funding. At the same time, the system provides council members with assurance that the promised levels of performance will actually be delivered; it also allows council members flexibility in making requests for service levels. Performance budgeting allows elected officials to choose between a particular level of service at a given cost and quality and some other level of service at a different cost and quality. Unless a local government uses performance budgeting, these choices are not readily available.

Reporting

Performance reports should be presented to the chief executive, the council, and the public; but in practice, performance reports are more likely to be circulated to managers than to the public. As Boston's budget director noted, performance reports are distributed to the department heads, but city government doesn't "put out much publicity" about the reports. The city may be reluctant to publicize the reports because of concern about how the information may be perceived or used—if, for example, the media were to focus on failings while ignoring accomplishments.

Lest shortcomings be used against them in a political campaign, elected officials are often reluctant to make performance reports public. According to a longtime observer of the budget process in one city, the mayor had used the city's performance reports in her election

---

Performance budgeting in Tampa

Tampa, Florida, has had a performance budgeting system for many years, and the problems Tampa has encountered are typical of those that other local governments may encounter. The system requires the mayor to attend to routine departmental matters that are not politically exciting; it also requires discipline on the part of elected officials, who must resist asking for increases in service levels without commensurate increases in funding.

Elected officials have, in fact, been reluctant to match allocations to increased demand; nor do they necessarily make appropriate trade-offs when it is necessary to cut one service to expand another. A public works staffer in Tampa explained that projects were sometimes added without changes in budget targets:

The first question the council always asks is, "Can you do it without any more money?" You can ask for a little more and you may get an adjustment. Additional equipment is easier than additional staff. It's difficult to get additional people. You may have to double up, get more productivity or overtime, do a productivity study. If we change the work method, maybe we can do more. We do heuristic routing, targeting to specific areas.

Managers accept this pressure to do more with less and do the best they can to comply. Another Tampa staff member described wrestling with service delivery and the mayor's priorities.

The mayor says, "I want the streets swept twice a week all over town—and cut the budget." It's difficult, but the mayor reflects public interest, what the public wants, and I believe in that as much as in management.

The mayor's requests may cause managerial havoc in many departments, but because they reflect the public interest, the requests are not only particularly difficult to resist, but particularly likely to occur.

campaign—and was therefore extremely sensitive to the fact that they could be used against her by political challengers.

Partly because some portions of performance reports can be politically sensitive and partly because some measures are of greater interest to some levels of the organization than to others, a fully developed reporting system may have multiple sets of goals and objectives aimed at different audiences. Dayton uses four different reporting levels: one internal to the departments, one shared by the departments and the city manager, one that circulates to the council (and hence presumably to the public), and one that refers only to the strategic plan—and is therefore directed primarily to the press, the public, and the business community.

The Dayton system demonstrates that performance can be reported to the public, but it also suggests that other levels of reporting are valuable. In communities that cannot implement reporting on the fourth level— that is, communicating to the public about larger community goals—the first three levels of reporting may still be useful.

Integrating performance measurement

Although a number of local governments have used performance budgeting for years, it would be naive to assume that once the system is developed and implemented, it remains unchanged. Because the performance measurement system must not only win but maintain the support of department heads and elected officials, it has to be capable of adjusting to differing (and sometimes conflicting) sets of interests. Performance measurement systems are also subject to change as a consequence of a shift in leadership: the system may have been initiated and sustained by a particular chief executive, who is eventually replaced. A third source of change in the system is the violation, by elected officials, of their agreement with the departments (i.e., to allocate so much money to the provision of so much service of a given quality); political pressures may sometimes cause officials to revert to across-the-board or incremental budgeting.

Combining managerial and political needs To survive, performance budgets have to address both the routine needs of departments and the policy goals of elected officials. Performance measures for routine activities can be devised by department heads and the chief executive. Elected officials' interests are often twofold: to make departments more responsive to policy guidance and to make the elected officials appear more responsive to the public. One way to address elected officials' concerns is through a citizens' commission, which can work out a short list of community goals; staff can then develop measures to document progress toward these goals. Another approach is for the mayor's staff to come up with a list of politically relevant goals and let the departments determine how to measure progress toward them.

Suppose that the highest citizen priority is reducing violent crime. The performance budget can highlight what the local government is doing to accomplish this goal. For example, the police department can describe its programs to control gangs and to prevent students from using drugs. The mass transit department might report on its program to notify police of any suspicious activity bus drivers witness while on their routes. The housing department might report on its efforts to organize an escort service for seniors who are out after dark. The performance budget can then show progress toward safer streets in measurable terms, such as declines in the number of reported crimes and increases in the number of citizens who feel more secure. The number of people willing to walk outside at night in various neighborhoods can also be used as an indicator of success. Thus, public officials can tie together the efforts of several departments and demonstrate that government is doing what the public requested.

Figure 5–2 shows how citizens' goals for the community can be translated into strategies, objectives, targets, and achievements. (The actual report would probably include several goals.) The summary that appears in the budget need not be this detailed, but the reports coming from program managers might be similar to the figure.

Performance reporting, when linked to goals articulated by citizens, can be a powerful tool to gain public confidence. In Dayton, Ohio, a financial crisis required the city to ask voters to approve new taxes. In exchange for public approval of the tax increase, the city promised to accomplish certain goals that were based on citizens' recommendations. The city routinely evaluates and publicizes progress toward these goals. The citizens, in turn, have to vote regularly to maintain the higher level of taxes. Dayton's compact with the public has been successful: citizens regularly approve taxes by wide margins.

Because that is what elected officials are interested in, Dayton's performance measures include citizens' satisfaction with the quality of services. According to the former budget director, performance measures have to be "both statistical and perceptual":

> From the politicians' perspective, if you don't provide perceptual data, you've missed it. It's not just actual crime rates that are important but how safe people feel. Perception is probably the more important of the two.

In addition to reporting public satisfaction with particular services, Dayton's budget highlights key issues that may have been identified by staff or by citizens and elected officials. The budget describes programs that address these high-visibility issues and tracks progress in solving

---

Figure 5–2 Sample goals, strategies, objectives, targets, and achievements.

Citizen goals
1. Make the community safer.

Strategies
1. Reduce teenage drug use.
2. Establish a service to escort elderly residents after dark.

Objectives and targets
2a. Establish an advisory panel by August 15.
2b. Recruit eight volunteer escorts by September 1.
2c. Solicit donations for vehicles by September 1 for receipt by October 1.
2d. Establish a dispatch system by October 1.
2e. Advertise the service beginning September 15.
2f. Begin service October 5.
2g. Begin evaluation of service November 1; prepare initial report by November 30.

Achievements
2a. Achieved on time.
2b. Six recruits selected by September 1; lack of advance publicity slowed down the recruitment.
2c. Two vehicles promised by September 1 for delivery October 1; did not arrive on time.
2d. Achieved on time.
2e. Advertising began early to help recruit additional volunteers.
2f. Service could not begin until vehicles were delivered and inspected; actual beginning date October 17.
2g. Evaluation pushed back to November 15 because commencement of program delayed.

these problems. To measure the impact of Dayton's "war on drugs," for example, the budget includes the number of narcotics arrests for the previous five years; the amount of revenue the city has taken in under racketeering laws (which enable the government to confiscate wealth owned by drug dealers); and the number of incarcerations for drug use.

In Rochester, New York, the need to incorporate politically relevant information into performance measures is handled a bit differently. To maintain the balance between information needed for management and for political purposes, the budget director chooses from an overwhelming number of measures those that departments liked and used and those that the mayor is interested in. Where a department's performance measures obscure politically important information, the budget director adds his or her political judgment or clarifies the measures so they yield more politically useful information.

For example, when budget analysts argued that on the basis of performance measures, the cost of the mounted police patrol was too high, the budget director added what he knew about public satisfaction with the program. When the performance measures produced information about the cost per pothole fixed, the budget director added to the measures the number of potholes filled. Such changes were at the request of the mayor, who wanted to be sure that what interested voters was included in the budget. According to the former budget director (a political appointee), there was a clear link between performance measurement and reelection.

Reelection is the result; citizens showed that. For example, if you get twenty-five calls for potholes, you filled them, used X tons of fill, each cost $100—but so what? You filled twenty-five potholes. That is what matters to citizens.

In Boston, performance measures are developed and monitored in two different offices that coordinate their activities only loosely. The policy office focuses on short-term goals that the mayor wants to achieve; the budget office focuses on longer-term measures of managerial interest to the departments and tries to coordinate the whole process. One part of the process allows the mayor to include in the budget any indicators with political importance, to see how well the departments are complying with his policy. The other part of the process allows department heads to select measures to monitor workload and efficiency in service delivery.

The process thus combines the mayor's goals, which the departments determine how to measure, with departmental goals. For example, because one of the mayor's goals was to be responsive to the neighborhoods, he set up a hotline to take complaints addressed to the departments. The budget office then set up a reporting system to find out how long it took for these complaints to be resolved, setting as a target the resolution of 95 percent of all complaints within a certain number of hours.

Because both department heads and the chief executive have reason to support the system, this two-track approach appears to be a relatively stable combination. In general, a performance reporting system that satisfies department heads and program managers on the one hand and elected officials on the other is likely to be stable. Nevertheless, in Boston, more systematic coordination is needed between the budget office and the mayor's policy office, and a more explicit mechanism is needed to relate the mayor's goals to the activities of several different departments, each of which has various programs related to the goals.

Shifts in leadership   A performance budget that is designed to satisfy one chief executive may not satisfy a successor; budget systems have to match the management style of the chief executive. According to one staff member in Boston, the mayor's support was desirable, but not absolutely necessary:

It helps if you have the mayor's active support. But it's unrealistic to expect the mayor to care much about the process, as long as it's fair and informative. If the mayor is an advocate, it's easier. So the system will likely survive a change in mayors. I don't kid myself about institutionalizing it, but it does have widespread support in the departments, and the bureaucracy lives on. The next mayor should see the benefits compared to the previous system, which was a straight, line-item budget. So chances are good that it will live on.

In Tampa, there was considerable concern about the survival of the budget system when the new mayor demanded that the old system be abandoned. The old system had emphasized systematic review of all projects and programs. The new mayor, who was more interested in having the budget reflect public goals, wanted to create a list of community goals and use them as the basis for determining whether spending requests should be honored. Nevertheless, it seemed likely that some of the old system would survive because it served departmental needs. The budget director commented that regardless of the budget system imposed by the mayor, some departments would continue to keep performance measures. Otherwise, he said, "How can you tell how you are doing?" In short, even if elected officials abandon a performance measurement system, it may continue to exist if it continues to meet organizational needs and to be of value to departments.

Incremental budgeting   When performance budgeting is fully implemented, budget allocations are based on agreements as to what needs to be accomplished and the cost of doing so. However, since much of the budget is routine, there is a tendency to treat it incrementally, giving focused attention only to those areas that are of interest to elected officials. Increases may come to depend on last year's service levels, plus an amount to be determined by the amount of revenue available, rather than on a negotiated level of performance. If elected officials perceive the budget as routine or become frustrated by the difficulty of making trade-offs, they may lapse into across-the-board cuts or allocate increases that have little to do with changes in demand or service levels. If budget allocations become incremental or across-the-board, the linkage between the allocation process and the performance measurement process is gradually dissolved, and the system may lose credibility and departmental support—without which it is likely to deteriorate entirely. Nevertheless, if incremental budgeting is not applied for too long, performance budgeting can survive it. In a robust system, the degree of integration between performance measures and allocations can vary over time, as can the amount of attention that elected officials pay to performance measures.

In short, once performance budgeting has been implemented, it is not necessarily stable. Performance budgeting usually needs the support of both elected officials and department heads, but political and managerial needs may sometimes be in conflict. Moreover, a program and performance budget that satisfies one chief executive or group of elected officials may not satisfy another. If elected officials find it tedious or stressful to follow management issues closely or to make policy choices, they may revert to incremental allocations, severing the relationship between performance reporting and budgeting; and department heads may come to perceive performance measurement as a waste of time.

Summary

The budget can provide a great deal of information that is useful for management; line items can be used to monitor trends over time and give warning of potential problems, and performance budgets have even broader managerial applications: they can be used to measure and monitor productivity, to link performance to allocations, and to encourage innovation by decentralizing decision making. Under performance budgeting, detailed monthly or quarterly reports reveal managerial problems and help focus attention on finding solutions.

Although program and performance budgets have a number of advantages, they can be difficult to implement and institutionalize. Common problems include poorly or hastily designed measures, difficulties with data collection, and departmental resistance. Implementation may also be hampered by the departments' tendency to set defensively low targets or to turn in unreliable or unusable reports—and by elected officials' failure to maintain their implicit contracts with departments (i.e., so much funding in return for an agreed-upon level of service).

Although the implementation of performance budgeting does pose problems, the good news is that the whole system need not be in place to be managerially useful. Managerial concerns (e.g., identifying future problems, increasing productivity, and maintaining service quality) require particular information in the budget document, and even a little bit of that information can be helpful. Because different kinds of performance measures and their purposes seldom contradict each other, they can be combined.[5] In short, even if a program and performance system is not fully implemented, it is likely to be managerially useful.

Whether it is implemented throughout the organization or program by program, performance budgeting should be designed to serve both policy and managerial goals. While there is some natural tension between a policy and a managerial orientation, there is also a natural interrelationship. If policy goals are overemphasized, the opportunity to improve management through performance budgeting may be lost. On the other hand, if performance budgeting addresses only managerial issues, elected officials may not support the system—and without their support, performance measurement may not become a regular feature of the budget.

1   Richard C. Tracy and Ellen P. Jean, "Measuring Government Performance: Experimenting with Service Efforts and Accomplishments Reporting in Portland, Oregon," *Government Finance Review* (December 1993): 11.

2   Paul D. Epstein, *Using Performance Measurement in Local Government: A Guide to Improving Decisions, Performance, and Accountability* (New York: Van Nostrand Reinhold, 1984); Irene Rubin with Gloria Simo and Deborah Clayton, "Performance Budgeting in Cities: Problems and Solutions" (paper presented at the annual meeting of the Association for Budgeting and Financial Management, Washington, DC, October 1994).

3   Harry P. Hatry et al., *How Effective Are Your Community Services? Procedures for Measuring Their Quality*, 2d ed. (Washington, DC: The Urban Institute and ICMA, 1992).

4   Tracy and Jean, "Measuring Government Performance," 13.

5   For an illustration of how multiple performance measures can be combined in one system, see James R. Griesemer, "The Power of Performance Measurement: A Computer Performance Model and Examples From Colorado Cities," *Government Finance Review* (October 1993): 17–21.

6 Budgeting and financial control

The budget implementation system
    The approved budget
    Apportionment and allotment controls
    Encumbrance controls
    Position controls
    Budget amendments
    Rescissions
    Closing the accounts at year end
    Line-item controls
    Budget transfers
    Budget reserves

The accounting system
    Accuracy in recording transactions
    Chart of accounts
    Fund structure
    Reconciling budgeting with accounting data

The financial reporting system

Summary

Budgeting and financial control

The two preceding chapters examined the budget as a tool for shaping policy and improving organizational performance. This chapter examines the oldest and most basic function of the budget: financial control. As budget scholar Allen Schick observed almost two decades ago, "Control is the first requisite of budgeting. Control must take precedence because a government's budget cannot be reliably applied to upgrading the efficiency or effectiveness of public service if it does not accurately account for the expenditure of funds."[1] Financial controls help prevent overspending, ensure budgetary balance, and guarantee that money is spent in accordance with the approved budget.

Elected and appointed officials, citizens, investors, bond-rating firms, and higher levels of government are entitled to accurate information about how a local government has spent the public's money. These multiple claims for accountability have increased the number and complexity of financial controls. Council members typically approve highly detailed budgets and require a separate, year-end financial report that compares actual spending to the budget passed a year or more earlier. The chief executive wants to ensure that department heads keep expenditures within legal limits and that revenue collections keep pace with budget expectations. The interim financial report, usually prepared monthly in larger governments, allows management to monitor progress toward these objectives. Investors and bond-rating firms are more interested in the year-end financial report, which tells them whether a government has reliably balanced its budget over a number of years.

The budget document itself incorporates many elements of financial control. For example, the document usually includes a comparison of budgeted figures for the forthcoming year to actual figures for the preceding year. It often includes a set of accounting categories, so that spending can be easily tracked and compared with budgeted amounts. And it may include line items showing, for example, the amount of money allocated for office supplies for the police department. Department heads may change detailed line items only a little, if at all; expenditures must comply not with just one aggregate figure, but with many line-item totals within the budget allocation. To demonstrate that earmarked revenues have been spent as intended, budgets may also reflect the fund structures that underlie them. When this is the case, the budget shows the source of money for each major expenditure, project, department, or program.

The financial control measures commonly used by local governments fall into three categories: budget implementation, accounting, and financial reporting (see Figure 6–1). Budget implementation begins when the budget office interprets the new budget and ends after the end of the fiscal year, when financial accounts for that year are closed.

During the implementation phase, the budget office records financial transactions, makes sure the numbers are accurate, and aggregates the details into reports that match the budget and can be used to point out

Figure 6–1 Systems and participants in budget implementation.

Financial control systems	Key participants	Methods of financial control
Budget implementation	Budget office	Estimates revenue and makes appropriations Controls apportionment and allotment Approves transfers Provides position controls Recommends budget amendments and impoundments Monitors budget reserves Closes accounts at year end
Accounting	Accounting unit	Enters approved budget into accounting system Maintains accounting records Creates and closes accounts and funds Maintains chart of accounts Reconciles accounting records with budget
Financial reporting	Comptroller's office	Prepares interim financial reports Maintains internal controls Prepares annual financial report Prepares additional financial reports Works with external auditor

where problems are occurring. Keeping a running tally of how much money is unobligated and available to be spent helps provide financial control; an accounting system with sufficient financial controls can make it impossible to overspend the budget.

The comptroller's office or chief accountant, working closely with the budget office, is charged with the task of preparing an annual financial report that discloses the results of operations and the financial position for the preceding fiscal year. One purpose of this report is to ensure that funds were spent in compliance with the budget and the law. A second purpose is to ensure that revenues did indeed cover expenditures—that the budget was balanced at the end of the fiscal year. Deviations from law or from balance are reported to the council.

These three systems of financial control—budget implementation, accounting, and financial reporting—complement one another. Budget controls, for example, prevent overspending by allowing departments to make purchases only after budget office scrutiny and approval. Local government budget directors keep the budget in balance and ensure that legislative intent is fulfilled during budget implementation.[2] The accounting system provides the information necessary to make midcourse corrections—if, for example, revenues are lower than anticipated or the spending rate is faster than planned. The financial reports allow the budget office to monitor any inappropriate choices or patterns that emerge during the year. For example, if there were instances in which the fund balances had been drawn down, suggesting that revenues had not covered expenditures, these would appear in the financial reports. Figure 6–1 summarizes the three overlapping systems of financial control and the tools commonly used by each one. The rest of the chapter describes these three sets of financial controls and illustrates how they are intended to work.

The budget implementation system

If the budget office could allocate money to each department and program as specified in the budget, without deviation, budget implementation would be a cinch. But that is not how budgeting actually works: budget implementation involves fine-tuning the financial plan to fit reality. In its effort to balance plans with reality while following the intent of the council, the budget office makes use of a number of tools—"administrative technologies," in the words of noted public administration scholar Dwight Waldo. This section of the chapter examines the controls that have evolved to aid the budget office in this politically sensitive but fiscally critical task.

The approved budget

Budgets at the local level are generally revenue driven, meaning that the amount of spending approved in the budget must be less than or equal to the amount of expected revenue. If actual revenues turn out to be higher than budgeted, the budget can be modified; alternatively, any amounts beyond estimated revenues should be set aside in the fund balance. If revenues fall short of budget estimates, the local government must reduce spending or draw down the fund balance to cover the gap.

Historically, one of the merits of the property tax is its capacity to bring revenues into balance with expected expenditures. When preparing the operating budget, the budget office typically compares anticipated general fund expenditures to general fund, nonproperty tax revenues (sales tax, excise taxes, service charges, and miscellaneous revenues) and makes up the difference by adjusting the property tax rate. Increasingly, however, state and local property tax limits have made this process problematic, particularly if changes in tax rates are prohibited or restricted. Typically, the ordinance levying the property tax is approved concurrent with council's adoption of the budget. (These ordinances vary considerably in form; an example is provided in Figure 6–2.)

The budget as passed represents permission to spend up to the amounts specified, assuming that (1) anticipated revenues come in at the appropriate times in the expected amounts and (2) unexpected expenditures (e.g., floods, hurricanes, civil unrest, bridge collapses, major equipment failures, or any other technological or natural disaster) do not intervene. However, despite emergencies, changing priorities, and revenues that are slow to come in or lower than expected, the budget has to be implemented more or less as passed, and balance has to be maintained. Although the budget office tries to minimize the destabilizing effects of shortfalls by estimating revenues as accurately as possible, the exact amount and timing of revenues cannot be known in advance; actual spending must therefore be held up and matched to the revenues as they come in.

The more uncertain the revenue and the more contingencies that occur, the more changes there will be from the original plan. Before a department or program can enter into an **obligation**, the budget office must approve actual spending for new and replacement personnel and for many capital items. This scrutiny prevents departments from spending money that is not currently available, even though the item was approved in the budget; it also prevents spending for nonapproved items.

The council formally approves the budget by adopting one or more appropriation laws—that is, ordinances granting the chief executive and his or her designees legal authority to enter into financial obligations,

Figure 6–2   Property tax ordinance, Bellaire, Texas.

ORDINANCE NO. _96 - 056_

AN ORDINANCE FIXING THE TAX RATE AND TAX LEVY FOR THE CITY OF BELLAIRE, TEXAS, FOR THE FISCAL YEAR ENDING SEPTEMBER 30, 1997, UPON ALL TAXABLE PROPERTY IN SAID CITY.

BE IT ORDAINED BY THE CITY COUNCIL OF THE CITY OF BELLAIRE, TEXAS:

1. There is hereby levied and shall be assessed and collected for the year 1996 an ad valorem tax of 51 cents of each $100.00 worth of property located with the City limits of the City of Bellaire, Texas, made taxable by law, which said taxes when collected shall be apportioned among the funds and departments of the City of Bellaire, and for the purposes hereinafter set forth, as follows, to wit:

For the General Fund:	$0.32
For the purpose of paying the accruing interest and to provide a Sinking Fund for payment of the bonded indebtedness of the City of Bellaire:	$0.12
For the purpose of paying the cost of or a portion of the cost of such capital improvements as shall from time to time be authorized by the Council:	$0.07
Total:	$0.51

2. The Director of Finance is hereby directed to assess, extend and enter upon the tax rolls of the City of Bellaire, Texas, for the current taxable year, the amounts and rates herein levied, to keep a correct account of same, collect the same, and when so collected to be distributed in accordance with this ordinance.

PASSED AND APPROVED THIS 16TH DAY OF SEPTEMBER , 1996.

_____
Mayor, City of Bellaire, Texas

Attest:

_____
City Clerk

Source: City of Bellaire, Texas, *Adopted Budget for Fiscal Year Ending September 30, 1997*, 4.

such as contracts and purchase orders, that will result in the disbursement (payment) of money. Most Western democracies require some sort of legislative approval before the executive (or any other branch of government) may enter into a financial commitment. In the United States, the origins for legislative approval are in the Constitution, which specifies that "no money shall be drawn from the Treasury, but in consequence of appropriations made by law."[3] The practice of legislative enactment of appropriations has become universal among states, localities, and even nonprofit organizations with a governing board.

An appropriation does not grant agencies money; rather, it grants them budget authority—authorization to enter into binding agreements. Program managers who incur obligations greater than the amount authorized by the appropriation act may be personally liable for such excesses unless the council acts to amend the budget. While an appropriation is the most common means used by governing bodies to grant budget authority, spending authority may also be given through more indirect means; for example, to pay a debt or to pay for contracted services prior to the approval of an appropriation, the council may grant a department borrowing authority or contract authority.

Appropriations may be for one year, multiyear, sum sufficient, or permanent. Most appropriations granted by a municipal or county governing body are for one year. That is, at the end of the fiscal year, any unused budget authority lapses. Thus, program managers closely monitor their available spending authority to ensure that it is used fully by the end of the fiscal year; otherwise, unused appropriation authority lapses—meaning that it can be redirected in the following year to other priorities of the governing body.

Multiyear appropriations, a strategy occasionally used by Congress, typically give agencies or grant recipients budget authority for two or three years. Multiyear appropriations allow program managers more latitude for planning and enable them to make longer-term commitments to suppliers and contractors. A sum-sufficient appropriation grants a specific amount of budget authority to a project, regardless of the length of time it takes to complete. As noted in Chapter 7, some local governments approve their capital budgets on this basis, which enables project managers to enter into contracts that will run for the duration of a construction project.

Permanent appropriations are more likely to be found at the federal level: authorization for payment of social security benefits and interest on the federal debt are examples of permanent appropriations. For permanent appropriations, the authorizing legislation includes budget authority that does not lapse at the end of the year but continues as long as the authorization is in force or until the legislation is amended—such as whenever Congress must raise the national debt ceiling.

The governing body's most direct means of maintaining control over the budget is through the level of detail in the appropriation legislation. For example, virtually all states approve appropriations at an agency or program level, and at least twenty-three provide additional appropriations detail at the line-item (or object-of-expenditure) level.[4] At least twenty-one states also include in the appropriation act the number of staff positions approved in each agency or program. At the local level, the appropriation ordinance may specify a lump-sum amount of budget authority for each fund, then incorporate by reference the detailed executive budget with council's amendments.

Although this rarely occurs at the local level, governing bodies may also adopt separate riders to their appropriation legislation that restrict (or, less frequently, supplement) departments' spending discretion. For example, a state legislature may approve several million dollars in appropriations for a university but then require the university to match the state's contribution for employee retirement benefits using "local" (nonstate) funds. Following budget adoption, budget offices are kept busy interpreting the budgetary implications of legislative riders included with the appropriation bill.

In some states, an additional layer of oversight is provided through state review of local budgets prior to implementation. New Jersey, for example, requires municipalities to submit their budgets to the state's Local Finance Board for review prior to implementation. Any amendment to the approved budget must first be approved by the Division of Local Government Services. State-level reviews are usually for the purpose of ensuring compliance with state law, especially laws requiring balance.

Apportionment and allotment controls

Because revenues come in unevenly during the year, the budget office must monitor revenue receipts continuously. So that the availability of funds is somewhat predictable, the budget office may allot several months of revenue at a time: releasing funds gradually prevents departments from spending a year's allocation in the first or second quarter and then coming back for more money; it also leaves enough time for midcourse corrections if revenues lag behind expectations.

In the federal government the disbursement of actual monies during the year is called **apportionment**. (This vocabulary is not standard; at the state and local levels, the word **allotment** is sometimes used.) State and local governments that receive federal grants may receive grant funds on a quarterly basis, rather than in a lump sum, because that is the way the agency dispensing the funds receives its funding.

Encumbrance controls

Another device that helps prevent departmental overspending is a system of **encumbrances**. An encumbrance is a way of marking off part of a department's budget that has not yet been spent but that is obligated. The accounting system divides up a department's budget into two general categories: one that is set aside (encumbered) to pay for items that have been ordered but not yet received (or billed), and one that is available (unencumbered) for expenditure. Each time the budget office approves a purchase order or contract, it shifts funding from the unencumbered to the encumbered column, from which bills are paid. Once the unencumbered portion is reduced to zero, no further spending will be approved.

To make the system work, budget offices require departments to prepare **purchase orders** (or POs) or contracts, which are reviewed by the purchasing office; those that are approved are sent on to the budget office for final approval. The budget office checks to see (1) whether the unencumbered budget total available in the department's allocation is sufficient to pay for the request and (2) whether the spending is authorized in the approved budget. Encumbrances are an accounting control device, but because spending requests must be approved by the budget office, they also serve as a budgetary control measure.

Position controls

The approved budget may detail the number and level of positions authorized for each department. Such detail is quite common in local government budgets, since personnel expenditures represent as much as 80 percent of the costs for general government operations (e.g., public safety, health, and recreation). Regardless of whether the approved budget includes position details, the budget office reviews requests to make new hires, fill vacant positions, or reclassify existing positions. Given the long-term budget implications of creating a new position or reclassifying an existing one, the budget office carefully scrutinizes such requests.

The budget office must ensure not only that position expenditures reflect legislative intent but also that sufficient cash is available. This control function can be especially important during periods of fiscal stress, when positions are sometimes frozen as a means of curtailing expenditures. For example, although the budget may have granted approval to hire an additional person, the budget office may delay approving the hire on the grounds that the money is not currently available. Although it will follow the budget insofar as is possible, the budget office must always balance the permission that is in the budget against actual funding availability—with the latter taking priority.

To create a small body of savings for reallocation during the year, budget offices sometimes hold up permission to hire even when the money is available. In addition to creating some flexibility and allowing adaptations during the year, such funds can also be reallocated by the council to meet an unexpected political need.

Budget amendments

Another approach to financial control is the budget amendment, a formal process requiring legislative approval. When amendments are made, any changes necessary to make the budget adapt to current circumstances and remain in balance are retroactively incorporated into the legally passed budget. Budget amendments may reflect labor negotiations that were not completed in time for publication in the budget; amendments may also reflect the costs of land purchases that were not known when the budget was adopted. Budget amendments may occur if, for example, a new chief executive wishes to redirect certain spending priorities. The budget can also be formally modified to account for revenues that are lower or higher than anticipated. When revenues in the state of Georgia were growing faster than expectations, the legislature routinely adopted a midyear budget amendment: all spending increases for the fiscal year were deferred to that time and were then funded from revenues in excess of projections.[5]

In some local governments, amendments may be made several times in a single year, whenever a major change in the budget requires formal ratification and public scrutiny. However, some local governments make informal budget changes throughout the year, then at the end of the year make a single, omnibus change to formalize the previous informal changes. Although this procedure seems more efficient, it means that the changes are not exposed to public view until long after the fact. Some state laws make it difficult to amend the budget; although restrictive legislation encourages communities to make fewer formal changes in the budget, some adaptation is inevitable, and communities nevertheless continue to make informal changes.

Rescissions

When it becomes clear that revenues are not keeping pace with projections, something must be done fairly quickly if the government is to end the budget year in the black. Since there is not enough time to mobilize support for, pass, and implement a tax increase, the only realistic option is a midyear spending reduction. Spending may be deferred or actually denied, reducing budgeted expenditures.

A midyear spending reduction is called, after federal practice, a **rescission** (the budget authority is rescinded, or taken back). At the federal level, rescissions can be initiated by either Congress or the president and must be passed by both houses. At the local level, a rescission may be less formal. The chief executive or the budget office determines that revenues will be inadequate to end the year as planned and cuts the remaining quarters' allotments to make up the gap. Because rescissions often occur late in the year, after most obligations have already been made, the budget office is likely to sweep up all loose or uncommitted resources—which may have a disproportionate effect on departments whose spending cycles leave some money uncommitted late in the year.

At the state level, it is usually the governor's right and responsibility to pare down expenditures if revenues don't show up on time. Such mid-year reductions can have significant implications for the operating budgets of local governments that depend on state aid. Fifteen states place no restrictions on the governor's authority to reduce appropriations.[6] Nine states grant the governor authority only for across-the-board reductions. In six states, the governor may make reductions up to a specified percentage; in Connecticut, for example, the governor can cut up to 5 percent of an appropriation. In the remaining states, the governor's authority is a variation of one of these three approaches, or the governor has no authority to impose rescissions.

One arrangement at the state level worth instituting at the local level is legislation granting the governor authority to make any changes necessary to balance the budget—up to a given percentage (say, 5 percent) of a department's budget. Granting similar powers to the manager or mayor combines fiscal control and accountability: it ensures budgetary balance during the year without risking delegating too much budgetary power to the chief executive. Any changes larger than 5 percent would be brought to the council for formal approval.

Closing the accounts at year end

At the local level, at the end of the fiscal year, any unobligated balances in accounts are moved to the fund balance and become available for reappropriation in the following year. Though this feature of public budgeting has often been criticized because it may encourage wasteful spending toward the year's end (program managers must use funds or lose them), the idea makes sense from the perspective of fiscal control. A budget requires department heads and program managers to estimate how much work they can do in a year at what cost. Once the work for the year is already done, if it turns out to have cost less than anticipated, then the estimate was wrong, and the department is not entitled to that money. Hence, leftover money reverts to the fund balance.

If the only purpose of returning leftover funds to the fund balance were to save money, it would not be a very effective device, because program managers can find ways to spend it. However, the closing of accounts at the end of the year has a second and more important function. Each fiscal year, all expenditures incurred are attributed to that year, and all revenues levied during the year are attributed to the same year. When the revenues for the year are matched to the expenditures, the budget office's success or failure in maintaining balance becomes clear. In order to determine whether budgetary balance was maintained, the budget office establishes a cutoff date toward the end of the fiscal year to receive purchase orders. Any encumbrances incurred before that cutoff date are charged to the current year, and any received after that deadline are charged to the following budget year. Department heads and program managers also provide projections of unspent funds, which then lapse into the fund balance. Lapsing funding and closing accounts help enforce the end-of-year deadline.

Line-item controls

Line items—detailed lists of expenditures such as personnel, supplies, insurance, and vehicles—provide spending justification by specifying what acquisitions need to be made to accomplish a given amount of work; line items are also used to control the quantities purchased. Each item of expenditure is placed on a separate line of the budget, as in Figure 2–4. Budgets vary widely in their level of line-item detail.

In the second decade of this century, line items were considered a desirable innovation; before long, however, some public officials came to see them as obstacles to good management. What if there were too much funding in one line item and not enough in another? Not every contingency could be anticipated. Moreover, as the number of line items multiplied, budgets became unwieldy and unreadable.

Even more important, line-item budgeting became entangled in a series of political changes. The first was an effort to disempower legislative bodies, which were often perceived as inept and inclined to unbalance budgets. Thus, around the turn of the century, state or local laws often denied city councils the prerogative to increase the executive's proposed budget, although they were generally permitted to reduce line items.

Efforts were being made not only to limit the power of legislative bodies, but to increase the chief executive's power over the budget as well. Reforms intended to make executive budgeting more widespread gained prominence during the teens of this century, roughly at the same time that line-item budgeting was growing in popularity. Reformers who favored executive budgeting argued that councils used line items to curtail the executive's budgetary power, locking the executive into adhering to the original budget in minute detail and forbidding any changes.

Thus, although it was initially conceived as an important tool of financial control, line-item budgeting became part of the struggle between the legislative and executive branches for budgetary power. Implementing the line-item budget often meant implementing the legislative budget.

Emmett Taylor, an early observer of budgeting, wrote in 1925 that "segregated budgets" (the old term for line-item budgets) had been widely adopted in larger cities, but that the result had been an increase in transfers, which were used to get around the controls.[7] The practice Taylor observed continues today: although many budgets still use line items for financial control, the constraints they impose encourage the use of various techniques to increase flexibility and make it easier to rebalance the budget during the year; **transfers** and discretionary accounts are two such techniques. Shifting money between funds or between accounts is called a transfer; discretionary accounts are monies set aside in the budget for unanticipated contingencies.

Budget transfers

Transfers at the local level are of two types. One constitutes a reimbursement for services, such as the police department paying central supply for rental of a photocopy machine.[8] Typically, a department head can initiate this type of transfer on his or her own authority, usually with an **interdepartmental order** (IDO). The second type of transfer occurs between funds—for example, from a water fund to the general fund. Such transfers often have policy implications that require council review and approval. Because transfers are sometimes abused, some state legislatures either forbid them or require that they receive council approval.

Since local governments are forbidden to run deficits, legal transfers from a fund running a surplus to one with a deficit may be important in balancing the budget. But because even legal transfers have policy implications, chief executives are rarely granted unlimited discretion to change the approved budget through transfers, particularly interfund transfers. The National Conference of State Legislatures reports that in only four states does the governor have broad authority to make such transfers.[9] At the local level, state statute, local charter, or ordinances may define the extent of the chief executive's authority to make transfers. Typically, interfund transfers are highly circumscribed, although many chief executives have the authority to move funds within a department from one division to another (such as from police patrol to dispatch) or from one line item to another (such as from salaries to maintenance). Transfers out of earmarked funds are usually tightly controlled, lest the money be spent for a purpose other than that specified by law.

Another kind of problem occurs if the executive withholds a portion of the budget for some favored program, such as a capital construction project. Since these projects never appear in the operating budget, withholding these funds is, in effect, a transfer, with policy and political implications. The most effective control over such transfers is to require legislative approval.

Battles between council members and the mayor are another potential source of transfers. For example, when the council eliminates items, the mayor may restore them through transfers, negating the council's power over the budget. This kind of transfer is especially likely to occur in communities where the council has little power and is permitted to cut or reduce items but not increase them. In St. Louis, for example, a council member complained that the mayor had used transfers to restore all the council's cuts.

If the council controls the executive too tightly through detailed line items, the executive may respond with excessive numbers of transfers, and the legislative body (either at the state or local level) may react in turn by forbidding or tightly restricting transfers. In that case, the need for flexibility may generate contingency funds that can be drawn down in case of an emergency. To permit some flexibility while ensuring that the budget as implemented will not deviate excessively from legislative intent, transfers out of a contingency fund may require council or board approval.

Budget reserves

There are different kinds of **budget reserves**. Some are relatively informal: for example, a local government may gradually release funds designated for other purposes (e.g., snowplowing) or hold back commitments for a short time (e.g., delay awarding a contract for a renovation project). Others, sometimes called rainy day funds, are formally established to protect against emergencies, to satisfy the requirements of bond-rating companies, or to cope with the uneven flow of revenue.

In the northern part of the country and in the mountain states, snowplowing is one source of informal fund reserves. Money is set aside for this purpose; as it becomes clear that not all the money set aside in the snowplowing account will be needed, transfers can be made from this account. Another informal source of budgetary slack is **salary savings**, the funds that become available when a position is vacated and not filled right away, or when a senior person quits or retires and a more junior person is hired as a replacement at a lower salary.

The other kind of budget reserve is a more formal arrangement in which an account or fund is set up explicitly to deal with unexpected events. Such reserves may be (1) located in the budget of each major department, (2) centralized under the manager or mayor, (3) put in a segregated portion of the general fund balance, or (4) established as a separate fund.

During the 1970s and 1980s, as states increased their dependence on sales and income taxes, which fluctuate with the economy, they began to establish budget stabilization funds (rainy day funds) to protect against midyear spending reductions in the event of an economic slowdown;[10] forty-four states now have such funds. As local governments continue to reduce their dependence on property taxes and increase their dependence on sales taxes, they, too, have become more vulnerable to downturns in the economy.

Providing a cushion against the vagaries of the economy is only one reason for state and local governments to establish budget reserves. Local governments maintain reserves for a host of contingencies, including adverse court decisions involving cash settlements, natural or technological disasters, unanticipated delays in receiving state or federal aid, or the need to accumulate sufficient funds to replace a building or a large piece of equipment. Whatever the reason, budget reserves are an essential part of a local government's budget control strategies. Bond-rating agencies place considerable emphasis on reserves to ensure the timely payment of debt service (principal and interest), and governments that fail to maintain such reserves are given lower bond ratings. In addition, local governments maintain reserves because of the uneven flow of tax revenues. For example, while their fiscal year may begin 1 July, property taxes may not be due until the following 1 January. During the six-month lag, local governments must either borrow money in anticipation of the payment of taxes or maintain sufficient cash reserves to finance their operations.

Considerable discussion occurs among budget officers as to the appropriate size of reserves. For local governments, the most influential guidance comes from the bond rating firms, which use a "rule of thumb" figure of at least 5 percent of annual operating expenditures.[11] Other governments view from thirty to ninety days of operating expenditures as an acceptable level for reserves. Experts agree, however, that the more unstable a government's revenue base, the larger its reserves should be. For example, local governments that rely on revenues such as sales and excise taxes should maintain a higher level of reserves to compensate for fluctuation in the amount of revenue these sources produce.

In a discussion of budget reserves, public financing expert Ian Allan identifies three methods governments use to allocate resources to reserve accounts: a formula; a specified percentage of operating surpluses; or dedication of revenues from a particular source.[12] A formula approach is common, possibly because both Moody's Investors Service and Standard & Poor's Corporation, the two most influential bond-rating firms, emphasize this approach. For example, Dallas specifies a minimum of $5 million in its liability reserve and requires its emergency reserve to be equal to no less than 3 and no more than 4 percent of the general fund.

Elected officials need to decide whether to create separate reserve funds, set up reserve accounts within existing funds, or both. A separate fund is more visible and thus more likely to attract the attention of both citizens and the governing body. Citizens may want to know why a government is accruing a surplus instead of reducing taxes; council members may want to use the money for a more politically attractive purpose. The advantage of creating a separate fund, however, is that the purpose and the procedures for using the resources can be explicitly defined in law.

At the state level, segregated funds are commonly set aside to combat recessions. Local governments seem less disposed to set up separate, earmarked funds to combat recessions. They may, however, carry larger general fund balances to protect against revenue shortfalls. Because these monies are not officially earmarked for recessions, particular economic conditions need not be met before the money can be spent, and these fund balances are thus available for other purposes. Nevertheless, the size of the fund balance and the fact that it is maintained from year to year suggest that its principal function is as insurance against revenue fluctuations. A tightly earmarked separate fund might be more secure in time of need, but it would be less available for a variety of purposes in the interim. To deal with legal liability, storms, major fires, or other unexpected events, local governments also create less visible and less controversial contingency accounts within existing funds.

In most cases, tapping a state's budget reserves requires a legislative appropriation. In Kansas, a separate state finance council must approve withdrawal of resources from the budget stabilization fund.[13] In North Dakota, the governor may withdraw funds in order to avert a negative fund balance. At the local level, council approval is almost always required for the use of budget reserves that are part of the fund balance. Ideally, the chief executive or budget office should develop a policy on the creation and use of reserve accounts.

The accounting system

The accounting system, which records and reconciles transactions in accordance with rules promulgated by the governmental accounting profession, is the information system that continuously monitors revenues and expenditures so that they can be balanced in real time. The accounting system tells department heads how much money they have left to spend; it tells the budget office whether revenues are available to commit; and it tells everyone whether the government succeeded in balancing the budget and how closely budget implementation followed the budget as passed or as amended.

So that revenues and expenditures can be monitored, the accounting system provides a record-keeping framework to log the transactions authorized by the budget. Every financial transaction, whether it be a bank deposit, the receipt of property taxes from the county, or the payment of a bill for roof repair at the community center, is recorded. These individual transactions are aggregated in various ways and included in reports issued at intervals during the year. At year end, all the transactions are gathered up and reported in a traditional format called the **comprehensive annual financial report** (CAFR). The interim reports help maintain balance during the year, and the CAFR looks backward to determine how well the government maintained balance and how close actual figures were to the budget as amended.

According to Frederick Cleveland, one of the founders of public budgeting in this country, accounting and reporting together operate as a conning tower. That is, accounting and reporting provide accurate information about the government's financial position at any moment, and thus help identify trouble spots—where spending is getting out of control or exceeding allotments. Without the continuous flow of information from the accounting system, governments cannot know whether the budget is balanced and cannot take timely corrective action if necessary.

In order to carry out this reconnaissance function, accounting must be timely and accurate. In addition, it must be in a form that answers key financial control questions and must match the format used in the budget. It is entirely possible to imagine a **chart of accounts** (a way of recording expenditures) that includes all expenditures but that does not match either the budget format or the departmental structures. Such a system might be accurate but less than useful in maintaining control over departmental spending.

Accuracy in recording transactions

The first requisite of an accounting system is that it be accurate. In addition to being accurate, an accounting system must adhere to professional standards and ensure that the same types of transactions are recorded in the same way over time. Consistency in the treatment of particular kinds of transactions allows comparison with previous records and with financial reports from other jurisdictions; it also helps those who oversee the government's finances understand what they are reading. Auditors, state officials, and bond-rating houses are among the primary external users of financial accounting data.

The accounting system seeks to provide financial information that is understandable, reliable, relevant, comparable, consistent, and timely.[14] These six goals of accounting form much of the conceptual basis for the twelve standards—called **generally accepted accounting principles** (GAAP)—adopted by the accounting profession to guide the recording and reconciling of transactions in an accounting database. As a result of the growing acceptance of GAAP among governments, accounting information is much more standardized than is budgeting information.

The accompanying sidebar summarizes the twelve accounting principles adopted by the Governmental Accounting Standards Board (GASB), the five-person body of accounting professionals that is widely recognized as the official source of **accounting standards** for state and local governments. (The Federal Accounting Standards Advisory Board has been charged with the task of developing comparable principles to guide accounting practices in federal agencies.) Since GASB's creation in 1984, these principles have generated considerable discussion. Of particular concern have been principle 8, which deals with the basis of accounting, and principle 5, which deals with the treatment of fixed assets and long-term debt. One concern is that much of accounting practice is based on the private sector, where full accrual accounting is the rule and where reporting the depreciated value of fixed assets (land, buildings, and equipment) and reporting long-term liabilities (corporate bonds) is important both for tax purposes and for calculating returns on investments. Full accrual means that both revenues and expenses are recorded when anticipated and knowable. In the public sector, except in the case of enterprise funds, it is not important to estimate the value of fixed assets: since the assets are not earning money and governments do not pay taxes, tax breaks for depreciation of capital equipment are meaningless. Similarly, a local government needs to know only that portion of the long-term debt due this year, in order to set a tax rate and adopt a budget that covers both principal and interest. Moreover, estimating the worth of some capital assets, such as highways or storm sewers, is difficult and would require a lot of guesswork, possibly weakening the credibility of the entire financial reporting system.

Governments tend to be more fiscally conservative in accounting for revenues than private sector entities, an approach that helps prevent overestimation of revenue. Before recording revenue, local governments generally wait until they are sure they know exactly when and how much

Summary of the twelve generally accepted accounting principles.

Principle 1. Requires that accounts be maintained on a GAAP basis and demonstrate compliance with finance-related legal requirements.

Principle 2. Requires the use of funds in maintaining accounting records.

Principle 3. Specifies the seven specific types of funds to be used in governmental accounting.

Principle 4. Calls for governments to maintain a minimum number of funds and only those required by law.

Principle 5. Specifies how information about fixed assets (land, buildings, and equipment) and long-term debt should be maintained in the accounting records.

Principle 6. Specifies that fixed assets should be accounted for at cost.

Principle 7. Specifies how depreciation of fixed assets should be recorded in governmental accounting records.

Principle 8. Requires the use of the accrual basis of accounting for measuring financial position and operating results.

Principle 9. Requires the adoption of an annual budget; requires that budgetary control be provided by the accounting system; and requires that the budget be compared annually with the actual results of operations.

Principle 10. Specifies the accounting procedures for interfund transactions.

Principle 11. Calls for the use of a common terminology and classification system throughout all financial records.

Principle 12. Requires the preparation of interim financial reports and specifies the format of the comprehensive annual financial report.

Source: Adapted from Joan W. Norvelle, *Introduction to Fund Accounting*, 5th ed. (Eaton Rapids, MI: RIA Professional Publishing, 1994), 13–25. Adapted with permission of RIA; Resource Information Associates, Inc., 215 Dexter St., Eaton Rapids, MI 48827. All rights reserved.

revenue will be received—in short, until the revenue is available (or nearly so) to be spent. The GASB proposals to modify existing standards to include full accrual accounting would make public sector accounting less fiscally conservative. Although GASB was established to tailor accounting standards to the particular needs of governments, the organization's origins are in the accounting profession; as a consequence, the standards it generates are sometimes inappropriate to government.

The result is some inconsistency between the assumptions that underlie the budget and the standards that guide the accounting system and the reports that it generates. Budgets reflect the need to pay the bills incurred during the budget period—that is, the fund's cash condition; the value of fixed assets such as city hall or a water tower is of less importance, because the imputed value will not be available to pay bills. Accounting for governmental funds focuses on whether a fund's total revenues equal or exceed its expenditures—that is, its financial condition. (For proprietary funds, the focus broadens further to include the fund's economic condition—current and fixed assets, current and long-term liabilities.)

As a result of these differences in perspective, totals in the budget and in the annual financial reports based on the accounting data often differ—although intuitively, they should match, since the accounting records reflect every financial transaction. From the point of view of fiscal control, the summaries of assets and liabilities in the year-end accounting reports are less important than the continuing—even daily—reports of expenditures (and reductions of the available balance) that the accounting system provides.

Chart of accounts

While much of what accountants do is record financial transactions, some of their most important and creative work is setting up the chart of accounts, which groups transactions into meaningful categories. If each transaction were recorded without being put into a category, there would be hundreds of thousands, if not millions, of transactions, but no way of summarizing their effect. For records of transactions to be useful, similar transactions have to be grouped together (although, for financial control purposes, transactions that have been grouped together sometimes need to be broken apart). For example, property tax revenues need to be grouped together; payroll expenditures need to be grouped together; and office supplies sometimes need to be grouped together. To categorize every expense, accountants must have rules about how to treat ambiguous expenditures. Is disability compensation a salary expense or a benefit? What are the budgetary implications of treating it one way or the other? The rules that guide how information is classified in the budget must also guide the classification of transactions in the accounting system. A chart of accounts provides a framework that brings consistency to the way the budget and the accounting system classify transactions.

A chart of accounts organizes into categories all the items that might be purchased and all the transactions that might occur. All recording depends on the chart of accounts; if it does not contain useful categories, the accounting system will not produce useful information. Most important, the chart of accounts has to fit the organization. A chart of accounts that might fit one organization is unlikely to fit another exactly.

Although each local government's chart of accounts is unique, all such charts have one thing in common: they assign a unique identifier to each fund, department, and type of expenditure. In Figure 6–3, a simplified excerpt from a chart of accounts, the fund has a three-digit code, the department has a three-digit code, the subagency has a four-digit code, and the **object of expenditure** has a four-digit code. The combination of these codes makes up the account number for a particular type of transaction. In the figure, the code for budget office salary expenditures drawn from the general fund would be 100-201-3010-2100.

Figure 6–3 Deciphering an account code. The type of expenditure or revenue is identified by fund, department, and unit within the department.

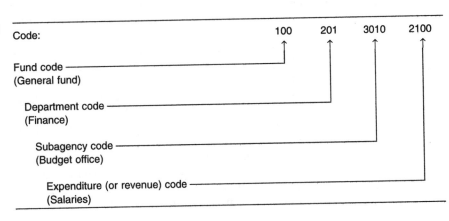

Code: 100   201   3010   2100

Fund code — (General fund)

Department code — (Finance)

Subagency code — (Budget office)

Expenditure (or revenue) code — (Salaries)

If the categories in the chart of accounts are small enough to be informative but large enough to be flexible, the chart can adapt gradually to changing purchases, revenues, or financial control requirements without being radically altered. Striking a balance between too little and too much detail is not always easy, however. For example, if the chart of accounts lumps together a number of different revenue sources under the general heading of miscellaneous income, the level of aggregation may be so high that it obscures important patterns—for example, increases or decreases in particular revenue sources; variations in the way that revenue sources respond to recessions; and decreases in revenue caused by collection problems. To obtain a level of detail sufficient for management's needs, it may be necessary to disaggregate the revenue sources categorized as miscellaneous income. At the same time, it is important to avoid creating categories that are too small and too numerous. Although a high level of detail in the chart of accounts may give management maximum flexibility, it may confuse departments and the budget office when they are preparing the budget.

Fund structure

Whereas a business combines the results of the operations of all its subsidiaries into one consolidated report, a local government creates a separate report for each of its groups of funds. A **fund** is an accounting entity with a self-balancing set of accounts. Each fund receives revenue from different sources and functions as if it were a self-contained business with its own set of accounts and financial report. The expenditures from each fund have to be covered by the revenues from that fund, plus any appropriate transfers of revenue from other funds. Because of the fund structure, governments do not have a single bottom line, but many bottom lines, one for each fund.

Funds are almost always created by law, seldom by executive order. A government may have anywhere from a half dozen to several hundred funds, depending on the size of the government and the complexity of its funding sources.

Funds have several functions: First, by ensuring balance of the parts, they ensure balance of the whole budget. Second, because it is more difficult to bury transactions in separate funds (each of which must balance and have its own report) than in one large, undifferentiated fund, segregated funds ensure that earmarked revenue is being spent appropriately. Finally, individual funds are smaller, less complicated, and easier to view than a whole consolidated budget.

The fundamental purpose of the fund structure, however, is fiscal control: not only must the entire budget balance, but every part of it—that is, every fund—must balance as well. Moreover, a surplus in one fund may not necessarily be available to liquidate a deficit in another. The fund structure thus forces governments to meet a more exacting standard of balance than private sector organizations.

Separating the budget into a variety of funds, each of which must balance, allows different types of funds to be treated differently from an accounting standpoint. Whereas the private sector uses only the accrual method of accounting, governments use the **modified accrual** method for governmental funds and the accrual method for proprietary funds. The use of separate funds, in combination with the use of these different bases for recognizing transactions, makes governmental accounting much more complex than its private sector counterpart. This complexity reflects the public sector's obligation to be accountable to a wide variety of constituencies with various information needs.

Figure 6–4 identifies the seven basic types of funds used in governmental budgets and accounting records and the three broad categories in which they are grouped—governmental, proprietary, and fiduciary

Figure 6–4 Types of funds used by local governments.

Fund category	Description	Example
Governmental funds		
General fund	The major fund in a government, used to account for all financial resources not accounted for in any other fund	General fund
Special revenue funds	A set of funds used to account for revenue legally earmarked for a particular purpose	Motor fuels tax fund
Debt service funds	One or more funds established to account for revenues and expenditures used to repay the principal and interest on debt	1991 Series A debt service fund
Capital projects funds	One or more funds established to account for resources used for the acquisition of large capital improvements, other than those accounted for in proprietary or trust funds	Mulberry Street reconstruction fund
Proprietary funds		
Enterprise funds	A set of funds used to account for a business-like service provided to the public on a fee-for-service basis	Water service fund
Internal service funds	One or more funds that account for the goods and services provided by one department to another within government on a cost-reimbursement basis	Data processing fund
Fiduciary funds		
Trust and agency funds	A set of funds used to account for resources held in trust by government on behalf of other individuals or governments.	There are four subtypes of fiduciary funds.
Nonexpendable trust funds	Endowment-like funds whose principal is never spent but is invested and whose interest earnings are expended	Endowed MPA scholarship fund
Expendable trust funds	Trust funds whose principal and interest may be spent	MPA scholarship fund
Pension trust funds	Funds established to receive and invest payments held in trust by government for its employees and to distribute benefits to eligible retirees	Municipal employee retirement fund
Agency funds	Funds used to collect and temporarily hold money for a third party, often another unit of government	Local sales tax fund

Source: Government Finance Officers Association, *Governmental Accounting, Auditing, and Financial Reporting* (Chicago: GFOA, 1994), 11–17. Reprinted with permission of the Government Finance Officers Association, 180 N. Michigan Ave., Suite 800, Chicago, IL 60601.

(the seven basic funds are those required by the third generally accepted accounting principle).

Governmental funds   The **general fund**, usually the largest and most important of the governmental funds, is the primary operating fund. Any transaction that cannot be accounted for in another fund must be recorded in the general fund.

Whereas a government will have only one general fund, it may have several **special revenue funds**, each with a particular name, such as the Hotel/Motel Tax Fund. Such funds are established to account for the proceeds of revenue sources earmarked or restricted by law for particular purposes. For example, use of revenues from a state or local hotel/motel occupancy tax may be restricted to historic preservation, economic development, and the promotion of tourism.

Local governments often use special revenue funds to account for grants used for operating purposes. Doing so enables governments to segregate revenues with restricted uses from those used for general operations; segregating the monies from such grants also provides a means of verifying that the revenue was used for the legally specified purposes.

Debt service funds, a third type of governmental fund, account for resources used to pay the principal and interest on long-term, general debt—for example, the annual debt service required on a general obligation (GO) bond. The purpose of establishing a separate fund for the bond repayment function is to demonstrate that money to pay back the debt has been set aside and will not be used for anything else. Governments may have one or more such funds, depending on their accounting preferences. For example, governments sometimes establish a separate fund for each GO bond series. (Debt service funds were formerly called "sinking funds," in reference to the process of sinking [retiring] a debt obligation.)

Capital projects funds, the final type of governmental fund, account for financial resources used to construct or acquire capital facilities. For example, the council may choose to create a separate fund—the Eagle Street Improvement Fund—for the reconstruction of this thoroughfare. Revenues flowing into the fund may include GO bond proceeds that were authorized for the project, state and federal grants, and current taxes. Expenditures flowing out of the fund are usually payments to contractors for project design and construction. Once the project is complete, the fund is closed and the remaining balance transferred elsewhere.

Capital projects funds help not only to account for, but also to control, the cost of large capital projects. By creating a separate fund, the local government makes more visible the amount of money flowing into the project as it progresses, as well as the total cost of the project. Because accounting within the general fund is not project-oriented, attempting to keep a detailed record of project costs within the general fund would be difficult, if not impossible.

Proprietary funds   There are two kinds of proprietary funds: enterprise and internal service. **Enterprise funds** account for government services that derive a substantial portion of their income from user charges. Such services include water and wastewater services, other utilities, and a range of governmental, quasi-business activities (toll roads, airports, public transit, docks, golf courses, and government-owned radio and television stations). Accounting for enterprises in separate funds makes it easier to see whether those enterprises are bringing in enough revenue to cover all their costs. The local government can then decide whether to increase fees or to subsidize the fund from general revenues.

Internal service funds are similar to enterprise funds, except that they account for the activities of government departments that do work for (or provide equipment to) other government departments, rather than to the public. For example, a motor pool, which provides vehicles for various departments and agencies, may be fully funded by the charges levied on other agencies. Its rates may include both operating and capital costs (e.g., the cost of replacing vehicles). Other government agencies or departments include in their operating budgets a line item for the rental charge to use motor pool vehicles.

One advantage of an internal service fund is that it encourages efficiency: if data processing is financed through the general fund and provided at no charge to departments, departments are more likely to overuse this "free" service. If the service is accounted for in an internal service fund and departments are charged on the basis of use, they are more likely to limit their data processing costs.

Fiduciary funds Fiduciary funds account for resources that governments hold in trust for individuals or other governments; with a few notable exceptions—such as the Social Security trust fund—fiduciary funds are typically excluded from the operating and capital budgets of governments. Fiduciary funds are of four subtypes (see Figure 6–4): A nonexpendable **trust fund** is one whose principal may not be spent— for example, an endowed scholarship fund. In the case of an expendable trust fund, both the principal and accrued interest may be spent. Pension funds, the third type, are treated like nonexpendable trust funds and held in trust for payment of employee retirement benefits. Agency funds are similar to expendable trust funds and are established by one unit of government to hold money in trust for another unit of government. If a state collects a sales tax on behalf of its municipalities and counties, the state may hold the money in trust in a local sales tax fund until disbursing it.

Interfund transactions Interfund transactions are one of the potential trouble spots in financial accountability. One of the purposes of the fund structure is to ensure that earmarked money has been spent appropriately, but interfund transactions can muddy the waters, making it difficult to determine what the money was actually spent for. If revenue is transferred twice—that is, from one fund to another and then from that fund to a third fund—the switch is virtually impossible to trace. Although the use of revenue in one fund to shore up a gap in another can help balance the budget, excessive interfund transactions can give rise to a number of problems and are therefore generally regulated by law, precedent, or both.

Generally accepted accounting principle 10 classifies interfund transactions into four types: equity, reimbursements, quasi-external transactions, and operating transfers.[15] An equity transfer is a nonroutine and nonrecurring transfer of resources between funds. For example, to provide start-up capital for the new venture, a local government will often make an equity transfer from the general fund to a newly created internal service fund. There is no expectation that the transfer will ever be repaid. Whenever a fund is discontinued, the transfer of the residual balance to the general fund is also categorized as an equity transfer.

Reimbursements pay back a fund for services or charges paid for by another fund. For example, an internal service fund should be reimbursed if it incurs an expense that is correctly applicable to an enterprise fund. A quasi-external transaction represents a payment by one fund for a service provided by another fund. For example, payment to the maintenance department for repair of a heating and air conditioning unit will result in a transfer of funds from the general fund to the maintenance department. Payment from the general fund to the water utility fund for the use of water in fire hydrants is another example of a quasi-external transaction.

Operating transfers, which tend to be ongoing, are much more common than other types of interfund transactions and can create complications for the chief executive. They may be required by charter (e.g., a return from a utility fund to the general fund), or they may be periodically required by the council as an interfund subsidy. Sometimes such transfers are made for convenience, because one fund has a surplus of cash and another a shortfall. Such transfers may or may not be financially justified, but they are an understandable response to the rigidity created by the fund structure, the sometimes excessive earmarking of revenues, and the imbalance between the demand for services and a fund's capacity to raise revenue.

Reconciling budgeting with accounting data

To operate as a control system, the accounting system must not only be accurate, but must also be linked with the budget in a way that permits the funding levels established in the legally passed document to be monitored. The accounting system provides information about the rate of spending and the rate of revenue receipts. It also shows whether spending is exceeding the budget in some lines or categories. Such information allows the budget office to make midcourse corrections, including amending the budget if necessary, to keep the budget in balance.

For the accounting system to perform this control function, the categories in which it records transactions have to match those that appear in the budget. The chart of accounts links the budget with the accounting system. Once the budget is approved, detailed information in the budget, such as the line-item appropriation amounts by department, are entered into the accounting records. This ensures that the budget matches the detailed records maintained in the accounting system. Moving from the budget to the accounting system sometimes requires some interpretation, especially if the budget shows lump sums rather than detailed line items. Nevertheless, as long as the budget matches the categories in the accounting system, that system can provide information for midcourse corrections.

To ensure that the budget and the accounting system match, budget items are assigned accounting codes that come from the chart of accounts: each fund has an accounting code, each department or program has a code, revenues have a code, expenditures have a code, and particular kinds of revenues and expenditures have codes. The accounting system can get quite detailed, but the budget document need not include all the detail. Some governments include the accounting codes in the budget document, while others just use the codes to keep track of transactions in a way that responds to the budget.

The heart of the accounting system is the recording and reconciling of transactions. Governments may maintain several specialized journals, such as a cash receipts journal or purchases journal, in which to log transactions. A journal is a chronological listing of transactions made throughout the fiscal year (see Figure 6–5). All transactions not logged

Figure 6–5 Sample page from a general journal.

Date	Account Titles	PR	Debit	Credit
19X4				
Tr 1	Taxes Receivable		50000—	
	Fund Balance			50000—
	To record levy of property taxes.			
2	Cash		10000—	
	Notes Payable			10000—
	To record loan from bank on tax anticipation notes.			
3	Cash		45000—	
	Taxes Receivable			45000—
	To record receipt of taxes levied.			
4	Fund Balance		25000—	
	Vouchers Payable			25000—
	To record preparation of voucher for payment of salaries.			
	Vouchers Payable		25000—	
	Cash			25000—
	To record payment of voucher.			
5	Fund Balance		21000—	
	Vouchers Payable			21000—
	To record preparation of voucher for materials and supplies.			
	Vouchers Payable		21000—	
	Cash			21000—
	To record payment of voucher.			
6	Notes Payable		7500—	
	Vouchers Payable			7500—
	To record preparation of voucher for notes payable.			
	Vouchers Payable		7500—	
	Cash			7500—
	To record payment of voucher.			

in a specialized journal are entered in the general journal. A record of a transaction always involves at least two entries. By convention, the first line is the debit, or left-handed entry, and the second line is the credit, or right-handed entry, which is indented. In other words, the same item is recorded twice, once positively and once negatively. (One way to think about this is that an expenditure increases the amount of money spent and reduces the amount of money available to be spent.) The sum of the debits must always equal the sum of credits. Each set of entries is followed by a brief explanation of the nature of the transaction. As organized in the journal, the information is not particularly useful. The accounting system aggregates the raw information into larger and more usable categories.

Interim financial reports are prepared periodically that compare the budgeted and actual amounts of revenues and expenditures for each account. This comparison is central to ensuring that receipts for each revenue source are keeping pace with estimates and that expenditures and encumbrances for each account do not exceed what is authorized in the budget.

The financial reporting system

The culmination of budget implementation is the preparation of interim (usually monthly) and annual financial reports. From a budget implementation perspective, the quarterly or monthly reports are more important. These reports, which generally originate as computer printouts of the expenditure and revenue ledgers for each fund, may, for example, be arranged as follows:

Budgeted expenditures	Current period expenditures	Year-to-date expenditures	Encumbrances	Unencumbered balances

The information may then be summarized graphically to give council members a pictorial representation of the trends in actual revenues and expenditures. Each department receives a more detailed report of expenditures. The report enables the budget office to monitor the budget status of each department—and of each line-item appropriation within the department—and to identify potential areas of concern. This information may then be summarized to show the proportion of the year that has elapsed and the proportion of the total budget that has been expended. For example, if 55 percent of the budgeted total has been spent or committed by the sixth month of the fiscal year, that figure may or may not represent a problem, depending on the department's seasonal spending patterns. If expenditures should be relatively constant throughout the year, the expectation would be that about 50 percent of the budget would have been spent halfway through the year.

For the interim revenue report, the budget office may organize the information for each account as follows:

Budget for current year	Actual revenue for current period	Percentage of year-to-date budget

If the expenditure and revenue reports suggest that revenues are falling seriously short and are not being made up by unexpected increases in revenues from other sources, the budget office will recommend corrective action.

The comprehensive annual financial report (CAFR), which is prepared primarily for use by external stakeholders, reports on all funds managed by a government for the preceding fiscal year. Information in the CAFR is organized by aggregating funds of a similar type, with more highly aggregated information presented first.

Unlike the interim reports, the CAFR is subject to examination by an external auditor who reports on its accuracy. Since the CAFR is prepared by the executive branch, the system of checks and balances requires an independent auditor to verify the accuracy of the report to the legislative body. The final version of the CAFR includes a copy of the auditor's report, usually one page in length, on the auditing firm's letterhead.

The **audit** often includes a management letter that identifies weaknesses in the control environment and makes recommendations for improvement. Because of the external auditor's influence, this letter can strengthen the hand of the budget office or finance department in recommending changes. The finance director may also ask the auditors to focus on issues on which it is difficult to obtain cooperation from department heads.

Although much of the information in the annual report is not useful for internal financial management or control, some of the figures may be of interest to department heads and program managers. For example, for each fund, the CAFR presents the beginning balance, revenues, expenditures, total transfers in and out, and the end-of-year fund balance. This part of the report shows not only whether the budget was in balance at the end of the year, but also whether operating revenues covered operating expenditures, whether the fund balance was drawn down to cover a revenue shortage, or whether transfers were used to balance the budget. In some local governments, this part of the annual report may be the only source for such information.

An annual report in compliance with GAAP will also include an estimate of unfunded liabilities—that is, amounts the government owes or is likely to owe in the future for which it has not put any money aside. Although these numbers do not appear in the budget, they are relevant to financial control because they indicate the cumulative effect of such liabilities and the amount of funding needed to handle the anticipated problems. For example, if employees are accumulating sick days, for which they are eligible to be paid if they leave the organization, is the government putting money aside to pay this benefit? Is the government putting enough money into its self-insurance fund and into its pensions? Again, the annual report may be the only place this information is presented—and unless officials specifically request the information, it may not show up even in the CAFR.

The annual report also includes a statement comparing the budget with actual revenues and expenditures. Because the CAFR is concerned with legal compliance, it uses the budget as amended, rather than the original budget, as the basis for this comparison. If, for example, the budget is amended the day before the books are closed, and the actuals are measured on the next day, the CAFR will make the government appear to have adhered closely to the budgeted figure. Although the actual figures may comply with the law, they may, in fact, diverge widely from the original budget. This part of the report would be more useful to management if it included the original budget along with the amendments.

One more piece of information that shows up in the annual report and that is useful for financial control is a list of interfund transactions. Although the list does not indicate precisely where transferred funds originated or ended up, it does note the total amounts of transfers into and out of each fund. These figures allow the reader to see at a glance which funds are importing resources and what the level of transfers is as a proportion of the fund totals. By comparing these figures across various annual reports, an analyst can determine whether the level of transfers is going up as a proportion of the budget—and if so, where the increases are occurring.

Summary

Budget implementation, accounting, and financial reporting are the three categories of financial control measures employed by local governments. Each category has its own financial control mechanisms: in the context of budget implementation, for example, the budget office uses apportionments or allotments to prevent departmental overspending, encumbrances to ensure that items are in the budget and that money is available before it is committed, and position controls to ensure compliance with the budget and to match spending to incoming revenues.

When excessive financial control renders it difficult to achieve balance, local governments often use operating transfers or contingency funds to increase budgetary flexibility. When transfers get out of hand, however, they may be sharply restricted. Although transfers between lines or programs within a fund usually do not require council approval, transfers across funds almost always do.

When state or local legislation puts extreme limits on transfers, local governments may use a variety of reserve accounts and funds to maintain balance in the face of unpredictable fluctuations in revenues and expenditures. Local governments also have access to a number of other mechanisms for revising the budget to accommodate changes that occur during the year, including rescissions (cuts in expenditures), and amendments, which change the original budget to reflect the new levels of expenditures or revenues.

By closing the books at the end of the fiscal year, the budget office matches revenues and expenditures for exactly the same period for all units, and is thereby able to determine whether the budget did indeed balance as planned.

The annual report provides an after-the-fact view of efforts to keep the budget in balance; it also provides warning of problems that may evolve over a period of one or more years, including the drawing down of reserve funds, excessive or increasing levels of interfund transfers, and excessive unfunded liability. By calling attention to such problems in a public document, the annual report can help pressure a local government to deal with the identified problems in future budgets.

1 Allen Schick, "Contemporary Problems in Financial Control," *Public Administration Review* 38 (November/December 1978): 513.

2 Thomas J. Kane, "A National Survey: Municipal Budget Directors View Budget Control," *Public Budgeting and Finance* 2 (summer 1982): 35.

3 U.S. Constitution, art. 1, sec. 9.

4 Corina L. Eckl, *Legislative Authority over the Enacted Budget* (Denver, CO: National Conference of State Legislatures, 1992), 10–11.

5 Thomas Lauth, "Midyear Appropriations in Georgia: Allocating the 'Surplus,'" *International Journal of Public Administration* (1988): 531–50.

6 Eckl, *Legislative Authority*, 35.

7 Emmett R. Taylor, *Municipal Budget Making* (Chicago: Univ. of Chicago Press, 1925), 25.

8 George E. Hale and Scott R. Douglass, "The Politics of Budget Execution: Financial Manipulation in State and Local Government," *Administration and Society* 9 (November 1977): 367–78.

9 Eckl, *Legislative Authority*, 25.

10 U.S. Advisory Commission on Intergovernmental Relations, *Significant Features of Fiscal Federalism* (Washington, DC: ACIR, 1994), 8–11.

11 Ian Allan, "Unreserved Fund Balance and Local Government Finance," *Research Bulletin* (November 1990): 5–6.

12 Ibid., 4.

13 ACIR, *Significant Features*, 8–11.

14 Government Finance Officers Association, *Governmental Accounting, Auditing, and Financial Reporting* (Chicago: GFOA, 1994), 200–1.

15 Joan W. Norvelle, *Introduction to Fund Accounting*, 5th ed. (Eaton Rapids, MI: RIA Professional Publishing, 1994), 72–75.

7 Planning and budgeting for capital improvements

A separate capital budgeting process

Developing a capital budgeting policy

Capital improvements plans
Time frame
Inclusiveness
Maintenance and renovation

Organizing the capital budgeting process
Oversight
Timing
Assignment of priorities

Identifying and selecting projects
Developing priorities
Conducting a needs assessment
Collecting and ranking requests
Developing and applying criteria

Funding: Policy issues
Debt
Revenue and general obligation bonds
Amount of debt
Misestimation of capital project costs

Preparing the capital budget
Preparing the capital budget manual
Determining project costs
Determining project funding
Bundling debt needs and planning a referendum
Holding public hearings
Appropriating for capital outlays

Summary

Planning and budgeting for capital improvements

Elected officials and citizens often take a keen interest in capital budgeting. The projects are usually large and expensive, with visible results—buildings, swimming pools, airports, and streets. When capital projects go awry, there are floods, water pressure is low, sewers back up, and traffic snarls. Where such projects will be located, how much traffic they will generate, and what they will look like are typical of the controversial issues that must be resolved. Neighborhoods may be cut in half by elevated highways or nearly destroyed by noise from jet engines or squealing brakes. The addition of turn lanes or the improvement of sight lines may make intersections safer, but homes may have to be torn down to make room for the changes.

Capital outlays are often budgeted separately from operating expenses. The operating budget covers routine costs for service delivery, while the capital budget covers the nonroutine costs of infrastructure, public buildings, equipment, and land purchases. Infrastructure refers to public investments such as streets, storm drainage, water and sewer lines, streetlights, and sidewalks. Examples of public buildings are government offices, courthouses, jails, schools, and airports. Equipment includes items such as computers, printers, patrol cars, telephone systems, and office furniture. Local governments often purchase land for airport construction, parking lots, parks, and landfills. To enlarge the tax base, municipalities—and occasionally counties—purchase and prepare for development land that would be too expensive for the private sector to develop.

Of these four types of public investment, infrastructure is the most important to the largest number of people. Everyone benefits from streets, storm drainage, water and sewer lines, and streetlights. Before communities began investing in infrastructure, towns were dark at night, roads were filled with mud during rainy seasons, homes and businesses flooded periodically, and water- and sewage-borne diseases were epidemic.

Infrastructure not only improves the quality of life, but also creates many of the conditions businesses require to operate. Historically, the business community was hard hit by disasters related to inadequate infrastructure: epidemics drastically reduced urban populations, and fires devastated areas where water pressure was insufficient or where fire hydrants were sparse. Business leaders often led the fight for improved infrastructure to resolve such problems. Businesses have also benefited economically from infrastructure improvements. Paved streets and highways stimulated the automotive industry and the ancillary businesses that service motor vehicles. More broadly, good roads reduce the cost and increase the speed of delivering finished goods, making it possible to distribute products to regional, national, and even international markets. If businesses can expand their markets, they can use their plant and equipment to capacity, thereby increasing their productivity.

The benefits resulting from the construction of public buildings, the purchase of equipment, and the acquisition of land are less dramatic and visible but nonetheless important. A new city hall may become a symbol of community pride; new computers may boost public sector efficiency; and the purchase of land for public purposes may create welcome open space that increases property values. Sometimes such capital outlays are necessary in order to provide services that the public has requested. For example, if a community wants publicly provided recreation services, then public officials may have to acquire land, build swimming pools and recreation centers, and provide office space for staff.

This chapter examines the process of budgeting for capital outlays in local government. The first section considers the advantages of separating capital budgeting from the operating budget. The chapter then describes the development of a capital budgeting policy, which can be used to guide budgeting deliberations. Particular policies are then considered in detail—whether to have a capital improvements plan and what to include in it; organizing the capital budgeting process; identifying and selecting projects; and funding capital improvements. The chapter concludes with a brief discussion of how to prepare the capital budget document for council review and approval.

A separate capital budgeting process

Most governments in the United States distinguish between capital and operating expenditures. In a survey of the 50 state budget offices, Lawrence Hush and Kathleen Peroff found that 42 states have capital budgets.[1] Of these, 40 either use a separate section in the governor's budget or submit a separate document with the capital budget requests. In California and Mississippi, capital requests are separate line items in an integrated budget; this is analogous to what is done at the federal level. In a 1992 survey of cities over 75,000, 73 percent of finance officers said that they routinely prepare a capital budget; 61 percent of the sample said that their capital budgets were separate from the operating budget.[2]

Governments at the state and local levels separate capital and operating spending for several reasons. First, capital outlays are often paid from one-time, earmarked sources such as debt proceeds and grants. Segregating capital items helps ensure that revenues earmarked for capital items are indeed spent for those purposes.

A second reason to separate capital and operating budgets is that their decision-making processes differ. Building a capital budget involves preparing a list of projects, then ranking them: projects are all—or nearly all—compared against each other. As projects are funded and built, new projects are added to the list, and the process repeats itself. In the operating budget, by contrast, most of the programs and projects will be continued from one year to the next. Except in zero-base budgeting, programs are not compared to each other and ranked; and because programs normally continue from year to year, there is little need to prepare a list of programs and assign priorities to them.

A third reason for a separate capital budgeting process is that the time frame for the capital budget differs from that of the operating budget. Everything that is in the operating budget occurs within a fiscal year; capital projects, in contrast, may take years to plan and implement. Extensive planning and review is required for several reasons: First, any errors in a capital project can be corrected only at considerable—and in many cases prohibitive—expense. An error in an operating budget, however, can be revised the following year or even amended during the current year. Second, capital projects—especially for infrastructure—tend to be linked, requiring careful attention to their sequencing. For example, a street resurfacing project may be preceded by replacement of water and sewer lines.

Time frames for the two types of budgets also differ because capital spending tends to be uneven. Projects are expensive and come in clusters, whereas operating expenditures tend to be smooth, marked by steady but gradual increases rather than peaks and valleys. A capital budget allows a government to plan much further ahead than the operating budget does, making it possible to save for large projects or to spread their cost more evenly over a period of years.

Finally, capital projects, which are often plagued by **change orders** and overspending, require closer monitoring than ongoing programs such as police or fire protection. A separate capital budget encourages careful monitoring of project implementation; moreover, it permits separate accounting for capital projects, which facilitates cost control.

Developing a capital budgeting policy

Capital budgeting requires a number of policy decisions, although not every government will want to adopt formal policy guidelines. Thinking about policy decisions in advance has a number of advantages: First, clarifying policy issues can help make conflict during budget deliberations more productive. Second, developing policy guidelines can help decision makers see a variety of options where they may not have realized there were choices. Third, drawing up a policy statement gives chief executives and council members an opportunity to think about decisions they may not have viewed as policy laden. Fourth, formulating a policy statement and getting it approved may help gain community consensus on good financial practice. A capital planning policy statement need not be followed rigidly, but it should make decision makers think about whether specific situations require an exception to policy—and if so, why, and whether a new policy should be formulated.

The accompanying sidebar lists possible elements for inclusion in a local government's capital budgeting policy.

Capital improvements plans

If a local government has a capital budget, why does it also need a capital improvements plan (CIP)? The capital budget lists only the projects and equipment to be undertaken or purchased during the budget year, as well as their sources of funding. The capital budget typically does not list projects that are planned to begin more than a year in the future.

A CIP, by contrast, lists projects and equipment purchases that are anticipated and scheduled over a period of five years or more (see Figure 7–1). A CIP forces local governments to look ahead, see what their needs will be, and plan for future projects. Is the population growing? Will more schools or roads be necessary? How will such projects be funded? Will funding the projects require a bond referendum? Large and expensive projects, such as drainage improvements, may need to be completed in segments, to hold down annual costs.

A CIP is a useful tool for any local government, even if there are not a lot of complicated projects. In addition to making officials think about

Potential elements of a capital budgeting policy statement

1. Preparation of a capital improvements plan (CIP)
   a. What is the planning period?
   b. How inclusive should the CIP be?
   c. Will expenditures for maintenance and/or renovation be included in the capital budget?
2. Organizational issues
   a. What unit will be responsible for preparing the CIP and capital budget?
   b. Should the capital budget be prepared concurrently with the operating budget or during the off season?
   c. Will a capital allocation committee be used to evaluate and recommend a ranking of proposed projects? Will the committee include citizens?
3. Project evaluation
   a. What procedures will be used to evaluate and rank proposed projects?
   b. What criteria will be used to evaluate and rank proposed projects?
4. Funding sources
   a. Will debt be used for capital projects, and under what circumstances?
   b. What type of bond (general obligation or revenue) will be used, and under what circumstances?
   c. How much debt, if any, can be incurred?
   d. How will unused balances in the capital project funds be used?

future capital needs, a CIP forces decision makers to review, compare, and assign priorities to projects. The first year of the plan is then included as the capital portion of the budget. Creating a CIP is simpler and more efficient than casting around each year for projects or equipment purchases.

Time frame

The typical CIP includes a five-year projection. As long as the priorities are not treated as fixed, some good arguments can be made for planning for longer than five years. Acquiring land for parks, airports, retention ponds, and public buildings is much less expensive when population density has yet to become a problem, and the land can be held in a relatively undeveloped state until needed. Long-term planning for water and sewer lines can also be helpful: if, for example, a look ahead reveals that future population estimates exceed current water production capacity, planning may be needed to expand and protect the watershed, build aqueducts, drill wells, or lay pipe to reach surface water. Such projects may require more than a five-year planning horizon.

Inclusiveness

To ensure the integrity of the CIP, all proposals for capital investment should go through the capital planning process. In its capital improvements policy, Fort Collins, Colorado, notes that "the City will make all capital improvements in accordance with the adopted Capital Improvements Program and the Capital Project Management Control System."[3] Ideally, local governments should avoid a two-track process in which some projects are subject to scrutiny and comparison in the CIP, while others—possibly with strong political backing—avoid such scrutiny. If

Storm Drainage
Capital Projects

	ADOPTED 1997	PROJECTED 1998	PROJECTED 1999	PROJECTED 2000	PROJECTED 2001
Revenue					
Basin Revenue	$1,328,806	$1,534,928	$2,025,727	$1,704,940	1,364,581
Reserves	9,000	9,000	9,000	9,000	9,000
Total Revenue	$1,337,806	$1,543,928	$2,034,727	$1,713,940	$1,373,581
Expenses					
Canal Importation Basin	0	267,828	143,015	50,000	50,000
Cooper Slough/Boxelder Basin	0	0	0	0	69,269
Dry Creek Basin Instream	651,834	32,000	123,000	33,000	33,000
Evergreen/Greenbriar Basin	33,000	69,800	179,600	178,000	49,000
Foothills Basin	0	122,000	451,000	550,000	136,000
Fossil Creek Basin	0	163,000	40,000	40,000	40,000
Fox Meadows Basin	128,000	33,000	102,000	34,000	65,212
McClelland/Mail Creek Basin	0	45,000	299,915	85,000	91,000
Old Town Basin	159,000	339,900	340,000	80,000	419,100
Poudre River Master Plan	9,000	9,000	9,000	9,000	9,000
Spring Creek Basin	187,900	356,400	200,000	308,000	338,000
West Vine Basin	169,072	106,000	147,197	346,940	74,000
Total Expenses	$1,337,806	$1,543,928	$2,034,727	$1,713,940	$1,373,581

Figure 7–1   Excerpt from a capital improvements plan, Fort Collins, Colorado.

Source: City of Fort Collins, Colorado, *1997 Annual Budget: Budget Overview*, vol. 1, 257.

elected officials can put forward proposals for consideration and revise priorities in the CIP, they are less likely to try to bypass the CIP approval process entirely.

The scope of the CIP may also be affected by the definition of capital items. Since it is difficult to come up with one definition that clearly differentiates capital from operating expenses, a community may want to use several definitions to cover a variety of situations. One definition of capital items is "fixed assets of considerable value." If the item or project is long lasting and costs more than a predetermined minimum amount, then it belongs in the capital budget. The minimum will vary, depending on the size of the budget and the preferences of the chief executive and the governing body. In smaller communities, the amount may be as little as $1,000, rising to $25,000 or more in larger jurisdictions.

Another approach to sorting out capital and operating items is to categorize expenditures as routine or occasional. Routine or recurring expenditures, such as those for heat and electricity or for consumable items that last less than one year, are normally considered part of the operating budget. Expenditures that occur episodically and items with a life expectancy of more than a year go into the capital portion of the budget. Thus, routine road maintenance would go into the operating budget and road reconstruction into the capital budget.

The distinction between operating and capital is less clear in practice than in theory. For example, if a police squad car is leased, is it part of the operating budget? If the chief's car is kept five years, is it a capital purchase? If all the cars belonging to the building department are kept more than a year, they would go in the capital budget—which would make the building department's operating budget look smaller than the operating budgets of departments that lease their vehicles or trade them in more often. Whether certain types of expenditures, such as those for automobiles, are classified as capital or operating will depend on the formal or informal policies (i.e., conventions) of the local government.

To complicate matters further, capital projects may involve some operating expenditures. Road resurfacing, for example, is normally considered a capital project, but it requires the time of the public works and engineering staff; because labor costs are recurring, they are normally defined as operating expenditures. If project costs are calculated in such a way as to exclude all costs for labor and consumable supplies, the project will appear much less expensive than it actually is. Since, however, all project costs must be covered (by bond proceeds, revenue transferred from the operating budget, or grants), it is essential to estimate the full project costs, including labor and consumable supplies. As a consequence, capital budgets may include some items ordinarily classified as operating.

The most common way to handle ambiguities related to categorizing costs is to divide capital outlays into two types: departmental capital and large capital projects. Departmental capital includes furniture, office equipment such as computers and photocopiers, and minor remodeling. For departmental capital, the criterion of lasting a year or more and costing more than some minimum number of dollars is appropriate. (In the case of motor vehicles, however, it may be easier to categorize all expenditures for passenger vehicles as either capital or operating, rather than to distinguish between automobiles that will last more than one year and those that will last less.) For large capital projects, whatever labor and supplies are used are considered part of the capital costs. The result may not be perfect, but it is clear and useful.

However ambiguities about assignment of costs are resolved, what is most important is that officials develop policies appropriate to the circumstances and then apply those policies consistently. Although it may be tempting to change the definition of capital and operating items according to circumstance, this practice confuses citizens and council members, and may lead to a lower bond rating or even to an adverse audit opinion.

Similarly, because increases in the operating budget quickly push up the property tax, whereas increases in borrowing have a more gradual impact, property tax limits may create pressure to put ambiguous items into the capital budget. On the other hand, legal limits on the amount of general obligation debt may create pressure to shift capital items into the operating budget; for example, through leases, capital purchases may be transformed into operating expenses. Because decision-making processes for capital and operating items usually differ, an item may fare better or worse, depending on how it is defined; this is especially true if there are ceilings on some portions of the budget.

Assigning expenditures inappropriately to the capital or operating budget is especially problematic if it results in the use of long-term debt to acquire short-lived assets (i.e., citizens are still paying for the project or equipment when it is no longer in use). Another potential difficulty occurs if capital items of relatively low priority evade the intense competition and scrutiny of the capital planning process by being funded through the operating budget. Other potential problems include evasion of regulations and excessive borrowing.

One way to help prevent abuses is to include in the capital budget policy statement a definition of a capital item. For example, road repairs may be defined as operating or as capital; or road repair projects intended to last less than a few years may be defined as operating, and those intended to last longer may be defined as capital. Whatever the definition, it should be used year after year, and the legal and policy implications of any deviation from this definition should be explored before a change is implemented. Another mechanism for preventing abuses is to establish a policy requiring that the duration of loans match the longevity of the projects funded by them.

Maintenance and renovation

Another policy consideration is the treatment of maintenance expenditures for existing capital facilities. A case can be made for treating maintenance and renovation as new capital expenditures. In their survey of state budget offices, Hush and Peroff found that thirty-six states included major maintenance expenditures in their capital budgets.[4] The logic of this approach is that it ensures that capital projects cannot be constructed unless there is sufficient funding for upkeep in the operating budget.

In an article on the state of research in capital budgeting, Michael Pagano recommends that the capital budget be linked annually, and project by project, to maintenance items in the operating budget; he also recommends that maintenance be funded through the capital budget— by means of long-term debt, if the benefits accrue to more than one year.[5] In Pagano's view, this strategy would help prevent the premature and costly deterioration of public facilities.

In short, there may be good reasons to include in the capital budget what appear to be operating items or to include in the operating budget what appear to be capital items. However, a clear justification based on policy guidelines should accompany such decisions. While most expenditures will clearly belong in either operating or capital, classification of ambiguous items depends on policy. As noted earlier, thinking these policies through and applying them consistently is preferable to continually changing definitions, which can confuse decision makers, render historical comparisons meaningless, and contribute to unwise and politically costly decisions.

Organizing the capital budgeting process

The three sections that follow discuss policy issues in the organization of the capital budgeting process: oversight, timing, and the assignment of priorities to projects.

Oversight

Interestingly, the literature on capital budgeting does not recommend that a particular unit within local government be responsible for capital budget preparation. Likely possibilities include the finance department or budget office, the planning department, and, in larger jurisdictions, a separate capital budgeting office.

Because many of the skills required to put together a capital budget are similar to those required to prepare the operating budget, the most logical location is the budget office. Like the operating budget, the capital budget (including the CIP) requires a timetable, forms, supporting documentation, executive budget hearings, and physical preparation of the final documents. Locating the capital budgeting function in the budget office also has another benefit: if the capital budget is put together somewhere other than in the budget office, its impact on the operating budget (and the operating budget's impact on the capital budget) may not be fully understood.

A second possible location for managing the capital budget is the planning department, which deals routinely with time horizons five, ten, or more years in the future. In addition, if the community has a comprehensive plan, locating capital budgeting in the planning department facilitates implementation of the plan. For example, if the ten-year population projections in the comprehensive plan suggest that water and sewer facilities will have to be expanded, the planning department can see to it that the CIP reflects these needs.

When the planning department has key responsibility for capital budgeting, the emphasis is likely to be on setting standards for service levels and generating projects on the basis of community needs; this is how planning departments normally function when preparing a comprehensive plan. Because this approach tends to emphasize anticipated needs rather than immediate demands, it may be more expensive than a demand-based system; it also raises a number of political problems. First, the public may resist tax increases to pay for improvements—for example, road widening—that are not yet necessary. Second, under a planning-dominated process, neighborhoods with higher needs—for example, those with fewer "tot lots" and more children—get more projects, regardless of councilmanic input. The planning model thus makes it more awkward for council members to ask for specific projects in their districts. Finally, giving the planning department responsibility for capital budgeting can also create conflict with department heads, who may feel that their role in generating capital projects and proposals is being usurped by the needs dictated by the comprehensive plan. For a number of years, the planning department in Tampa, Florida, had responsibility for generating and ranking capital projects, but the other departments asked the mayor to remove the planning department from this function. The planning department then shifted to advising the other departments on how to put together their own lists of capital projects, using principles similar to those that the planning department had used. That this shift reportedly worked well suggests that planning departments need not have overall responsibility for preparing the capital budget in order to be successfully integrated into the capital planning process.

A third option is to locate responsibility for capital planning in a separate office; this is the arrangement used in Boston. There are two principal disadvantages to this organizational location: First, departments may resent the fact that another office has authority over their capital requests. Second, the interdependence of capital and operating expenditures may not be fully recognized.

The location of responsibility for the capital budget depends to some extent on the circumstances the local government faces. If nothing out of the ordinary is happening, then it is perhaps best to house capital budgeting in the budget office; if capital budgeting and planning have been more or less ignored for a number of years and the infrastructure is in bad shape, then a planning orientation may be important. Locating the capital budgeting function outside the budget office has some advantages, but it may create problems that require explicit attention.

Timing

Concerning the timing of the capital budget cycle, little documentation exists on actual practice among local governments. On the one hand, preparing the operating and capital budgets concurrently has several advantages: First, the attention of department heads and council members is focused simultaneously on budget issues, without prolonging budget preparation. Second, the impact of capital spending on the operating budget (and vice versa) will presumably be more clear when the two cycles are concurrent. On the other hand, preparing the capital budget in the "off season" (alternating with the operating budget cycle) makes better use of staff time by distributing the workload more evenly throughout the year. Even under the best of circumstances, preparing an operating budget requires enormous amounts of energy and time; adding the task of drafting a capital budget may jeopardize the quality of deliberations on both budgets. If staff is limited and the capital budgeting process demanding, it may be necessary to prepare the capital and operating budgets separately; however, steps should be taken to ensure coordination.

Assignment of priorities

The identity of the participants in the capital planning process influences the outcomes. Under a planning-oriented capital budgeting process, the planning or capital budget office assigns priorities on the basis of need or technical standards. Citizens and council members may influence the ranking process, but usually at the margins. In less planning-oriented processes, there may be more councilmanic and community involvement. Yet another alternative is to have priorities assigned by a committee that includes both elected officials and technical staff.

One common approach is the creation of an interdepartmental capital allocation committee to review and rank proposals for inclusion in the CIP and capital budget. Dayton, for example, appoints a capital allocation committee "to guarantee that the city responds to all of its needs and works to achieve all of its objectives rather than reacting to the needs and objectives of a special interest group/department."[6] Membership on the committee includes the assistant city managers; the directors of urban development, budget (who chairs the committee), planning, and water; the city engineer; and the director of the city's development corporation. The committee reviews and ranks all proposals, applying the same criteria to each project. Members also visit proposed project sites, monitor project progress, and meet monthly to review issues or new projects. The capital budgeting office provides staff support for the committee. Comparable data do not exist for local governments, but in its survey of state budget officials, the National Association of State Budget Officers found that at least twenty states rely on an interorganizational board to review and recommend projects for inclusion in the governors' budgets.[7]

Hennepin County, Minnesota, appoints a capital budgeting task force made up of eleven citizens to make recommendations to the county commissioners.[8] Phoenix involves citizens in the capital budgeting process through a 250-member bond committee, which is divided into subcommittees with up to fifteen members each. Each subcommittee reviews the proposed list of capital improvements prepared by a particular program area (e.g., police or public works) and endorsed by the city manager. Each subcommittee recommends projects for inclusion in the bond package to be taken to the voters. The executive committee of the bond committee (which consists of the chairs of each subcommittee plus a few at-large citizens) then reviews the recommendations of all the subcommittees and recommends to the city council the projects to be included in the bond package. Once the council approves the bond referendum and voters ratify the package, the executive committee of the bond committee functions

Capital improvement policies, San Luis Obispo, California

A.   Construction projects and capital purchases (other than vehicles or equipment to be acquired through the Equipment Replacement Fund) which cost more than $10,000 will be included in the Capital Improvement Plan (CIP); minor capital outlays of $10,000 or less will be included with the operating program budgets.

B.   The purpose of the CIP is to systematically plan, schedule, and finance capital projects to ensure cost effectiveness as well as conformance with established policies. The CIP will reflect a balance between capital replacement projects which repair, replace, or enhance existing facilities, equipment, or infrastructure and capital facility projects which significantly expand and/or add to the City's existing fixed assets.

C.   Every CIP project will have a project manager who will prepare the project proposal, ensure that the required phases are completed on schedule, authorize all project expenditures, ensure that all regulations and laws are observed, and periodically report project status.

D.   A CIP Coordinating Committee, headed by the City Administrative Officer or designee, will review project proposals, determine project phasing, recommend project managers, review and evaluate the draft CIP budget document, and report CIP project progress at least annually.

E.   The CIP will emphasize project planning, with projects progressing through at least two and up to six of the following phases:

1.   Designation: sets aside funding for future project development under "pay-as-you-go" financing.
2.   Study: includes concept design, site selection, feasibility analysis, schematic design, environmental determination, property appraisals, scheduling, grant application, grant approval, and specification preparation for equipment purchases.
3.   Acquisition: includes equipment purchases and property acquisition for projects, if necessary.
4.   Design: includes final design, plan and specification preparation, and construction cost estimate.
5.   Construction: includes bid administration, construction, project inspection and management, and closeout.
6.   Debt service: installment payments of principal and interest for completed projects funded through debt financing.

Generally, it will become more difficult for a project to move from one phase to the next. As such, more projects will be studied than will be designed and more projects will be designed than will be constructed or purchased during the term of the CIP.

F.   Release of funding and related appropriations to project accounts will be made only upon completion and approval of the preceding project phase. Accordingly, project appropriations for acquisition and construction will generally be approved when contracts are awarded.

G.   Project phases will be listed as objectives in the program narratives of the programs which manage the projects.

H.   CIP projects will be evaluated during each phase to determine the feasibility and appropriateness of including public art.

I.   Supplemental information regarding the purpose, organization, and appropriation control for the CIP projects is included in the Capital Improvement Plan section of this document.

Source: City of San Luis Obispo, California, *1989–1991 Financial Plan & Approved 1989–1990 Budget*, B-9–B-10.

as a bond advisory committee, meeting annually to review progress on project implementation.

Involving citizens in the evaluation phase provides them with an opportunity for genuine participation and may provide the foundation for public support if a bond referendum is necessary. From the perspective of staff, however, involving citizens in the allocation process carries some risk. One study reported that with citizen involvement, the ability of operating departments to influence the council decreased, and the influence of neighborhood interests increased.[9]

The accompanying sidebar offers an example of one city's capital improvements policies, showing how the policies resolved many of the issues described above, including the requirement to draw up a CIP, the definition of capital items, and the organization of decision making.

Identifying and selecting projects

Project selection is the heart of the capital planning process. At one end of the continuum, projects are generated and ranked through a technical planning process, possibly overseen by the planning department. Under this approach, projects are evaluated according to professional standards. At the other extreme, projects are generated by departments and examined and ranked by variously structured committees. Political considerations normally dominate the deliberations at this end of the continuum. Many project evaluation processes fall between these extremes, making the planning-oriented model more politically accountable or the politically oriented model more technically justifiable.

Thus, selecting projects normally has a technical and a political side. Samuel Nunn, who has researched the capital planning process, has identified two competing policy procedures in capital decision making[10]: The first is formal policy making, which includes the selection of proposals on the basis of technical requirements and formal organizational procedures (e.g., the CIP, subdivision codes, and matching requirements for grants). The second procedure Nunn characterizes as informal policy making, which takes the form of ad hoc deals between government negotiators and private firms; such deals often result from an aggressive economic development initiative. The interaction between these two policy-making procedures often determines the selection of capital investment projects.

By examining the capital improvements associated with the Alliance Airport project in Fort Worth, Texas, Nunn highlights what can happen when the technical part of the selection process is overrun by political bargaining. In this case, significant portions of the resources planned for projects in the CIP had to be diverted to unplanned projects emanating from the informal process. In addition, because staff time was diverted to the unplanned Alliance projects, other projects in the capital budget suffered from neglect or insufficient funding. Because the developer used a "divide and conquer" strategy, the informal process also had a demoralizing effect on staff. Whenever negotiations with the staff reached an impasse, the developer would reveal that decision makers higher up in the organization had already endorsed the developer's position. As Nunn observes, "this cycle of proposal and counter-proposal eventually exhausted the city staff's reliance on formal policies."[11]

It is tempting to think that if project selection were based only on technical factors and politics were kept out of the process, the result would be better choices. The problem is that politics cannot be excluded from project selection; project choice has an embedded political dimension. Moreover, purely technical decisions may undercut the power of elected officials and their ability to be responsive to the electorate. The consequences of excluding politics from the process may be to reduce not only the responsiveness of government but also political support for the form of government. Capital budgeting *appropriately* combines political and technical factors. The issue is to determine what proportion of the process should be political and what proportion technical.

The planning model, for example, in its purest form, establishes service standards (e.g., so many square feet of park or open space for each citizen). By identifying those facilities that are furthest from meeting the standards, the planning model assigns implicit priorities to projects. The model also assumes that with respect to the supply and condition of public facilities, all neighborhoods should be equal. As a consequence, infrastructure improvements, facilities improvements, or open space acquisition may be more extensive in some parts of the community than in others.

Since a fully implemented planning model may not be sufficiently accountable to political considerations—for example, council members' demands that projects be distributed equally among districts—some local governments employ a modified approach, which begins not with the development of standards but with an inventory of existing assets and their condition. The inventory is then used to determine where capital investments should be made. Dayton prepares such an inventory, then uses it to negotiate standards for service. Having an inventory enables city staff to pose tough questions to council members. For example, "If the city has 2,000 lane-miles of streets and repairs 20 miles per year, it is on a 100-year replacement cycle. Is that enough?"[12]

Developing priorities

The capital improvements planning cycle often begins with the budget office's call for project proposals; this is followed by deliberations on project selection. At about the same time that proposals are being solicited, the chief executive, in consultation with the governing body, should develop broad priorities for capital allocation.[13] Every local government has its own traditions for establishing priorities. The leadership in one community may emphasize specific service areas, such as streets, storm drainage, or open space; in another community, officials may use broad categories to delineate priorities, such as service expansion, maintenance, and land acquisition. Yet no matter how priorities are ultimately described, each community should start the capital planning process with a general statement of priorities that reflects both political and technical concerns.

A great deal is at stake in project selection. The location of a new highway and its major intersections can produce windfalls for property owners whose land borders the project. The bid specifications for an expensive fire truck or for a fleet of police vehicles can affect the number of manufacturers willing to submit a bid.

Professional staff can examine campaign promises for political priorities relevant to the capital budget. For example, the mayoral campaign may have promised downtown renewal; council members may have promised to revitalize the neighborhoods or to improve the physical plant of the schools. Appointed officials are also likely to have some priorities, such as adequate funding of maintenance projects and compliance with state and federal mandates.

Conducting a needs assessment

The planning model places considerable emphasis on inventorying the current capital stock and determining its condition. The strength of this approach is that it provides a comprehensive, rather than scattershot, approach to capital needs. Even in a community where capital budgeting is not located in the planning department, evaluating the condition of capital assets has a number of benefits: First, it helps demonstrate to citizens and elected officials that previous investment in maintenance and repair is paying off; this gives legitimacy to the idea of investing in maintenance and repair. Second, because a comprehensive appraisal of the condition of capital assets allows the relative merits of new proposals to be judged in relation to the condition of current assets, it can help build consensus on spending priorities. Finally, because a needs assessment helps staff argue that those bridges, roads, or roofs that are in most urgent need should be repaired or replaced first, it helps reduce the "squeaky wheel" phenomenon in the allocation of limited funding for capital improvements. (Figure 7–2 shows a graphic summary of Dayton's assessment of the condition of its bridges.)

The functions of a needs assessment dictate that it be neutral and comprehensive; but in many communities, capital project proposals are put together piecemeal. A department may take a more or less comprehensive view of its own needs over a shorter or longer period of time; citizen advisory groups and council members may also generate projects with little attention to conflicting or competing needs. Instead of using needs to generate proposals, the tendency is to use demands—and demands are logically isolated from each other. When projects are put on the table willy nilly, the task of evaluating and ranking proposals becomes more burdensome and politicized.

Overstating the case a little to make a point, *needs* assessments should be done by neutral parties; by contrast, *demands* should be made by those interested in benefiting from the projects or delivering benefits to constituents. If the requests are generated piecemeal and with the interests of individuals, neighborhoods, and departments in mind, then it is essential that the evaluation and ranking process include community-wide considerations and a determination of financial feasibility.

(*continued on page 184*)

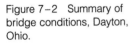

Figure 7–2   Summary of bridge conditions, Dayton, Ohio.

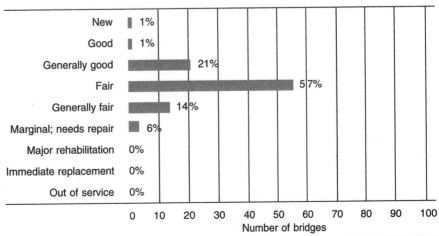

Source: Timothy Riordan, Maria E. Oria, and Joseph P. Tuss, "The Bridge from Dreams to Realities: Dayton's Capital Allocation Process," *Government Finance Review* (April 1987): 10. Reprinted with permission from *Government Finance Review*.

Figure 7–3 Request form for capital improvement projects, Skokie, Illinois.

Department _____ Dept. project no. _____

Division _____ Date _____

Department priority no. _____

I. **Project description**
   A. Project name _____
       _____
   B. Description _____
       _____
   C. Location _____
       _____
   D. Purpose _____
       _____
   E. A project request _____ was _____ was not submitted covering this project last year.

II. **Need**
   A. Who will derive the greatest benefit from this facility?
       _____ General citizenry
       _____ Commercial
       _____ Industrial
   B. What will be the scope of services provided by this facility?
       _____ Countywide
       _____ Community
       _____ Neighborhood
   C. Comment on the needs to be met by this project.
   D. How are needs currently being met?

III. **Cost**
   A. Approximate total cost   _____
   B. Cost already incurred   _____
   C. Balance   _____
   D. Detailed cost estimates
       1. Planning
           a. Engineering   _____
           b. Architectural   _____
       Total   _____
       2. Land
           a. Site already acquired _____
           b. Site to be acquired   _____
           c. Area required (acres) _____
           d. Estimated cost   _____
       3. Construction
           a. Estimated cost   _____
       4. Equipment and furnishings
           a. Equipment   _____
           b. Furnishings   _____
           c. Other   _____
       Total   _____
       TOTAL COST   _____

IV. **Proposed expenditures by years**
       Prior _____   4th   _____
       1st   _____   5th   _____
       2nd   _____   Later _____
       3rd   _____

V. Construction data
   A. Estimated construction period _____ months
   B. Proposed manner of construction:
      Contract   _____
      Force account   _____
      Other (describe)   _____
   C. Status of plans and specifications
      _____ Plans not needed
      _____ Nothing done except this report
      _____ Preliminary engineering estimate received
      _____ Plans and specs. in preparation
      _____ Plans and specs. complete
      _____ Sketches in process
      _____ Sketches complete
      _____ Surveys complete

VI. Estimated effect of completed project on operating budget of this department
   A. Increased revenue   _____
   B. Decreased operating expenses _____
   C. Number of new positions   _____
   D. Additional salary costs   _____
   E. Additional other expenses   _____
   Net effect on operating budget _____

VII. Estimated effect of this project on operating budgets of other departments
   Department affected   General effect on their budget

   Comments:

VIII. Relation to other projects
   A. Of this department   Yes _____   No _____

   Name of project   How related

   B. Of other departments   Yes _____   No _____

   Department   Name of project   How related

IX. Priority
   A. What priority number does your department assign to this project among
      those being requested at this time? _____
   B. What are your reasons for attaching this priority rating to this project?

X. Recommended financing
   _____ Federal aid   _____ Lease-purchase
   _____ State aid   _____ Bonds
   _____ Special assessments   _____ Motor fuel tax
   _____ Current revenue   _____ Capital reserve
   _____ Other

   Comments:

Source: Village of Skokie, Illinois.

Collecting and ranking requests

Suggestions for capital projects to include in the CIP can come from inside or outside the organization, but all requests for inclusion in the CIP should be submitted on standardized forms. (Figure 7–3 shows the form used by departments in Skokie, Illinois, to submit their requests.) Most of the proposals come from departments in the executive branch, particularly public works (street improvements), utilities (water, wastewater, sanitation), and planning (as part of the master plan). Citizen complaints are a second source of requests for capital spending, although these may be funneled through departments or council members. A third source is the campaign promises of elected officials. Community-based interest groups may also be an important source of proposals for projects. Normally, the cost of all these proposals far exceeds available financing.

Once all requests have been received by the budget office, the task of ranking proposals begins. If there is a capital allocation committee, it should establish criteria to judge each proposal. (The next section discusses the development and application of criteria in detail.) If the procedure for ranking is relatively informal, more projects may be approved than there is money to fund. Which projects are actually funded during the year may depend on how much pressure supporters of the project are able to muster. When the ranking process is more formal, the process moves along because ranking does not get bogged down in a morass of political pressures and counterpressures.

Once the ranking of projects for the CIP is complete—and before the plan is final—citizens should be given the opportunity to make recommendations to ensure that the plan meets with their approval. Although legislative approval is not required, it is recommended that the CIP be submitted to the governing body for review and approval. Legislative approval does not authorize money for any of the projects in the plan, but it adds credibility to the planning process and legitimizes the work of the capital allocation committee and chief executive. If the CIP has received legislative approval, it is a relatively straightforward matter to take the first year of projects from the five-year plan and put it in the budget as the capital portion. The capital budget, which does require legislative approval either as an independent document or as part of the operating budget, should generate little dissent or discussion, given the previous discussion and consensus building.

Developing and applying criteria

In an article on criteria used to evaluate capital projects, Annie Millar identified the eleven factors that she found in use by a sample of local governments. (These factors are listed in the accompanying sidebar.)[14] One factor Millar does not mention, that should perhaps be included, is whether the project is being done to meet a state or federal mandate.

The city of Dayton, Ohio, uses a rating sheet (see Figure 7–4) to score each project on ten basic criteria. Each member of the capital projects committee rates each project from 0 to 10. The scores given by each committee member are then summed, and the projects are ranked on the basis of total score. In local governments that do not use a capital projects committee, staff or other raters can use a similar approach.

A slightly more complicated rating process allows a capital projects committee to assign greater weight to selected criteria, such as safety, compliance with mandates, or economic development. In Denton, Texas, which uses a system like this, each committee member completes a rating sheet, then multiplies each score by the appropriate weight. (See Figure 7–5.) For example, let's say that a committee member awards 6 points to drainage improvements for the downtown mall, which is considered an economic development project. If economic development projects are weighted 0.7, then that committee member's score for that project is 4.2 (6.0 x 0.7). The weighted scores from all the committee members are totaled, yielding a final score for each project. The projects are then ranked according to the number of points earned. The weights can be altered as the priorities of the community and elected officials change.

After the initial round of rankings, members of the capital allocation committee may discuss the merits of each request with each other, and may alter the rankings of some projects on the basis of these discussions. In the case of Dayton, a high score does not guarantee that a project will

Criteria for selecting capital projects for inclusion in the CIP

1. Fiscal impact: (1) capital costs for the current and future years, and whether the proposed project will reduce future capital costs; (2) year-by-year estimates of the additional operating and maintenance costs or reductions in these costs because of the new project; (3) year-by-estimates of the revenue impact from the project (either increases or decreases due to loss of taxable property); (4) impact on energy requirements (may be separated from operations and maintenance estimates if particularly high); (5) potential legal liabilities and costs in undertaking or rejecting the project.
2. Health and safety effects: impact on traffic accidents, injuries, illness due to poor water quality, or health hazards due to sewer problems.
3. Economic effects: impact on property values, tax base, additional jobs, and the stabilization or revitalization of neighborhoods.
4. Environmental, aesthetic, and social effects: how does the project affect the quality of life of the community, including noise, air, and water pollution and the impact on households, commuters, and recreational opportunities.
5. Disruption and inconvenience: an estimate of the impact (inconvenience or disruption) on the public while the project is in progress.
6. Distributional effects: how will the project affect various geographical areas, low-moderate income areas, or other disadvantaged groups in the community?
7. Feasibility: extent of public support for the project, compatibility with the master plan, and whether the project is a continuation of an earlier effort.
8. Implications if the project is deferred: what is the impact if the project is deferred due to insufficient funds, including higher future operating and maintenance costs, and inconvenience to the public?
9. Amount of uncertainty: an educated guess of the likelihood that changes will occur in any of the foregoing factors, such as a change in the cost of the project.
10. Effect on surrounding cities: possible beneficial or adverse effects from the project on surrounding cities or quasi-governmental agencies.
11. Impact on other capital projects: whether the proposed project has a beneficial or adverse impact on other projects; for example, a street resurfacing project may precipitate the need to install new underground water and sewer pipelines.

Source: Annie Millar, "Selecting Capital Investment Projects for Local Government," *Public Budgeting & Finance* 8, no. 3 (autumn 1988): 66–68. Reprinted by permission of Transaction Publishers. All rights reserved.

Figure 7–4   Project rating sheet, Dayton, Ohio.

Member's name _____

Project name _____

No. _____

	Score range	Rater's score
A. Impact on Dayton's goal of economic vitality. The major objectives are:		
Major impact on 1 or more objectives	6–10	
Minor impact on 1 or more objectives	1–5	
No impact	0	

1. Increases available prime commercial/industrial land.
2. Increases the amount of first-class office space downtown.
3. Increases the number of first-class hotel rooms downtown.
4. Increases the number of market rate housing units downtown.
5. Improves/encourages development of health care industries.
6. Increases development along the rivers.
7. Improves Dayton's position as a hub for commerce, culture, and history.
8. Leverages private at a minimum ratio of 4:1.

	Score range	Rater's score
B. Impact on Dayton's goal of neighborhood vitality. The major objectives are:		
Major impact on 1 or more objectives	6–10	
Minor impact on 1 or more objectives	1–5	
No impact	0	

1. Improves the variety of housing stock opportunities through new construction and adaptive reuses.
2. Increases the rate of home ownership.
3. Increases the number of neighborhoods with special designations.
4. Improves neighborhood appearance.

	Score range	Rater's score
C. Impact on Dayton's goal of conserving its infrastructure and heritage. The major objectives are:		
Major impact on 1 or more objectives	6–10	
Minor impact on 1 or more objectives	1–5	
No impact	0	

1. Reduces urban sprawl.
2. Promotes Dayton's aviation/inventor heritage.
3. Encourages reconstruction, rehabilitation, and efficient use of capital.
4. Pursues alternative sources of energy in public facilities.

	Score range	Rater's score
D. Project implements an element of an approved plan(s).		
Major element	8–10	
Moderate element	4–7	
Minor element	1–3	
No element	0	
E. Priority board ranking.		
First priority	10	
Second priority	8	
Third priority	6	
Fourth priority	4	
Fifth priority	2	
F. Departmental ranking.		
First priority	10	
Second priority	8	
Third priority	6	
Fourth priority	4	
Fifth priority	2	
G. This project *directly supports existing neighborhood and economic development efforts* in areas with a majority of low- and moderate-income households.		
Yes	6–10	
No	0	
H. Impact on expenditures/energy consumption.		
Major decrease	6–10	
Minor decrease	1–5	
Remains the same	0	
Increases	2 1/2 5	
I. Project is specifically included in an approved replacement/maintenance schedule.		
Yes	6–10	
No	0	
J. Rater's general appraisal	0–10	

Project notes:

Source: City of Dayton, Ohio, *Capital Funding Request, Application Preparation Manual.*

Note: The City of Dayton no longer uses this particular form but now groups projects into six categories—housing, human services, industrial and commercial development, leisure and amenities, public facilities, and transportation—each with its own set of criteria and weights.

be funded, only that it will receive careful scrutiny from the committee.[15] After completing its deliberations, the committee submits its list of proposed projects to the chief executive.

One of the most noticeable and fundamental differences between government and business procedures for making capital investment choices is that the private sector relies much more heavily on economic criteria. Finance and accounting scholars have repeatedly called for governments to make greater use of such techniques as cost-benefit analysis, **net present value** (NPV), and **internal rate of return** (IRR), yet surveys show such criteria to have little bearing on public officials' choices of projects to fund.

For example, Robert Kee and his associates found that one-third of the cities responding to their survey used no quantitative method to analyze capital proposals.[16] Of the quantitative procedures that cities did use, the cost-benefit ratio and the **payback period**, the two simplest measures, were used most frequently. Less than 5 percent of the respondents used either NPV or IRR to rank projects. When respondents were asked why they chose not to use these widely accepted measures, the two most frequently cited reasons were political considerations (27 percent) and the inability to factor nonfinancial criteria into these procedures (26 percent). Commenting on the implications of the survey, Kee et al. note that "many proposals are accepted because of factors such as voter approval, municipal need, and the extent of outside funding. Whenever these factors become the decision criteria, sophisticated quantitative procedures lose their usefulness."[17]

For public officials, the important question is to what extent economic criteria should be a part of the calculus in project selection. In the case of projects such as infrastructure, which have no direct, income-producing capability, the utility of economic measures is nil. The benefits of such projects elude easy quantification and may even be intangible. Economic criteria may have greater merit in evaluating income-producing projects, such as those associated with public utilities. Here, determining a clear net income stream for the life of the project and estimating the NPV is relatively straightforward. However, even in the case of income-producing projects, measures such as NPV and IRR are of little merit when the goal is to compare projects with differing objectives—for example, expanding a water treatment plant versus increasing the capacity of a landfill. On the basis of projected demand, both projects will probably be necessary; given limited capital, the issue is not whether to construct the projects, but which to construct first.

				Impact on					
Project number	Project description	Estimated cost	Sources of funding	25% Public safety, life, health	22.5% Legal requirement, mandate	20% Quality of current services	17.5% Economic growth and development	15% Recreation, cultural, aesthetics	Total weighted score

Figure 7–5   Weighted capital budget rating sheet, Denton, Texas.

Source: Internal correspondence, Finance Department, City of Denton, Texas.

Applying sophisticated economic techniques to the evaluation of all projects is inappropriate. Instead, public officials need to balance economic and political criteria. Computing the NPV for a utility project can inform discussion of the project's merits and relative priority. At the same time, the decision requires a careful assessment of the community's needs and preferences among projects. Officials must also take into account the potential for citizens' objections should the project not be undertaken in a timely way. In short, local officials should use economic analyses when and where they make sense. When officials have to make tough choices, sound judgment is more important than sophisticated analysis, and economic analyses are unlikely to be helpful.

Funding: Policy issues

To some extent, selecting funding sources for capital projects is a matter of piecing together the funds that are available in any one year. For example, a project may be funded from a mix of current revenues, state or federal grants, bond proceeds, intergovernmental contributions (e.g., from a county or from other communities benefiting from the improvement), reimbursements, and builder contributions. Improvements to utility services may be financed through grants, the sale of revenue bonds, and service charges levied on users.

Whatever the mix of funding sources ultimately applied to capital improvements projects, there are underlying policy issues that must be dealt with—preferably through an explicit debt policy statement. A policy statement protects the operating budget from being overwhelmed by debt service and sets a limit on the amount (and type) of borrowing. The statement may deal with issues such as

What combination of pay-as-you-go (current revenues) and pay-as-you-use (bond proceeds) financing to use

What type of bond repayment guarantee to offer investors

How much borrowing to allow

What to do if actual expenditures are higher or lower than the funding set aside for the projects.

Debt

As a general policy, a local government should decide whether to pursue a **pay-as-you-go** or a **pay-as-you-use** strategy (see accompanying side-

---

Strategies for financing capital improvements

1. Pay-as-you-go financing:
   Current taxes, especially those linked to a particular service, such as motor fuel taxes earmarked for highway improvements
   Federal or state grants
   Other own-source revenues, such as utility charges
   Reserves accumulated in a replacement fund or as retained earnings in a utility fund
   Leases or lease-purchase arrangements

2. Pay-as-you-use financing:
   Bonds or other debt instruments issued by the local government
   Special assessments on property owners benefiting from the improvement
   Mortgages or bank loans

bar.) The pay-as-you-go approach relies on current revenues to pay for capital improvements; the pay-as-you-use approach relies on debt to pay for capital outlays. Governments that choose not to issue debt need to pay particular attention to the timing of project initiation if tax rates are to remain stable.

Under pay-as-you-go financing, current taxpayers bear the burden of financing improvements, and future residents reap the benefits. As long as the repayment of the debt does not exceed the life of the asset, a pay-as-you-use strategy may be more equitable than pay-as-you-go. However, debt funding of capital projects does have some disadvantages. Borrowing costs more than paying for projects or equipment with current revenues. In addition, state law may require a voter referendum to obtain citizen approval for issuing bonds, and that approval may be difficult or impossible to obtain. In some states, local governments have to get state approval before entering the bond market. Some communities face legal limits on the amount of debt that can be backed by the full faith and credit of the local government.

Nevertheless, local governments sometimes choose to take on debt: especially in jurisdictions experiencing rapid population growth, the need for public improvements often outstrips the current revenue available to fund projects. In such cases, governments may borrow, paying back the loan during the life of the project or equipment. A local government that chooses to use debt financing of capital projects should be aware that annual debt service obligations (principal and interest) must be met before all other obligations, including payroll. Failure to make a debt payment on time constitutes a **default** on that debt, and a government that defaults loses the confidence of investors and will find it difficult to issue debt in the future. In order to create greater assurance that the debt will be repaid on time, local governments usually establish **debt service funds,** in which they deposit money that will be used to pay interest and principal as they come due. These funds are replenished annually, as part of the operating budget process. The local government must set aside enough money in the debt service fund to cover the obligations for that year.

Long-term debt should be used only to acquire long-lived assets—not for operating expenses or to cover an operating deficit. The rule of thumb is that long-term debt should be used only to acquire assets with a useful life greater than two years, and repayment of the debt should not extend beyond the life of the asset. If a resurfaced street is expected to last ten years, then the bonds used to finance that project should be paid off in ten years or less.

Revenue and general obligation bonds

If bonding plays a role in a community's funding plan, officials need to decide when to use **general obligation (GO) bonds**, which are backed by the taxing power (sometimes called "full faith and credit") of the local government, and when to use **revenue bonds**. GO bonds are usually used for public facilities or equipment that benefits everyone and that has no revenue-producing capabilities—such as streets, school buildings, storm drainage, sidewalks, local government buildings, and public safety vehicles.

Revenue bonds can be used only to finance revenue-producing projects, such as public housing complexes, hospitals, toll roads, water or wastewater facilities, airports, and parking garages. Revenues earned from the project are used to repay the bonds used to build the facility. Because state referenda requirements and limits on GO bonding make revenue bonds comparatively easier to issue, governments often use revenue bonds whenever a project produces revenues that can be used to pay off the bonds.

Although revenue bonds are ordinarily backed only by the revenue-producing capacity of a particular project, local governments issuing revenue bonds do have some policy options. For example, a local government can sometimes pledge its full faith and credit to the repayment of revenue bonds. This pledge means that in the event that revenues from the project are insufficient to cover the annual debt service requirements, the local government will draw from other sources—including taxes—to pay the debt service obligation. Putting the full faith and credit of the community behind a particular project can be risky, but it does make the project more secure for investors, thereby keeping down the cost of borrowing. Another policy option is to use general tax revenues—especially during the development phase—to subsidize a project funded by revenue bonds.

Amount of debt

Another policy issue related to the funding of capital projects is the maximum amount of debt that will be permitted. As a rule of thumb, the annual cost of servicing GO debt (principal and interest) should not exceed 20 percent of the operating budget, a guideline that is reportedly used by the credit-rating industry. The more a government spends on debt service, the less it has for other purposes. If a jurisdiction is experiencing rapid population growth, it may need to exceed the 20 percent limit temporarily. On the other hand, communities whose tax base is shrinking or that are experiencing little or no population growth should consider reducing their debt service obligation to 15 percent or less of the operating budget.

Because it depends on the revenue-producing capabilities of each project, the question of debt capacity is more complex in the case of revenue bonds. Obviously, annual debt service must not exceed what the facility is capable of generating in revenue over and above operating costs. For services such as water and wastewater facilities, prices can be set to cover annual operating costs (treatment, pumping, labor, storage, and supplies) plus debt service. In other cases—parking garages, for example—the facility may be in competition with nongovernmental providers, and the local government may therefore be unable to raise fees beyond a certain level. To determine the limits of revenue—and hence the maximum amount of debt service the facility can afford—the local government must undertake a careful analysis of the market and of users' willingness to pay.

In short, debt can be a legitimate tool in the financing of capital improvements if used appropriately. To keep debt within manageable bounds and to retain investors' confidence in a government's commitment to repay its obligations, officials may find it helpful to adopt and implement policies that specify (1) when and for what purpose debt will be used and (2) the maximum amount of debt that can be incurred.

Misestimation of capital project costs

Local officials developing a policy on funding capital projects should determine the best course of action in the event that the costs of capital projects are under- or overestimated. If a government borrows more than it needs for a capital project, how should the extra money be used? Should it be used toward debt service; for other, related projects; or for unrelated projects? In the bond prospectus, the official document that explains to creditors how their money will be spent, how narrowly or broadly should officials word the section that describes the purposes of the bond proceeds? For the government issuing debt, it is most convenient to say that it will spend the money on whatever it chooses, but potential lenders may find such vagueness unacceptable.

Money that is left over from earmarked grants or intergovernmental funds normally remains in a special revenue fund if it is not spent that year. The fund balance can be spent the following year on similar items or projects. If a capital project fund incurs a deficit, which sometimes happens because of a cost overrun, the government may have to borrow against revenues expected in the next fiscal year. Assuming such a practice is legal, it may be more cost-efficient to use an interfund loan to ensure that a large project is completed on time. For example, a local government may lend a street improvement fund enough money from the motor vehicle gas tax fund to finish a project, then use the next year's allocation from the state to pay back the earmarked tax fund.

If a local government has earmarked general revenue for capital purposes, and the year's projects and capital purchases end up costing less than estimated, officials may be able to spend the **unreserved fund balance** on something else, depending on how the capital project fund was set up. If it has no restrictions, officials may wish to preserve the money in a capital account rather than transfer it back to the general fund. Because such decisions structure the legal freedom to move money around later, should a specific request arise for the council to consider, these decisions need to be thought through in advance.

Preparing the capital budget

While the CIP provides a rolling, five-year inventory of proposed projects and financing sources, the capital budget—the first year of the CIP—provides detailed information on the design, cost, and financing of improvements recommended for the forthcoming year. The **appropriation** adopting the capital budget gives the executive branch the same type of authorization for capital improvements that the operating budget gives for recurring expenditures.

If a CIP is maintained, the tasks that must be completed to annually update the plan and prepare a capital budget include:

1. Preparing a capital budget manual and calendar that contains instructions and forms for departments to use when completing their budget requests
2. Determining the costs of each project as precisely as possible
3. Providing a detailed estimate of the revenues, both recurring and from bond sales or other sources, that will be available for the period
4. Bundling debt needs and obtaining voter approval on bond sales, if required
5. Holding a public hearing on the proposed capital budget
6. Appropriating the capital budget.

Preparing the capital budget manual

The capital budget manual, like its counterpart in the operating budget, provides departments with forms and detailed instructions on how to complete their capital spending requests. The manual also includes a calendar outlining the timetable for budget preparation. Figure 7–6 shows the capital project request form for the city of Garland, Texas; Figure 7–7 shows the calendar used by Broward County, Florida, to guide its CIP and capital budget preparation. Like the operating budget calendar, this timetable includes a call for proposals, a review of those proposals by the budget office (and planning department, in the case of Broward County), executive-level review and hearings, and a budget workshop for elected officials.

Determining project costs

Up to the point of inclusion in the capital budget, the project cost estimates used in the CIP are based primarily on departmental projections, sometimes with the aid of preliminary engineering studies. The longer proposals remain in the CIP and become likely candidates for funding, the more detailed cost estimates must be; the local government may then hire a consultant or engineering firm to prepare detailed cost estimates. If the project involves constructing a new building or renovating an existing one, by the time the project reaches the capital budget, the government will have hired an architectural firm to prepare drawings of the facility.

Calculations by the budget office should include not only gross cost

PAGE NO.
P40

CITY OF GARLAND - CAPITAL PROJECT REQUEST

* ALL AMOUNTS ARE IN 000'S DOLLARS

RESPONSIBLE DEPARTMENT	PROJECT TITLE	CIP NO.	ACCOUNT NO(S).
ENGINEERING	KINGSLEY ROAD - GARLAND ROAD TO SATURN ROAD	08014	303-181-1207

PROJECT DESCRIPTION

This project involves the reconstruction of Kingsley Road to a Type "D1" thorough-fare, two 25' sections (four-lane divided) with a 13' median. The approximate length of the project is 3,500 feet.

FUNDING SOURCE

1991 Bond Fund	$3,005,000
Impact Fees	45,000
	$3,050,000

IMPACT ON OPERATING BUDGET

Project will decrease current maintenance costs associated with Kingsley Road. Adds 0.99 acres to Park Department's median maintenance program.

STRIP MAP

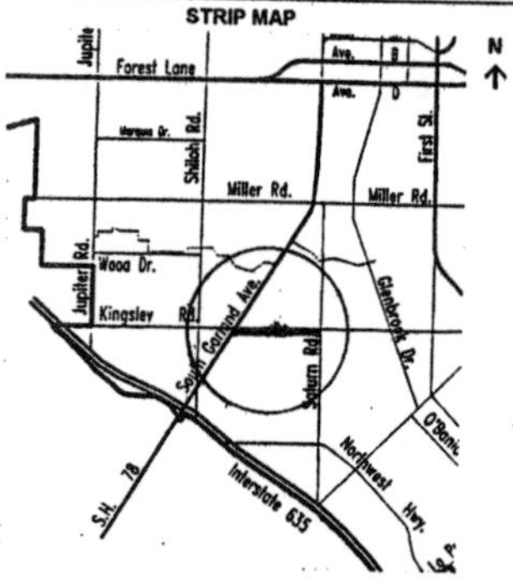

PROJECT COSTS	THRU 12-95	1996	1997	1998	1999	2000 to Completion	TOTAL
DESIGN	132	40					172
LAND/RIGHT-OF-WAY	378						378
UTILITY RELOCATION							
CONSTRUCTION		2,500					2,500
LANDSCAPING							
EQUIPMENT & FURNISHINGS							
OTHER							
TOTAL COSTS	510	2,540					3,050

SOURCE OF FUNDS	THRU 12-95	1996	1997	1998	1999	2000 to Completion	TOTAL
CURRENT FUNDS							
BONDS VOTED	510	2,495					3,005
BONDS NOT VOTED							
OTHER - (IMPACT FEES)		45					45
TOTAL SOURCE	510	2,540					3,050

PROJECT SCHEDULE	START	FINISH
DESIGN	12/91	10/94
LAND/RIGHT-OF-WAY	5/93	10/95
UTILITY RELOCATION		
CONSTRUCTION	1/96	12/96
TOTAL PROJECT	12/91	12/96

Figure 7–6 Capital project request form, Garland, Texas.

Source: City of Garland, Texas, *Garland Capital Improvement Program, 1996*, P40.

(the outlay required to purchase the land or equipment or complete the project) but also net cost (the immediate costs, minus savings over the long term, plus added operating costs). If a piece of equipment is less expensive to operate than its predecessor, it can pay for itself over a period of time. In addition, the budget office should determine whether a capital improvement will increase or decrease operating costs—and if so, by how much. For example, a new garbage truck that requires fewer workers to operate can reduce labor costs. On the other hand, capital spending may increase future operating costs: a new fire station will

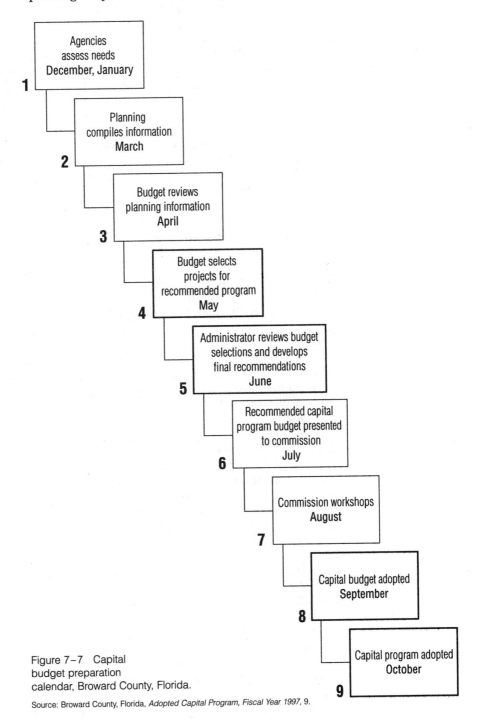

Figure 7–7 Capital budget preparation calendar, Broward County, Florida.

Source: Broward County, Florida, *Adopted Capital Program, Fiscal Year 1997*, 9.

require outlays for staffing and utilities. There may be enough revenue to acquire or construct a capital facility, but not enough to staff and maintain the facility when it comes on line.

When Robert Bland and Samuel Nunn examined the impact of capital spending on a variety of departmental operating budgets, they found that capital outlays generally increased future operating costs, but that the effect was most marked in the case of labor-intensive services.[18]

Capital-intensive services showed the least sensitivity to capital investment. In fact, in response to capital spending in prior years, operating expenditures for highways showed no significant change, and expenditures for sewer services showed only a small change. However, in the case of labor-intensive services, capital expenditures often increased capacity, thus creating a need for more labor. The effect of capital outlays was greatest for police protection: for every dollar per capita spent on capital items in the current year, future operating outlays for police protection increased by almost $2.50 per capita. Such effects linger over an extended period.

The chief executive's budget request should include the gross and net cost estimates, drawings of the location of the project, and, where appropriate, the payback period. It is also helpful to provide a completion schedule for the project, a year-by-year breakdown of project costs, and a list of funding sources. Figure 7–6 shows the level of detail on costs and financing that some local governments use in their capital budgets.

Determining project funding

To the extent that current revenues are used to finance at least part of the capital budget, the revenue forecasts prepared for the operating budget affect the capital budget. Thus, during the capital budget preparation phase, the budget office must develop detailed estimates of expected current revenues, including those from taxes, fund balances, grants, special assessments, and service charges. After estimating current revenues available for capital spending, the local government must decide how much money it plans to borrow to fund capital projects in the forthcoming year. (For smaller local governments that enter the bond market infrequently, the projections for borrowing needs may cover several years.)

As the budget office and chief executive begin to prepare the final capital budget request for legislative consideration, the accuracy of revenue estimates becomes increasingly important because capital budgets, like operating budgets, are revenue driven: the amount of funding determines the number of projects authorized. In the case of capital projects such as public housing or utility system improvements, updated estimates of consumer demand are essential to predict how much revenue will be available to service future debt obligations.

Bundling debt needs and planning a referendum

Issuing debt is costly because it involves preparing documentation and consulting financial advisors and attorneys. If there are a number of small projects for which a local government plans to sell bonds, it is usually less expensive and more efficient to bundle these projects together and issue one bond to pay for them. The cost of selling several small issues is disproportionately high compared with the cost of selling one larger issue. Larger projects may be financed separately, and utilities and other enterprises usually market bonds separately.

If a local government is planning a bond issue that requires a public referendum, funding will remain tentative until approval for the issue is obtained. Typically, the government budgets as if the referendum will pass, but the projects are not funded unless voters approve the measure. Once a bond referendum has failed, it is tempting to substitute forms of funding that do not require public approval. Such a move is politically risky, however, since the voters have already indicated an unwillingness to pay for the proposed projects. It is more important to mobilize support for a project through an information campaign than to develop a backup funding plan in case the public votes down the referendum. Even in the best of circumstances, it takes time to hold a referendum and additional time to market a bond; it is thus unlikely that funds will be available in the fiscal year in which the project is approved.

Holding public hearings

Public hearings on the capital budget are common and appropriate, whether required by law or not. These hearings may be combined with those on the operating budget or with a hearing on the CIP. The hearings should be timed to permit changes to be made on the basis of citizens' comments; otherwise, hearings are little more than a publicity exercise. Hearings on the capital budget sometimes occur just before review and approval by the governing body, but that is often too late for citizen participation to be meaningful or useful.

Appropriating for capital outlays

The governing body must approve the capital budget. John Vogt, a scholar of budgeting practice, describes three methods for adopting the capital budget.[19] In one method, the capital budget is adopted as part of the annual (or biennial) operating budget. Under this approach, multi-year projects may be funded only one year at a time, which creates potential uncertainty in project financing. In the second method, the governing body adopts a separate capital budget, and the amount appropriated is sufficient to see the projects through to completion. Under the third method Vogt describes, the governing body approves a bond referendum, although a separate approval for each project is usually still required by law.

Summary

Ideally, the foundation of the capital budgeting process is the creation of a capital improvements plan (CIP). The CIP typically covers a five-year period, and the first year of the CIP becomes the annual capital budget —the financing plan for those projects that will be carried out in the next fiscal year. Each year, the CIP is updated, revenue and expenditure estimates are revised for the remaining years in the planning period, and a new (fifth) year of projects is added. This "rolling" process forces public officials to evaluate projects more than once and to judge the merits and urgency of new proposals against those already in the CIP.

In addition to providing a year-by-year inventory of proposed projects, the CIP provides policy makers with a plan for financing those projects. Local governments rely on shared taxes, grants, special assessments, own-source revenue, and municipal bonds to fund capital acquisitions. To successfully establish a market for their bonds, governments must assure investors of the security of their investment by (1) paying debt obligations promptly, (2) creating a separate debt service fund in which to account for current-year payments of principal and interest, (3) restricting long-term debt to long-lived assets, and (4) adopting a policy statement that clearly describes the standards and procedures for issuing debt. A policy statement should address such issues as the following: whether projects will be financed on a pay-as-you-go or pay-as-you-use basis; what type of credit backing will be used for various types of projects; the maximum amount of debt that will be incurred; and how deficits or surpluses in capital projects funds will be handled.

Proposals for capital allocation may come from elected officials, department heads, neighborhood representatives, and members of the business community. Politicians express their views on the community's capital needs in the course of the campaign process and as representatives of the electorate. Departments routinely project their capital needs—first as part of the CIP, later as part of the annual budgeting process. Bringing citizens into the decision-making process is useful not only to obtain ideas and recommendations but also to gain support should public approval of bonding be required. There are many ways to rank proposals, but one of the most successful is a broad-based capital allocation committee, which ranks each proposal according to agreed upon criteria and prepares the proposed CIP for review by the chief executive.

As a project moves from the CIP to the capital budget, it is necessary to refine and update the costs, detail the revenues intended to pay for the project, and determine the amount of bonds to be sold. Like the operating budget, the capital budget is usually the subject of a public hearing before it is adopted. The capital budget must be formally approved by the legislative body before it takes effect.

1   Lawrence W. Hush and Kathleen Peroff, "The Variety of State Capital Budgets: A Survey," *Public Budgeting & Finance* 8, no. 2 (summer 1988): 71.

2   John Forrester, "Municipal Capital Budgeting: An Examination," *Public Budgeting & Finance* 13, no. 2 (summer 1993): 85–103.

3   Fort Collins, Colorado, "Budget Overview," in the *1990 Annual Budget*, vol. 1, C-24.

4   Hush and Peroff, "State Capital Budgets," 74.

5   Michael Pagano, "Notes on Capital Budgeting," *Public Budgeting & Finance* 4, no. 3 (autumn 1984): 31–40.

6   Timothy Riordan, Maria E. Oria, and Joseph P. Tuss, "The Bridge from Dreams to Realities: Dayton's Capital Allocation Process," *Government Finance Review* (April 1987): 7–8.

7   National Association of State Budget Officers, *Capital Budgeting in the States: Paths to Success* (Washington, DC: NASBO, 1992), 16.

8   Hennepin County, Minnesota, *Budget 1990*, 20.

9   Margaret A. Corwin and Judith Getzels, "Capital Expenditures: Causes and Controls," in *Cities under Stress*, ed. R. Burchell and D. Listokin (Piscataway, NJ: Center for Urban Policy Research, Rutgers Univ., 1981).

10 Samuel Nunn, "Formal and Informal Processes in Infrastructure Policy-making," *Journal of the American Planning Association* (summer 1991): 273–87.

11 Ibid., 283.

12 Riordan, Oria, and Tuss, "Dreams to Realities," 9.

13 William Lucy, "Capital Budgeting and Priority Planning," ch. 5 in *Close to Power: Setting Priorities with Elected Officials* (Washington, DC: American Planning Association, 1988), 139–41.

14 Annie Millar, "Selecting Capital Investment Projects for Local Government," *Public Budgeting & Finance* 8, no. 3 (autumn 1988): 63–77.

15 Riordan, Oria, and Tuss, "Dreams to Realities," 12.

16 Robert Kee, Walter Robbins, and Nicholas Apostolou, "Capital Budgeting Practices of U.S. Cities: A Survey," *The Government Accountants' Journal* (summer 1987): 16–22.

17 Ibid., 20.

18 Robert Bland and Samuel Nunn, "The Impact of Capital Spending on Municipal Operating Budgets," *Public Budgeting & Finance* 12, no. 2 (summer 1992): 32–47.

19 A. John Vogt, "Budgeting Capital Outlays and Improvements," in *Budget Management: A Reader in Local Government Financial Management*, ed. J.H. Rabin, W.B. Hildreth, and G.J. Miller (Athens, GA: Univ. of Georgia Press, 1983), 140.

8 The budget document

Legal requirements

Content and structure of the budget
    Budget message or transmittal letter
    Table of contents
    Introduction
    Summary tables
    Expenditure details
    Capital outlays and debt
    Supporting material
    Number of volumes

Budget reforms and budget formats
    Line-item budgets
    Program budgets
    Performance budgets
    Target-based and zero-base budgets
    Selecting and displaying information

Budget design
    Uses of graphics
    Designing tables, charts, and graphs

Making budgets readable: GFOA standards
    The budget as a policy guide
    The budget as a financial plan
    The budget as an operations guide
    The budget as a communications tool

Summary

The budget document

Budget documents vary widely in style and content, but *good* budgets have a number of characteristics in common. In addition to meeting basic legal requirements, good budgets (1) include all the necessary components, (2) focus on information essential to decision making, and (3) present information in a clear and accessible way.

This chapter provides guidelines for the contents, format, and design of good budgets. The chapter begins by examining legal requirements and budget content and structure. Next, the relation between budget format, budget process, and the selection and presentation of information is considered in detail. The chapter then discusses budget design, including the uses and design of graphic elements. Finally, the chapter summarizes and explains the criteria used by the Government Finance Officers Association (GFOA) to evaluate local government budgets.

Legal requirements

Above all, a budget document must conform to the law. A local government's charter may include detailed budget provisions—requiring, for example, the use of a line-item format and the inclusion of personnel lists by position. The charter may also require an executive budget process and specify (1) the date for transmission of the proposal to council and (2) the date by which council must approve the budget. A charter may even specify the different parts of the budget.

Some state governments require particular financial information in the budget and may even provide the forms on which the budgets are to be filled out. Fortunately, requirements included in state laws have served primarily as a minimum for budget documents. Once they have complied with state law, local governments are generally free to set up more sophisticated budgeting systems if they wish. Similarly, once charter requirements have been met, a local government can add more up-to-date, user-friendly features.

Content and structure of the budget

In addition to conforming to the law, a good budget document must include all the requisite components. Not every budget document will have every component, but most good budgets contain the following:

1. A letter of transmittal or a budget message
2. A table of contents
3. An introduction
4. Summary tables showing the balance of revenues and expenditures for each fund
5. A detailed section on expenditures for each fund
6. A section on capital outlays and debt
7. Supporting material.

The sections that follow describe the contents of a typical budget and discuss the advantages and disadvantages of a single-volume and multi-volume budget structure.

Budget message or transmittal letter

A budget typically begins with a budget message or a letter of transmittal. A budget message, usually a fairly long (say, five- to ten-page) document, describes the proposed budget to the council or board that is about to consider it. The budget message is likely to include a summary of the government's financial status, a list of policies reflected in the current budget, and a list of major accomplishments achieved during the past year; it will also note the overall size of the proposed budget and the tax level necessary to pay for it. If the budget reflects cutbacks, the budget message usually describes the cuts.

By contrast, a letter of transmittal may be brief and formal: "I herewith transmit the budget proposal for fiscal year 1999 to the council. The total budget is $15,234,670. The property tax levy will be $3,245,000." Even a brief transmittal letter usually includes the size of the proposed budget and the tax rate, but it may contain little more. If the mayor writes a brief transmittal letter, the budget director may write a budget message describing the important elements of the proposal.[1]

Table of contents

The table of contents that follows the budget message or transmittal letter should divide up the budget document into main sections—for example, overview of financial conditions, revenues and expenditures by fund, expenditure details by department, capital projects, debt repayment plans, personnel detail, and glossary. If the budget includes an index, a fairly general table of contents may work; but if there is no index, the table of contents should be detailed enough to indicate, for example, the page on which the police department expenditures can be found.

Introduction

After the table of contents, there may be an introduction—a section including general information that sets the context for the rest of the budget. The introduction may list goal statements and describe both the budget process and the policies that shaped the budget. If the local government uses a target-based or zero-base budget, the results may be summarized or laid out in detail.

One city that uses target-based budgeting lists in its introduction the total for the funded requests, then describes the criteria used to determine whether supplementary requests would be funded (e.g., whether the project would reduce operating costs within a relatively short period, whether the project fit in with the city's current goals). The descriptions of the target-based budget outcomes show the trade-offs made during the budget process and link spending to city goals to show citizens what is being achieved.

Some budget introductions include a detailed description of revenues by source and a history of the local government's finances. The revenue section of the introduction describes each of the local government's major revenue sources in lay terms, showing the estimate for each revenue source and the reasons for that estimate. For example, the section on sales taxes should briefly describe the law that enables the jurisdiction to raise sales taxes, including any limits, exemptions, or mandates, then describe projected sales tax revenues for the upcoming year and the assumptions underlying the projection. The discussion of sales tax revenue in the budget of St. Charles, Illinois, reads, in part, as follows:

During the last ten years ending April 30, 1994, sales tax receipts have averaged a growth of 9.9%. The last five years' average annual growth has been at a rate of 7.1%. In FY 94/95 sales tax revenues are projected to increase 8.6% over FY 93/94. We anticipate an increase of 23.6% in FY 95/96. This is a large increase. However, 17.3% of the increase is the result of the Council approving a local sales tax of .25%. . . . Normal increases due to smaller businesses opening, increased business activity and inflation are projected to increase sales tax revenue by 5%. As our past experience shows, this 5% increase appears to be conservative.[2]

Tables showing the proportion of tax revenue generated by each major revenue source over time can help highlight trends. If, for example, the proportion of total tax revenue generated by property taxes is dropping and the proportion generated by sales taxes is increasing, the local government may be increasingly vulnerable to recessions. Tables showing trends in the level and proportion of total revenues generated by state and federal grants and payments can also be useful in signaling dependence on an unreliable source.

If the local government has a property tax, a table showing the assessed valuation, tax rate, and tax levy over a ten-year period should be included in the revenue section of the introduction. Also useful is a chart showing the portion of the property tax that the local jurisdiction receives, in comparison with the portions received by overlying districts and governmental units. Citizens often blame local governments for high or increasing property tax rates, even when their jurisdiction receives only a small share. Clearing up this misunderstanding can help build trust between citizens and local government.

The budget introduction should have a section on the local government's recent financial history. If the government has been running deficits, a description of the origin of the deficits and of efforts to eliminate them should appear here. If the jurisdiction has been struggling to deal with tax limits, the introduction should describe the results of efforts to diversify the revenue base. If the community has been growing quickly in area or population, graphics can be used to map out that growth, showing the jurisdiction's boundaries at intervals of five years, for example, or depicting the rate of population growth at regular intervals (see Figure 8–1). This section is a natural location for attractive graphics.

Less common, but also appropriate for the budget introduction, is a list and explanation of interfund transfers included in the proposed budget. The budget office can include historical data, which makes large increases or decreases in transfers visible and requires explanation of the changes. A comparison of last year's planned and actual transfers, with explanations for any discrepancies, can also be useful. Clear descriptions of transfers may reduce the temptation to balance one fund at the expense of another fund without identifying and resolving underlying problems. Reporting on transfers takes very little space and helps ensure (1) that earmarked money, such as utility revenue, is spent for the designated purposes and (2) that enterprise fees are set to cover expenditures. Any subsidies to or from enterprise funds should be a matter of policy and clearly described as such; they should not be the result of unreported interfund transfers during the year.

Figure 8–1   Phoenix growth, 1881–1993.

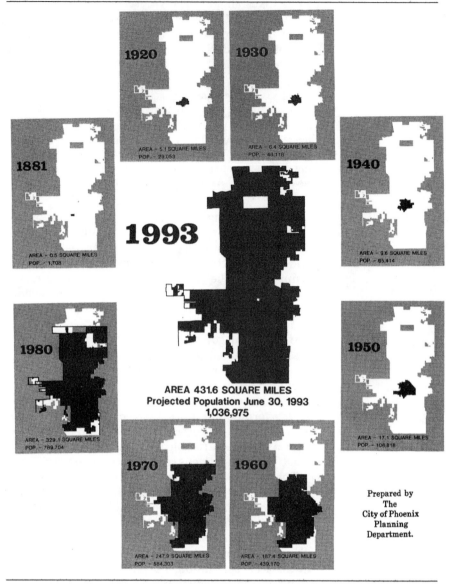

Source: City of Phoenix, Arizona, *Phoenix Summary Budget, 1996–97*, 10.

Summary tables

The next major section of the budget should include at least two summary tables: one table should show total revenues and expenditures for each fund; a second table typically lays out, for the general fund, (1) projected revenues by source and (2) expenditures by department. A similar table can be included for each fund outside the general fund; if this information is not included here, it should be included later in the budget.

Expenditure details

The next section of the budget usually presents detailed information on proposed expenditures: by department, by program, or by both department and program. This section usually includes some historical data comparing prior years' proposed and actual spending and proposed and estimated spending for the current year to the budget request for the next budget year. Personnel summaries by department and program can be included here, as can descriptions of performance goals, prior year's accomplishments, and explanations for changes from year to year. The departments' explanations for year-to-year changes are often called "budget highlights."

A line-item budget might list for each department personnel costs, insurance, training, travel, and equipment, or it might break down these costs into more detailed items. A program budget usually divides departments into programs; the police department might include programs for the recovery of stolen goods, drug prevention, and traffic safety. Examples of programs that cross departments include policy making, resource management, and health and safety. For each program, **full-time equivalent** staffing and total dollar costs should be listed. A hybrid of line-item and program budgeting breaks out program costs into line items.

In a performance budget, each program has a series of measures to describe demand, workload, output, outcome, and impact. Program managers build in particular workload levels and promise a particular quantity and quality of outputs for a particular level of budget allocation. Prior years' promises and actual levels of service can be reported here, so that the council can judge the likelihood that the promises underlying the current budget proposal will be fulfilled.

Most local governments present a greater level of detail for the operating departments in the general fund than they do for enterprise funds, possibly because these funds usually pay for themselves. However, because the lack of detail provided for enterprise funds sometimes contributes to a notion that they are secret, local governments that have financial responsibility for enterprise activities would be wise to provide an amount of detail for those funds that is parallel to that provided for the general fund.

Similarly, because pension and insurance funds are often simply described as revolving funds and are rarely given detailed treatment, it is difficult for the reader to learn anything about their costs or their soundness. More detail about how these funds are operating may be necessary—especially as more and more local governments choose to self-insure. Milwaukee's unusually thorough and easy-to-understand description of its pension funds includes the following elements: a mission statement; objectives and prior years' performance on those objectives; a discussion of the structure and coverage of each pension fund; a description of recent changes affecting the city's contributions; proposed revenues and expenditures; actual revenues and expenditures for the previous year; and budgeted revenues and expenditures for the current year.[3]

Capital outlays and debt

After the detailed description of expenditures, there should be a section on capital outlays. This section should include a description of debt and debt repayment schedules and a summary of major projects planned for the budget year. The detailed description of specific projects may be presented as an appendix or as a separate document.

The description of the debt outstanding should list, for each bond and note, the date the money was borrowed, the due date, the interest rate, and the principal and interest payments by year until maturity. All the local government's debt, including revenue bonds from enterprise funds, should be listed in this section, but revenue bonds should be distinguished from general obligation (GO) debt. While this information always appears in the annual financial report, it shows future obligations and should therefore appear in the budget as well. It is misleading to borrow money and not show that it must be repaid in the future, just as it is misleading to show the costs of only one year of an installment contract to purchase a fire truck or one year of a multiyear lease agreement. While the focus of a budget proposal is on obligations for the coming year, if expenditures are now being incurred that will have major implications in several years, those implications need to be presented. One place to do that is in the section on debt.

The debt section can also include the amount of short-term debt that is being carried over from one year to the next. The amount of short-term debt outstanding at the end of the year should be carefully scrutinized, and putting these figures in the budget calls attention to them.

Either in the appendix just after the description of debt outstanding, or in a separate volume, the budget should list capital projects planned for the upcoming year. If project detail is listed in a separate volume, it may be useful to include a brief summary in the main volume and point the reader to the additional volume for more detail. Otherwise, a reader might mistake the operating budget for the total budget.

Although this is not common practice, it is a good idea to identify those capital projects under contract with the private sector and those that are to be undertaken by government employees. Local governments may, for example, contract out some or all of their road rebuilding work, while continuing to perform smaller projects themselves. Because these capital contracts are, in a sense, outside the department's budgets, they will not show up anywhere unless they are listed and detailed with the capital projects. Unless the budget includes the history of the decision to contract, the expectations for the contract, and any history of costs and performance (e.g., whether promises were kept over the long term), there is often no basis on which to judge the wisdom or appropriateness of contracts. Some office at city hall may record such information, but unless it is in the budget, it is not readily available to council members, news media, or citizens.

Supporting material

The budget may include supporting or explanatory material of various types—for example, a detailed position classification (this may be mandated by law), a glossary, an index. Some local governments include a brief statistical section listing the number of lane-miles of streets, fire and police stations, squad cars, books in the library, and movie theaters and restaurants. The statistical section may also include demographic data as general background for policy making.

A glossary, commonly included, defines many terms that appear in the budget. The GFOA has worked out a typical glossary that a local government can use as a pattern, then modify to fit its particular needs. Because a local government can use the same glossary year after year, it becomes a source of a great deal of information for very little additional work or space. A glossary is often located at the end of the budget, but some local governments prefer to put it in the introduction, so that the reader has some grasp of the technical terms before trying to read the budget.

Although few local governments offer an index to the budget—probably because it seems like a lot of work—it is not hard to draw up a simple index with the assistance of a word-processing program; specialized computer programs can also create indexes. The additional ease an index provides may make investing in this software worthwhile.

Number of volumes

Whether the budget is consolidated or broken into separate volumes depends on a community's needs. The second volume, if there is one, often contains the capital budget for the forthcoming fiscal year and the multiyear capital improvements plan (CIP) discussed in Chapter 7. The multiyear perspective is helpful because many projects extend over several years, and it may be difficult in a one-year budget to show the entire costs of a multiyear project.

If a local government has a long-term capital program that it needs to begin implementing, devoting a separate volume to the capital budget may make sense. On the other hand, if the local government has little money for a capital program, if there are not many projects jostling each other for priority, or if capital projects are intensely political and battled out every budget year, then there is little need for a long-term capital plan.

When there is a separate volume for the capital budget, one key question is whether the other volume will contain only an operating budget or separate sections on operating and capital expenditures. If one volume contains only the operating budget and the second volume only the capital budget, the reader may have to read both—despite the fact that they have very different focuses and time frames—to understand the local government's total expenditures (operating and capital). If, on the other hand, the main volume includes both an operating and a capital section, then the separate volume describing the capital program becomes an appendix, providing more detail for the proposed capital budget—plus the CIP for outlying years. There is no firm rule as to which way to go. The most important thing is to make clear whether the main volume is just the operating budget—and hence incomplete—or whether it represents a consolidated budget (i.e., one that includes all revenues, including those from borrowing and grants, and all expenditures, including capital and operating).

Although either a one-volume or a two-volume arrangement is possible and may work well, there is something to be said for the idea of consolidating expenditures in one document so that whoever picks up the budget gets the whole picture. Since a consolidated budget may not be highly detailed, supplements can provide more detail for those who want it. One supplement that some local governments offer is a volume with the departmental budget requests or justifications in it. This volume, which requires very little preparation by the budget office, gives the council the same evidence to work with as the mayor or manager had.

Other possible supplements include separate volumes for goals statements, budget policies, external support (federal and state grants that are kept apart from general revenue), and performance reporting. Ideally, grant funding would be integrated into a comprehensive budget or divided between the capital and operating budget documents as appropriate, but grant funding is sometimes reported separately because the money is handled separately. (Some local governments have a separate decision-making process for grant funding that occurs at a different time of year from the budget.)

Given their potential political sensitivity, performance reports are often presented in a separate volume so that circulation will be limited.

Although it is probably better to integrate at least selected performance indicators into the consolidated budget or operating budget, publishing a performance report in a separate volume is better than not publishing it at all. Whether performance reports are distributed directly to the press will vary from community to community and possibly from one administration to another. Even without direct distribution to the press, a report that has been released to the council may be made public if council members choose to release it to reporters.

Many local governments have developed a short version of their budget to hand out to citizens and the press. If the budget is long, multivolume, and difficult to understand, then such a summary may have a number of advantages: First, giving away multiple copies of the budget-in-brief is less expensive than distributing the whole budget. Second, it is always easier to speak to one audience than to multiple audiences, and the intended audience for the budget summary is clear. A third advantage of such a publication is that it can be lighter in tone, with lots of graphics, without giving the impression that officials do not take governing seriously.

In summary, a budget can be presented in many volumes or in one single volume. The volumes may be of roughly equal weight, or some may be major documents and others supplementary. One of the advantages of multiple volumes is that each volume can have a different distribution list. A budget summary intended for the public can be widely distributed; a comprehensive main volume can be distributed to department heads, the governing body, and the press. (A few copies of the main volume can be set aside for the general public, to respond to requests and to comply with the law, but they need not be automatically distributed to all residents.) Departmental requests can be distributed to the council or board, either with the general budget or on request. Each department's performance report can be distributed to the appropriate departments and programs; summary versions that reflect council interests can be distributed to the council.

While multivolume budgets allow different kinds of information to be included in each volume and add flexibility in distribution, a single-volume, comprehensive budget is easier to understand. In fact, if the information in that one volume is attractively laid out and clearly explained, there may be less need for separate handouts. In addition, a single, comprehensive volume may best serve the goal of accountability. Other documents that are used in preparing the budget can be made available on request; they need not be included in separate volumes that appear to be equal in importance to the main document.

No matter how attractively a budget is laid out and how well it is explained, it is unrealistic to assume that many citizens will read and understand the entire document. To reach citizens, staff and elected officials have to prepare a message and take it to the public, to organized groups, and to the press.

Budget reforms and budget formats

In addition to conforming to the law and including the necessary components, a good budget document will highlight information that will help improve decision making and explain to the public how its money is being spent.

Since the early part of the twentieth century, a series of reforms have influenced both the budget process and the presentation of information in the budget. Reforms such as target-based and zero-base budgeting are primarily process reforms and may have little effect on the way the budget is displayed. Line-item, program, and performance budgets, in contrast, were intended to have a major impact on the way information in the budget is reported. The five sections that follow outline the ways in which various reforms have affected the presentation of budgetary information.

Line-item budgets

Line-item budgeting, a reform adopted in the early teens of the twentieth century, was designed to hold down departmental expenditures. The details of spending were supposed to emerge from a work plan that listed the items needed to carry that work plan to fruition. A list of specific items to be purchased made it possible to compare the costs of these items to the costs of similar items purchased elsewhere—which, in turn, helped determine whether a funding request was too high.

Line-item financial control may still be necessary in some situations, but overspending for routine items is no longer a major issue in most local governments. Nevertheless, line-item budgeting has survived for many years because it provides the impression of financial control and a crude budget justification. Moreover, line items provide a way to obscure the policy implications of cuts, offering a kind of protection to politicians who do not wish to be called on to justify decisions. Further, line items have the advantage of familiarity; elected officials are often reluctant to change to other forms of budgeting for fear that new budget systems will provide less detailed information for decision making. However, the disadvantages of line items weigh heavily against the advantages: First, the details of line-item budgets often obscure the whole; second, the more detailed the line items, the less flexibility managers have.

Rather than disappearing, line-item budgeting has evolved. Detailed line items have often given way to highly aggregated functional categories such as personal services, supplies and materials, capital expenditures, internal services, and miscellaneous. The village of Carol Stream, Illinois, which is a suburb of Chicago, uses the following categories: salaries and wages, contract services, commodities, capital outlays, and recurring capital expenditures.

Detailed line items may interfere with managerial flexibility, but they do provide information that managers can use. Less detailed aggregates are less managerially constraining—and, if cleverly designed, can still provide managerially valuable information. The categories should, for example, allow monitoring of important ratios such as personal services to capital expenditures, operating to capital expenses, or contractual services to wages and salaries. The categories should also allow monitoring of change over time. For example, how has inflation affected commodities purchases versus wages and personal services? A reader cannot pick up enough detail from these aggregate categories to compare the price of pencils in one town with the price of pencils elsewhere, but he or she can ask why the cost of office supplies is increasing more quickly than staffing levels.

Chicago continues to budget with a line-item approach, although it has been struggling to modernize its budget. The city uses the aggregate categories of personal services, contractual services, travel, commodities and materials, equipment, and contingencies. Personal services is broken into four categories: (1) salaries and wages (on payroll); (2) contract wage increment (salary); (3) scheduled salary adjustments; and (4) overtime. The contractual services category includes a wide range of items, including telephone expenditures, equipment leasing and repair, maintenance of city-owned vehicles, and advertising. In the office of budget and management, telephone costs are broken into equipment charges, Centrex billing, and telephone relocation charges. These line items are detailed enough to provide some meaningful comparisons and some budget justification, but they may be too detailed to provide administrative flexibility (unless they are ignored). Moreover, the level of detail tends to be overwhelming for nonspecialist readers.

Program budgets

Because much of the focus of line items is on controlling departmental spending, line items are typically drawn up for each department. When local governments began organizing the budget along programmatic rather than departmental lines, they gradually shifted from an emphasis on inputs (line items) to an emphasis on outputs (performance).

A program budget is designed to answer two principal questions: (1) What are we trying to accomplish? and (2) How much does it cost us to provide this service? In program budgeting, the program outputs and outcomes are what the local government is buying. Because it is total cost and performance levels that matter—not the costs of the components of service delivery—allocations should be lump sum rather than by line item, although this is not always the case. Program budgeting gives program managers the flexibility to achieve service targets in any way that works, as long as they stay within the budget allocation.

A program budget assigns costs to programs on the basis of both dollars and staffing levels: that is, instead of saying, "We have a police department and spend $1.2 million a year on it," a program budget might say, "We spend $500,000 a year on our traffic safety program and assign twenty full-time-equivalent positions to it. We spend $200,000 a year on our program for the recovery of stolen goods and assign the equivalent of ten full-time staff to that program."

Because it emphasizes the quality and cost of services (as opposed to the costs of things purchased without regard for quality or quantity of output), program budgeting is often accompanied by various kinds of performance measures, in a formal or informal agreement to provide services at a particular level and quality; when program budgeting and performance measures are linked in this way, a work plan is, in effect, incorporated directly into the budget.

Performance budgets

The aims of a performance budget are (1) to produce a work plan that justifies the budget total, (2) to provide a basis for comparing the cost and quality of services, and (3) to provide a running check on whether programs are achieving their goals. Workload measures help justify the budget; cost and output measures help evaluate whether service delivery is efficient and economical; and outcome and impact measures reveal to what extent programs are achieving their goals.

Workload measures are often included in the budget document, and output and outcome measures should be as well—though they are often left out. Although it does not include outcome measures (which reveal whether a program is achieving overall goals), the Oklahoma City budget does, at least, emphasize the quality, rather than the amount, of the work being done. For example, for 1996–97, the following performance measures appeared in the water department's budget:

Repair main breaks in an average of 4.5 hours or less.

Replace services in an average of 3.5 hours or less.

Update computerized inventory within 24 hours of issue.

Maintain fleet downtime at 2% or below.

For each of these objectives, the budget presents actual figures for previous years and projections for the budget year. Thus, the department's performance is compared to its previous performance (see Figure 8–2). (An alternative is to compare performance to a benchmark or to performance in other jurisdictions.)

The specific content and organization of performance budgets vary. For each program, the budget usually lists functions, budgeted expenditures

Figure 8–2 Performance measures for water utilities and line maintenance, Oklahoma City, Oklahoma.

The City of
OKLAHOMA CITY
ANNUAL BUDGET

LINE MAINTENANCE DIVISION

Summary of Divisional Responsibilities

The Water Line Maintenance Division is responsible for the repair and maintenance of the water distribution main lines, service lines, valves, fire hydrants, and manholes. Major activities include digging up and repairing or replacing leaking or burst main and service lines, including service connections; operating and repairing inoperable or malfunctioning fire hydrants and water main valves; and adjustments in the height of water meters, main valves, and fire hydrants. This division operates a central warehouse providing parts and equipment in support of the fleet.

1995-96 Accomplishments

Repaired 1304 main breaks.

Installed 22 valves, 6 hydrants and 12 mains.

Completed 8,976 jobs for the year.

1996-97 Objectives

Provide an effective water distribution system while minimizing loss of service and related expense.

Provide effective support of divisional activities through the efficient operation of the central warehouse and the equipment maintenance program.

Establish an effective customer service relationship with the public.

Identify problems within the distribution system and assist in finding solutions to the identified problems.

Performance Measures

		Actual FY 94-95	Actual FY 95-96	Target FY 96-97
1.	Repair main breaks in an average of 4.5 hours or less.	4.3	4.4	4.5
2.	Replace services in an average of 3.5 hours or less.	3.3	3.4	3.5
3.	Maintain fleet downtime at 2% or below.	0.68%	0.77%	2%

Source: City of Oklahoma City, *Annual Operating Program, Fiscal Year 1996/97*, 341.

and personnel levels, and some performance measures. The performance measures may be grouped along classic lines (demand, workload, output, outcomes, and impacts), or they may be organized into measures of quantity and quality. (Chapter 5 discusses performance measure design in detail.) Ideally, the budget should compare the performance level budgeted for the coming year with actual performance levels for prior years (see Figure 8–3). If prior performance is not reported in the budget, it may be difficult for readers to accept performance objectives as genuine budget justifications.

Target-based and zero-base budgets

Line-item, program, and performance budgets necessarily affect what information is presented in the budget and the way it is presented, particularly in the section of the budget that details expenditures. Reforms

Figure 8–3   1989 objectives and results, development services, Dayton, Ohio.

Development Services	1989 Objectives	1989 Results
	City Manager's Office	
	1. To satisfactorily complete all 1989 *Program Strategies* and strategic planning tasks assigned to the Development Services Group.	1. Objective achieved.
	2. To assist directors in the Development Services Group in achieving at least 90% of the 1989 high priority departmental objectives.	2. Objective partially achieved. Fifty-eight percent (58%) of the Development Services Group's high priority objectives were achieved.
	CityWide Development Corporation	
	3. To improve 167 occupied dwellings.	3. Objective exceeded. Improved 201 dwelling units.
	4. To achieve rental occupancy of 76 vacant dwelling units.	4. Objective partially achieved. Twelve vacant dwelling units occupied. Program was run from the Acquisition/Renovation Program which was taken over by the banking consortium under the Neighborhood Lending Program.
	5. To construct 12 homes at the Madden Hills Tomorrow site with purchase contracts.	5. Objective partially achieved. Four homes were sold and two sales are pending.
	6. To implement The Landing project in conjunction with the City of Dayton.	6. Objective partially achieved. Financing in progress and is anticipated to be in place by April, 1990. Construction is expected to begin in May, 1990.
	7. To assist in the creation of and/or retention of 1,500 job opportunities through financial counseling and direct lending.	7. Objective partially achieved. A total of 605 jobs were effected; 437 jobs were created and 168 retained.
	8. To coordinate with the City administration the development of the Omni Hotel and the expansion of the Stouffer Hotel.	8. Objective not achieved. Private financing for Omni Hotel is still being marketed. Construction for the expansion of Stouffer's is anticipated to begin in September, 1990.
	Economic Development	
	9. To manage the Enterprise Zone Program, monitoring all agreements.	9. Objective achieved.
	10. To assist in the attraction and expansion of businesses which create new jobs.	10. Objective achieved.
	11. To assist property owners of developable land adjacent to the City in the annexation process to offset the loss of developable land resulting from the City's Well Field Protection efforts.	11. Objective exceeded. One hundred sixty-two acres of development land were annexed.
	Housing Development	
	12. To determine locations and create development plans for two special projects which include rehabilitation and new construction.	12. Objective achieved. Developer for Westwood to be selected in January, 1990.
	13. To manage the Neighborhood Development Corporation Housing Production Support Program.	13. Objective exceeded. Seven new Neighborhood Development Corporations were certified.

Source: City of Dayton, Ohio, Office of Management and Budget, *1990 Program Strategies*, 135.

such as target-based and zero-base budgeting, which are essentially process rather than format reforms, need not affect the choice of information or manner of display used in the budget.

The question then becomes, how—if at all—should the results of a target-based or zero-base budgeting process be displayed in the budget? If the budget message, transmittal letter, or introduction discusses the budget process, major reductions in spending, or changes in priorities, then the zero-base or target-based budget should be described at that point.

The budget message, transmittal letter, or introduction can also summarize the results of the budget process; for example, some local governments include in the introduction a ranked list of funded and unfunded projects that shows how the use of a target-based or zero-base process affected the budget. Cincinnati, Ohio, included in its 1990 budget a list

---

1990 GENERAL FUND DISCRETIONARY REQUESTS VERSUS RECOMMENDATIONS

CITY MANAGER (CM) PRIORITY DESCRIPTIONS:

A: High Priority—ranked because the recommendation directly reflects the support of the ten service areas (safety, administration, infrastructure, housing, economic development/employment, environmental resources, leisure time, transportation, health & human services, and community relations) and maintenance of operating capacity to support the capital program.

B: Medium Priority—ranked because the recommendation indirectly reflects the support of the above service areas.

C: Low Priority—ranked because the item is either not recommended or, if recommended, does not reflect support of the above service area.

Note that fringe costs associated with each requested and recommended item are not calculated within the departmental total. Fringe costs are calculated within the recommended base non-departmental account or as a separate discretionary recommendation in the fringe benefit section.

Department	Division	Dept Priority	Discretionary Description	REQUEST		R E C	RECOMMENDATION				CM Prior
				Total	Posit'n		Personal Services	NonPerson Services	Total	Posit'n	
City Council	City Council	1	Office Formula	31,340	0.0	Y	0	31,340	31,340	0.0	B
Clerk of Council	Clerk of Council	1	Info Retrieval	33,750	0.0	N	0	0	0	0.0	C
		2	Portable Sound Sys	18,000	0.0	N	0	0	0	0.0	C
				51,750	0.0		0	0	0	0.0	
Mayor's Office	Mayor's Office	1	Mayor Formula	4,630	0.0	Y	0	4,630	4,630	0.0	B
CHRC	CHRC	1	Disabled Affairs	27,300	0.0	Y	0	27,300	27,300	0.0	B
CCY	CCY	1	Program Support	74,800	0.0	Y	0	49,800	49,800	0.0	B
RCC	RCC	1	FSP Production	491,110	0.0	N	0	0	0	0.0	C
RCC	RCC	2SB	IBM Operations Support	65,980	0.0	Y	0	65,980	65,980	0.0	C
RCC	RCC	3SB	FSP Phase II	46,380	0.0	Y	0	46,380	46,380	0.0	C
RCC	RCC	4SB	Information Ctr CADD	112,740	0.0	N	0	0	0	0.0	C
RCC	RCC	5	FSP Purchasing Support	60,330	0.0	N	0	0	0	0.0	C
RCC	RCC	6SB	Document Imaging	23,800	0.0	N	0	0	0	0.0	C
RCC	RCC	7SB	Labor Distribution	103,420	0.0	N	0	0	0	0.0	C
RCC	RCC	8	Unisys Dis Recovery	22,280	0.0	N	0	0	0	0.0	C
RCC	RCC	9SB	IBM Dis Recovery	69,420	0.0	Y	0	69,420	69,420	0.0	A
RCC	RCC	10SB	CASE Tools	18,240	0.0	N	0	0	0	0.0	C
RCC	RCC	11SB	Project Management	112,940	0.0	N	0	0	0	0.0	C
RCC	RCC	12	IBM Cap Mainte	9,250	0.0	Y	0	8,290	8,290	0.0	C
				1,135,890	0.0		0	190,070	190,070	0.0	

Figure 8–4   Rankings of some items from the supplementary request list, Cincinnati, Ohio (target-based budget).

Source: City of Cincinnati, Ohio, *1990 City of Cincinnati Budget: Comprehensive Overview*, xxxvi.

of all discretionary items requested by each department; the list also showed the priority (low, medium, or high) that the city manager had assigned to each item (see Figure 8–4).

It is not unusual for local governments that use a target-based budget to include in the budget a ranked list of unfunded items, but Cincinnati includes much more information: in the spending detail for each program, the program managers describe the criteria they used to determine whether an item would be part of the base or whether it would be left "unprotected" (i.e., appear as a discretionary spending request). Justification is given for each item on the unfunded (discretionary request) list, along with the city manager's recommendation. Thus, the reader knows exactly what each program manager requested, why it was requested, and how much of each proposal the manager approved. In other words, the target-based budgeting process is reflected in the published version of the budget.

Including such detailed information in the budget clarifies the criteria being used to fund proposals and shows how those criteria are linked to overall community goals. However, including such detail on departmental requests may give program managers a way to bypass the manager and, in effect, communicate directly with the council. In some local governments, such a process would seriously undermine the manager's role in financial matters. On the other hand, this process involves the council directly in the assignment of priorities to the unfunded list, which is certainly a legitimate function for a council.

Although local governments that use zero-base budgeting can summarize the process in the budget introduction, some local governments go much farther: Mecklenburg County, North Carolina, which has been using zero-base budgeting for many years, devotes nearly an entire volume to reporting on the zero-base rankings. One section of this volume lists service-level proposals and costs in rank order. Other columns show (1) the staffing implications of each proposal, (2) the funds requested from the county, state, and federal governments to pay for the proposal, and (3) the cumulative totals for staffing levels and dollars (see Figure 8–5). At the beginning of the volume, the county manager gives a figure that reflects the total budget he is recommending to the board. One particular year, that figure translated into funding for roughly the first 500 of 648 items; items 501 through 648 remained unfunded.

A detailed representation of the results of a zero-base budgeting process may be useful to persuade council members and citizens that the local government did, in fact, use a zero-base approach. However, unless the budget also includes the criteria used to rank projects and service level proposals, such detail has little context and may therefore be of limited use. In Mecklenburg's budget, the council's priorities are stated at the beginning of the first volume, and all service improvements approved by the manager are cross-referenced to demonstrate how council priorities shaped the budget.

Describing target-based and zero-base budgeting processes in the budget document creates an opportunity to make two important points: First, the budget was carefully scrutinized, proposals were assigned priorities, and lower-priority items were eliminated; second, the goals and objectives formulated by elected officials and the public were the criteria used to allocate funds among discretionary items. In other words, reporting on the target-based or zero-base process helps demonstrate how resources are being allocated. How many of the actual rankings to print in the budget is a discretionary decision; it may be best to print them in a supplementary volume that is available on request.

Figure 8–5 Budget submission, Mecklenburg County, North Carolina (zero-base budget).

```
SERVICE LEVEL ANALYSIS - FISCAL YEAR 1994-1995

SERVICE LEVEL  2 of  2 (C)     DEPARTMENT RANK  4 of  4     COUNTY RANK   402
DEPARTMENT NAME/NO:             County Commissioners/County Manager [050]
BUDGET UNIT NAME/NO:            Office of Productivity Improvement [074]
SHORT DESCRIPTIVE TITLE:        Additional Pursuit of Excellence Activities (Current Level)
STATEMENT OF PURPOSE:   To work in partnership with county leadership in creating an environment that
builds and sustains a culture of continuous improvement.
```

FUNDING	FY 95 THIS LEVEL	FY 95 CUMULATIVE	FY 94 AMENDED	FY 93 ACTUAL
COUNTY	45,572	416,119	400,238	403,722
FEDERAL	0	0	0	0
STATE	0	0	0	0
OTHER	0	0	0	0
TOTAL	45,572	416,119	400,238	403,722
	FT PT TP	FT PT TP	FT PT TP	FT PT TP
POSITIONS	1 0 0	7 0 0	7 0 0	7 0 0

```
DESCRIBE SERVICES PROVIDED: This level provides an additional Internal Consultant.  This level allows
the addition of another department redesign project.  Major activities in the redesign project are development
and training of an additional departmental Steering Committee, and the creating of a Redesign team.  The
consultant provides technical expertise to the Redesign Team in the form of Process Design Techniques,
Organization Structure Analysis, Information Systems Analysis, Human Resource Systems Development to include
selection, placement, training, development, appraisal, and rewards.
```

PROGRAM MEASURE DESCRIPTIONS	FY 95 THIS LEVEL	FY 95 CUMULATIVE	FY 94 ESTIMATED	FY 93 ACTUAL
1. DEPT. SYSTEMS REDESIGN PROJECTS	1	5	3	3
2. STRAT. QLTY. PLAN TASK TM. CONSUL.	0	3	3	0
3. SENIOR LEADERSHIP TM. CONSULTATION	0	1	1	1
4. SENIOR SUPPORT TM. CONSULTATION	0	1	1	1
5. SPECIAL CONSULTATION PROJECTS	0	2	2	2
6.				
7.				

JOB CLASS	POSITION TITLE	FT PT TP	JOB CLASS	POSITION TITLE	FT PT TP
E3598	INTERNAL CONSULTANT I	1 0 0			

```
Form B                                        4                                        04-94
```

Source: Mecklenburg County, North Carolina, *Proposed County Manager's Budget and Work Program, FY 94–95*, Form B.

Selecting and displaying information

To a significant degree, budget format will determine what information is reported in the budget and how it is displayed. In a line-item format, for example, tables are usually laid out to enable the reader to compare proposed spending with spending in the current and previous years' budgets. Only estimates are available for the current year, but actual figures may be used for preceding years. Examples of commonly used column headings are "last year's budget," "last year's actuals," "this year's budget," "this year's estimated actuals," and "next year's proposed." Variations include (1) actual data for an additional prior year and (2) actual data for the current year to date. If the local government uses a wide-page (horizontal rather than vertical) format, it may be possible to include one or two "shadow years"—that is, one or two years of projected budgets beyond the upcoming one.

Presenting information in this way invites council members to ask why a particular line item increased so much from last year to this year, or why the estimates for an item were off by so much. The answers should help the council decide whether the proposed line items are adequate or overly generous, in light of prior experience. When several out-years are included in the budget, the discussion can include the impact of current decisions on future expenditures.

When historical data are presented by line item, policy issues are often obscured. To help focus the discussion more on policy issues (e.g., Is this program doing what we want it to do?), historical data can be presented in a program or performance format, without reference to line items. A historical presentation is especially important in performance budgets because it enables readers to compare promised and actual accomplishments with budget allocations over time.

A full program budget—such as that used by Dayton, Ohio—de-emphasizes departmental lines. The budget is broken into functional areas such as economic vitality, neighborhood vitality, professional management, and urban conservation; the functional areas are then broken into programs. In the professional management area, for example, programs include financial resource management, human resource management, communications and information systems, and judicial services. Each program is further subdivided into activities: financial resource management is broken into general accounting, cash management, income tax collections, water revenue, purchasing, and debt service.

In one section of the budget, Dayton lists specific projects and objectives that each program manager has promised to try to achieve during the budget year. Although this section deals more with special projects or additional activities than with routine services, it does provide a partial justification for the budget. For each program, this section of the budget lists the previous year's stated objectives and the level of compliance with those objectives. Such information encourages council members to ask whether a program can be expected to achieve its goals—for example, whether it is well managed, inefficient, or too ambitious, given its staffing level. Council members may also be led to ask whether the objectives for the budget year are sufficiently closely related to communitywide goals or otherwise appropriate.

In various budget tables, Dayton provides much—but not all—of the traditional information that council members might expect to see; for example, Dayton's budget indicates how much money is being proposed for each program and how much money was spent on it in the current year. What Dayton does not provide is line-item detail; council members cannot ask about expenditures for paper supplies or gasoline.

The layout of the tables can suggest different sets of questions to the reader. For example, Oklahoma City's budget provides highly aggregated historical data for the functional categories of personal services, contractual services, commodities, capital, and transfers—but provides line-item detail only for the budget year. This arrangement has two advantages: (1) it justifies the budget request, and (2) it ensures that the reader's attention is not focused on year-to-year changes in line items but on underlying policy questions (e.g., why personal services expenses are growing more slowly than inflation, whether enough money is being spent on capital projects in comparison to personal services).

Cincinnati's detailed expenditure tables focus on (1) the amount in each program's budget that can be funded within the target, (2) the amount approved from the discretionary list, and (3) the funding sources. There are no historical comparisons—no budgeted and actual figures from prior years and no estimated actuals from the current year. The tables include only the current year's budgeted figure and the percent change from this year's budgeted figure to the proposed budget for next year. Increases from year to year have to be justified on a policy basis; if the council wants to ask questions, it must question either departmental or the chief executive's priorities.

In short, how the information is presented affects budget deliberations.[4] Because council members can inquire only about what they see in the budget, the nature of the detailed support for budget requests is likely to frame any debate on the budget numbers. Tables showing historical data at the line-item level invite comparison of line items over time and tend to remove the policy content from decision making. Program- and performance-oriented budgets, in contrast, present council members with specific objectives and a brief past record indicating whether or not the objectives were achieved. The result is a strong—though not exclusive—focus on policy.

If a local government wishes to encourage the council to address policy issues in the budget, it would do well to shift entirely to a program and performance format: when budgets provide line-item information by department in addition to program and performance data, the council may continue to rely on the line items, which put budgetary information into a familiar framework and do not require council members to take uncomfortable stands on policy issues.

However, any change in the budget format should be preceded by an extensive education effort. To assist with the transition, crosswalks (special tables or charts showing how information in the old format is presented in the new one) should be included in the budget for several years, to give council members an opportunity to develop an understanding of the new format before the crosswalks disappear. Where possible, the old line-item format organized along departmental lines should eventually be dropped, rather than carried along beside the program and performance format. If line-item budget proposals are mandated by law or charter, they can be relegated to a brochure or to a supplementary volume.

Budget design

Because the appearance of the budget affects whether people read it and what they gain from it, the design of the budget is an important factor in its overall quality. In fact, poor design—confusing charts, page after crowded page of unbroken text—may ultimately interfere with the role of the budget in providing governmental accountability. It is not enough for information to be *present* in the budget—it must also be accessible.

Some basic guidelines can help make the budget more readable—for example:

Alternate charts, graphs, and illustrations with solid text.

Leave wide margins and a reasonable amount of white space around text; filling all available space may overwhelm the reader.

Keep the art simple.

Use illustrations to underscore the main points.

Coordinate the text and the graphics.

Although graphics are a valuable tool for making the budget interesting and accessible, local governments are sometimes reluctant to make use of this important resource. In some jurisdictions, the concern may be that graphics will create too light a tone in what should be a serious piece of work. Although a budget is a formal document, it need not be so dull that it discourages readers. Some jurisdictions may wish to avoid outright humor, but it is not difficult to design or obtain graphics that are both appealing and tasteful. In short, a budget need not consist of ponderous rows of numbers to be taken seriously; there is a great deal of room for creativity and visual appeal. The appropriate tone will depend on the community—and perhaps on the administration.

Although local governments may be concerned that graphics will increase the cost and the time for budget production, graphics need not be fancy or expensive to be effective. Many word processors—and all desktop publishing programs—can produce attractive graphics quickly and inexpensively. These programs allow nonartists to create graphs and charts, draw lines and boxes, shadow headings, change type sizes, and, in some cases, to use "clip art."

In fact, what is most difficult about developing graphics for the budget is not getting the computer to draw them—although that may have its challenges—but (1) ensuring that graphics are useful and appropriate and (2) identifying important points and determining how best to display them visually.

Uses of graphics

Graphics can play a number of different roles in a budget, and knowing how and when to use them can greatly improve clarity and accessibility.

Some graphics are designed to lead the eye to important parts of the page; such graphics may be decorative but should not be too fussy. For example, arrows can point to parts of a table that are discussed in the text. St. Charles, Illinois, highlights the first two columns of a table with a color and leaves the rest of the table in black and white. The reader sees instantly that the highlighted material is meant to be compared with the material in black and white. Surrounding information with a box calls attention to the box's contents. Outline sketches can also be used to frame material—for example, performance measures for the ambulance service might appear within the outline of an ambulance. Some local governments put a frame around each page; various frames can be used to distinguish one program, department, or type of information from another.

Graphics can also be used to capture the essence of a point and make it quickly and dramatically. For example, a bar chart showing the property tax yield and the total tax yield over time enables readers to grasp the relationship at a glance. (If charts and graphs require a great deal of scrutiny to be understood, they should probably be simplified.)

A third function of graphics is to make it easier for readers to find their way around what can be a large and confusing document. Pages (or page separators) of different colors can be used to distinguish between various sections of the budget; sketches on divider pages can also be used to indicate the contents of each section. In one city, an icon on each tab signals the subject of the section; for example, the tab for public works shows a construction horse with a warning light on top, and the tab for the water and sewer department shows several drops of water. (Such icons will not work unless they are immediately understandable.)

The shift to program budgets has made it necessary to distinguish between levels of aggregation: although many of the tables in a program budget are laid out identically, the contents may range from governmentwide summaries to departmental data, program information, and activity reports. In St. Charles, Illinois, various numbers of trees represent levels of aggregation: summaries across service areas are marked with three trees (the forest); broad service areas are marked with two trees (a grove); and individual services within a service area are marked with a single tree.

A fourth function of graphics is to increase visual diversity, which makes the budget easier to read. The particular choice of illustrations can also help reinforce for readers the budget's central focus: the delivery of local government services. A sketch of a snowplow in action can dramatize the work of city hall; a sketch of a visiting nurse caring for an elderly woman can bring home the connection between public health expenditures and everyday life. Such graphics need not be elaborate, just visually appealing and appropriate: a picture of the skyline is appropriate for the section on economic development but jarring in the section on tree trimming.

Designing tables, charts, and graphs

The single most important principle in designing graphics can be summarized as "form follows function": that is, the point being illustrated should dictate the type of illustration. When budgeters discovered computer graphics packages, the number of pie charts and bar graphs included in the budget increased: it was easy to do a pie chart on revenue sources, so a pie chart was drawn. However, the addition of a pie chart —or of any other graphic illustration—does not necessarily improve the quality or clarity of the budget: choosing the appropriate illustration is key. For example, if the point is that the local government's property tax rate is lower than that of other jurisdictions, then a bar graph (with each jurisdiction represented by a bar) would be a good illustration. If the point is that property tax revenue is declining in relation to sales tax revenue, then a line graph would be appropriate, with one line representing the yield of the property tax over time and a second line showing the yield of sales taxes over the same time period. In both these examples, the graphic presentation makes the main point immediately apparent.

In addition to being appropriate to the purpose, tables, charts, and graphs should be simple—with one or two clear points—and the main points should be repeated in the text. To avoid confusing or overwhelming readers, the number of columns in tables should be limited. Lines on graphs should be thick and dark and the key should be clear, so that the points stand out.

One way to make the budget more interesting is to use graphics of various types, including organization charts, bar graphs, pie charts, and maps. In the beginning of the budget, organization charts are frequently used to introduce city hall; more detailed charts are then used to introduce each department. Pie charts are common in the overview section, to help illustrate revenues by source and expenditures by type. Bar graphs can be used in the introduction to compare yields or levies over time or to compare the local government with other jurisdictions in terms of staffing, tax levies, or borrowing. Bar graphs are commonly used to illustrate performance results. In the statistical overview section, which generally appears at the end of the budget, maps can show area growth over time and the location of economic development projects or capital improvements. Social service providers may want to use maps to show where their clients live or where dislocated residents have been moved. In a section presenting long-term projections for revenue and expenditures, line graphs can be used to compare alternatives: one line on the graph can show where the community will be under current policy, and a second line can show the impact of adopting a different policy. A chart showing the timing of events—summarizing the budget process, for example—is another useful visual aid (see Figure 8–6).

Although graphs and charts can help break up the text and make a page more attractive, they can be tedious if they all look alike (e.g., if all use the same dotted lines or plus signs, the same faint type, and the same color, shape, and size). To vary line graphs, fill in the space under the line, which makes an interesting shape. Bar graphs can be filled in with shapes that represent the subject; for example, in a graph showing the volume of garbage picked up daily, barrels or dumpsters can be used as the bars. Or, to suggest amounts of money, dollar signs or stacks of coins can take the place of darkened bars. To transform a static picture

Figure 8–6 Timing of the budget process, Dayton, Ohio.

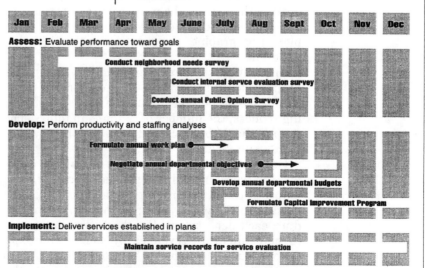

Source: City of Dayton, Ohio, Office of Management and Budget, *1995 Policy Budget*, 6.

into something that is moving and visually interesting, substitute an arrow for a line on a graph, pointing in whatever direction the line is headed.

Dayton's budget makes good use of such techniques: in a graph of narcotics arrests, the outline of a pair of handcuffs follows the trend line on the graph. To compare new office buildings in Dayton with those in other cities, the budget office used sketches of office buildings to represent the numbers (taller office buildings meant more square feet built). An illustration can also be used to bring home the meaning of a chart illustrating performance measures. In its chart showing the unemployment rate over time, the Dayton budget showed a sketch of a man in overalls leaning against the graph like an unemployed person waiting for work.

Making budgets readable: GFOA standards

Determining what to include in a budget and how best to present it is not an easy task. To assist local governments with this responsibility, the GFOA has established guidelines for public officials that explain what experts look for in good budgets. The GFOA also sponsors a budget awards program, which evaluates local government budgets according to how well they comply with these guidelines. The guidelines emphasize four kinds of information that should be included in the budget document:

1. Statements of policy
2. Information about the financial plan
3. Implications for managing the departments during the year
4. Information meant to help make the budget accessible to readers who are not trained in budgeting and finance.

The budget as a policy guide

According to GFOA guidelines, the policies that underlie and shape the budget should be stated clearly in the budget document. One way to highlight budgetary policies is to describe the criteria used to allocate resources. Local governments that use target-based or zero-base budgets often do so explicitly, by explaining how they chose among unfunded items.

A somewhat broader and more inclusive approach is to list communitywide goals or council members' goals and link them to departmental objectives and resource allocations. For example, the budget introduction might include a numbered list of six overarching goals. In the sections showing departmental objectives, the budget would then indicate which of these goals the objectives are designed to achieve. (Not all departmental objectives will speak to the overarching goals.) Whenever an addition to services is approved or a departmental request granted, the addition or request should be linked to the appropriate departmental objective and communitywide or council goal. For example, if increased citizen safety is communitywide goal number two, then an expenditure for an improved police dispatch system can be explained in the text as helping to achieve goal number two, increased citizen safety.

Another way to clarify policies is to summarize major policy issues in the budget message. For example, what were the major spending initiatives in the budget this year? What were they designed to achieve? Rather than simply say, "We are planning to finish the road reconstruction project this year," the budget can note that (1) it is a priority to bring all roads up to technical standards appropriate to the community's growing population, and (2) once that goal is realized, funds formerly used for reconstruction will be channeled into resurfacing and maintenance to prolong the life of the streets. Such a detailed explanation clarifies the local government's policy for citizens—and explains how a particular project fits into that policy.

Similarly, instead of simply noting that 1999 revenue will be $20,314,500 and 1999 expenditures $19,334,800, the budget message should explain the policy decisions that resulted in those totals. Budget deliberations may, for example, have been carried out under a number of policies—not increasing the property tax this year, trying to reduce the level of GO bonds outstanding, or maintaining general fund balances at 30 percent of general fund expenditures. Such policies should be described, and any deviations from policy should be fully explained. Requiring policy information to be included in the budget may press a local government to formulate its financial policies more clearly and think more explicitly about how it is implementing those policies.

The budget as a financial plan

Since the budget is a plan to balance revenues and expenditures, information about revenues and expenditures, by fund, should be prominently displayed. The document should also (1) note whether the proposal balances in the short term and (2) describe the prospects for balance in the future. The evaluation of longer-term prospects for balance should include (1) information on the amount and kind of debt outstanding (i.e., revenue or general obligation) and (2) a detailed description of revenues and expenditures over time.

Reporting on recent revenue trends can alert readers to the possibility of future financial difficulties. For example, if property tax revenue has been capped by law, the fiscal implications of the cap should be discussed. If the local government has increased its dependence on sales taxes (which increases its vulnerability to recessions), the budget should detail the performance of sales taxes during recent recessions and indicate whether declining yields have created a problem—and if so, how the government plans to handle this problem in the future.

In addition to reporting on revenues, the budget should report on planned expenditures for each department or program. It is important to note that the GFOA awards program urges local governments to use lump-sum allocations for programs where possible and to avoid detailed line items.

Capital spending should at least be summarized; ideally, the budget would list major capital projects and their costs. The budget should also outline the relationship between the capital and operating budgets: one way to do so is to show new spending in the operating budget necessitated by capital expenditures. Thus, if a new firehouse opens, the budget would show an increase in operating costs and an explanation for the increase—for example, "Twenty new firefighters were hired to staff the new building. Their salaries and benefits are included in the operating budget and account for the difference between current-year expenditures and the budget proposal." If capital projects result in a decrease in staffing, that should be explained as well.

The inclusion of one or two "shadow" years—projected expenditures for years beyond the budget year—can also help highlight the effect of budget-year capital outlays on future spending, especially if the numbers are supported by a brief explanatory narrative. Without such information, the reader might conclude that the increased operating expenditures that will result from capital projects are not being provided for—and that the budget is therefore not really balanced.

A financial plan takes on solidity and becomes more convincing when the budget proposal is put in historical context. If there is room for a clear display of several years' prior data for revenues and expenditures by fund, department, or program, these data should be presented for comparison. Many program budget formats and budgets that are designed for visual ease do not have room for three years of prior data, especially if both budgeted and actual figures are given for each year. If this is the case, comparative information can be presented in summary tables rather than in the expenditure detail. Presented in summary format, the comparative figures can go back even further than three years; the history of revenue sources, for example, often goes back ten years. The budget can also include revenue and expenditure projections for the coming five years, as well as a discussion of the assumptions underlying the projections.

The budget as an operations guide

The budget has been called a work plan with dollar signs: the estimated amount of work and the cost to each administrative unit for performing that work should underlie the budget, and this work plan should be presented somewhere in the budget.

One way to display the work plan is to show the spending plan, department by department, indicating which programs each department is responsible for and the level of service that will be provided for the amount budgeted. To describe the level of service being provided, the budget can list each program's objectives for the previous year and note the extent to which those objectives were achieved—for example, "Our objectives were to keep the grass on the medians to less than 2-1/2 inches, plant 25 replacement trees, and remove 3 tons of debris. We kept the grass under 2-1/2 inches for all but two weeks of the year, replaced 30 dead trees, and removed 2-1/2 tons of debris."

Performance objectives tell the reader what the administrative unit is promising to do with the budget allocation; they create a kind of contract and a justification for the budget. Information on actual performance in prior years tells the reader whether past contracts have been honored. Without such information, there is no way to judge compliance. Ideally, historical data should include several years of prior performance so that trends can be evaluated. An alternative to tracking trends in actual performance over time is to compare performance to a benchmark or other standard: "Did we do task X as well as the community that does it best?" "Did we do 50 percent as well as the standard?"

As a work plan with dollars attached, the budget represents not only estimated dollar resources needed to carry out the work, but also estimated staffing levels. As an operations guide, the budget should therefore include the staffing levels for each program—and there should be a clear relationship between staffing levels and objectives. Other things being equal, a program that is cut back in staff will be able to do less work, or the same amount of work at a lower quality; conversely, a program that is adding staff ought to be able to do more work, better work, or quicker work. Many jurisdictions list the staffing levels for the whole local government, but it makes more sense to list the staffing levels for departments and programs, to clarify the relationship between resource allocations and performance expectations.

The budget as a communications tool

One of the major functions of the budget is to provide public accountability. Although citizens pay taxes, they have no direct influence on the quality, quantity, and composition of local services they receive. At the very least, local governments need to give citizens a detailed accounting of how their money was spent. If the budget document is obscure or too technical, it will fail as a tool of accountability.

The requirement that a budget be understandable means that it must include certain components—such as a table of contents, a glossary, and an index. Other explanatory materials that can make the budget document more accessible include (1) a description of the budget process, complete with time lines showing who does what when, and (2) descriptions of the legal constraints that help shape the budget. Legal constraints such as tax limits, debt limits on GO bonds, and tax sharing arrangements may all be taken for granted by budget makers but unfamiliar—or unclear—to citizens. All such constraints—changes in state laws that affect revenue, charter requirements that affect budget format, provisions of a court settlement or a state debt bailout—ought to be explained in the budget. If a jurisdiction is setting up a tax increment financing (TIF) district, then the budget should describe not only the specific district being created, but also the laws pertaining to the operation of a TIF district.

As noted earlier, the budget's ability to communicate depends to a large extent on its physical appearance. At the very least, a budget document should not be a lengthy computer printout bound loosely into a folder. Whether it is spiral bound, paper bound, or circulated in a three-ring binder, a budget should have an attractive cover. It may include

---

Discarding unnecessary information
The budget office and the chief executive need to review the budget every year for clarity, purpose, and relevance. Budget documents sometimes include outdated information left over from experimental efforts or from earlier versions of current programs. For example, when local governments first begin to use performance measures, dozens of measures may be generated, only a few of which ultimately prove useful enough to retain. If no one thinks to eliminate useless measures, they may be maintained in the budget indefinitely.

Similarly, the budget should be reviewed to ensure that sections carried over from one budget to the next—program descriptions, for example—convey useful information. If the role of the fire department is described as "the protection of life and property,"
how does that differ from the role of the police department? Presumably, the two departments are doing very different things; those differences need to be clearly stated.

To help streamline the budget, the budget director should summarize where appropriate and note where additional detail can be obtained. Detailed line items, for example, can often be eliminated; less detailed line items, chosen to provide managerially relevant information, make much better reading. The aim of the budget should not be to provide overwhelmingly detailed information but to provide meaningful and useful information, offering backup details where necessary. If no one needs a given piece of information, it should be dropped. If only a few people need it, then it may belong in a supplementary handout.

sketches or be printed in colored ink (brown or dark green is a welcome change from black). Graphics—tables, charts, bar graphs, and line graphs—should be plentiful, clear, and to the point.

Creating a budget-in-brief, or a summary volume, with overview data and graphics is one way to increase the communication power of the budget. Such a document should (1) direct readers to other volumes that contain more detailed information and (2) provide instructions on how to obtain these other volumes.

Summary

As the GFOA criteria emphasize, the budget document has many different functions. To department heads, the budget represents an agreement to get a certain amount of work done at a particular cost; to the council, it represents information for policy making; to the budget office and chief executive, it represents good financial practice. To citizens, the budget offers a means of establishing accountability; it should be a clear statement of where tax money is going and a convincing demonstration that (1) the money is being well spent and (2) the local government's finances are in good shape. To the extent that it addresses debt and long-term fiscal health, the budget also speaks to the financial community.

Ensuring that the budget can perform so many different functions and serve so many different audiences takes considerable attention and thought, but the rewards of success are broader than GFOA recognition and higher bond ratings. A clear, well-designed budget document can become the basis for improved decision making, better departmental management, and greater public understanding—and appreciation—of local government operations.

1 For examples of transmittal letters and budget messages, see Dennis Strachota, *The Best of Governmental Budgeting: A Guide to Preparing Budget Documents* (Chicago: GFOA, 1994), 7–17.

2 St. Charles, Illinois, *Budget Plan, 1995–96*, I-21.

3 City of Milwaukee, *1994 Plan and Budget Summary*, 189–94.

4 Gloria Grizzle, "Does Budget Format Really Govern the Actions of Budgetmakers?" *Public Budgeting & Finance* 6 (spring 1986): 60–70.

Afterword

To enable readers to develop an understanding of the range of possibilities, this book explains how budgeting is done in a number of different local governments. The authors have sought out and described good practices that can be tailored to local problems and opportunities. None of the recommendations in this volume is abstract or theoretical: all of the approaches described have been tried out and are working somewhere in the United States—often in many places.

This volume is intended not only to address specific practical issues related to budgeting, but also to provide some overall recommendations for budget reform. First, local governments should attempt to develop an "open" budget process that allows problems, contradictions, and demands to surface; public officials should also learn to deal skillfully with controversy to prevent it from getting out of hand. Effort should go into creating a budget document that is interesting and intelligible—and that clarifies the legal and policy constraints under which the proposal was put together. In light of ongoing antigovernment sentiment, some sunshine is necessary to show the public how well managed and responsive local governments are. Budgeting can play an important role here.

Second, local governments should strive for open discussion and explicit articulation of the policies that underlie the budget; and once policies are adopted, any deviations should be formally proposed and debated. Open discussion of policy is likely to have a number of positive results: for example, on the basis of a better understanding of policy issues and policy decisions, citizens and elected officials are more likely to grant local administrative officials greater discretion in financial matters. Lack of understanding, in contrast, tends to breed mistrust—and mistrust often leads to the imposition of excessive external control. In addition, broad policy discussions and clear decisions are likely to yield a more lively budget process, engaging the interest of both citizens and public officials.

Third, local governments should seek to moderate the tensions that occur naturally in budgeting: budget office requests for departmental information should not be excessive; the influence of guardians and advocates should be appropriately balanced; and collective interests should be expressed with as much force and credibility as those of individuals and interest groups. Officials should design and monitor a suitable balance between democracy and bureaucracy and between accuracy and political expediency. Even if the outcome appears to be better or cheaper government, the chief executive should try to limit reliance on professional expertise, ensuring that it does not substitute entirely for demand: planners' service quality standards, for example, are not equivalent politically to the public's perceptions of need. Awareness of the tensions produced by budgeting and of the responsibility entailed in dealing with those tensions can help foster long-term solutions.

Fourth, local officials should encourage the budget office to abandon some of its old roles and adopt more contemporary ones—to shift, for example, from the role of naysayer to that of educator, adjudicator, and communicator. Budget offices still project revenues and monitor budgetary balance, but modern budget offices are less likely to micromanage and more likely to grant departments managerial discretion in meeting targets.

Why expend effort to change the budget process, budget policies, and the budget document? The need for reform is urgent, not because government is bad or corrupt, but because it is perceived as expensive and uncontrollable; this perception, in turn, renders the public overly willing to deny referenda and support overall tax limits. Approaches to reform have been working successfully in the field for years. What remains is for public officials to identify the problems in their jurisdictions and select the changes most suited to local circumstances. Where none of the existing tools seems to fit, local officials will do what they have always done: combine some, adapt others, and invent still more. The goal, overall, is to regain public support, enabling citizens and local governments to work together to solve collective problems.

Glossary

Account A separate financial reporting unit for budgeting, management, or accounting purposes. All budgetary transactions, whether revenue or expenditure, are recorded in accounts. *See also* **fund, chart of accounts.**

Accounting standards The generally accepted accounting principles (GAAP) promulgated by the Governmental Accounting Standards Board (GASB), which guide the recording and reporting of financial information by state and local governments. The standards establish such guidelines as when transactions are recognized, the types and purposes of funds, and the content and organization of the annual financial report.

Accrual basis of accounting A method of accounting in which revenues are recorded when measurable and earned, and expenses are recognized when a good or service is used. *See also* **cash basis of accounting, modified accrual basis of accounting.**

Activity A departmental effort that contributes to the accomplishment of specific, identified program objectives.

Allotment The distribution of budget authority by an agency to various sub-units or regional offices.

Apportionment The release of funds on a quarterly or project basis by the budget office. Apportionment is designed to prevent the premature depletion of a unit's appropriation and is more common at the state and federal levels than at the local level.

Appropriation Legal authorization to make expenditures or enter into obligations for specific purposes.

Assessed property value The value of property for the purpose of levying property taxes.

Audit An examination, usually by an official or private accounting firm retained by the council, that reports on the accuracy of the annual financial report prepared by the chief executive.

Balanced budget A budget in which current revenues equal current expenditures. The legal requirements for a balanced budget may be set by the state or local government.

Benefits received principle Principle under which users or those who benefit from a service pay for at least a portion of the cost of providing that service. Payment may be through service charges or earmarked taxes.

Biennial budget A budget that covers a two-year period.

Bond A promise to repay borrowed money on a particular date, often ten or twenty years in the future; most bonds also involve a promise to pay a specified dollar amount of interest at predetermined intervals. Local governments use bonds to obtain long-term financing for capital projects.

Bond covenant A legally enforceable agreement with bondholders that requires the governmental agency selling the bond to meet certain conditions in the repayment of the debt.

Bond ordinance A law approving the sale of government bonds that specifies how revenues may be spent.

Budget A spending plan that balances revenues and expenditures over a fixed time period—usually a year—and that includes, at least by implication, a work plan.

Budget amendment A revision of the adopted budget that, when approved by the council, replaces the original provision. Budget amendments occur frequently throughout the fiscal year, as spending priorities shift.

Budget calendar A timetable showing when particular tasks must be completed in order for the council to approve the spending plan before the beginning of the next fiscal year.

Budget cycle The recurring process—either annual or biennial—in which a government prepares, adopts, and implements a spending plan. The budget cycle consists of (1) preparation of a budget proposal, (2) legislative approval of the proposed budget, (3) executive-branch implementation of the proposed budget, and (4) preparation of an annual report detailing the results of operations.

Budget guidelines Guidelines developed by the chief executive, in consultation with the council, that describe the budget environment—i.e., revenue expectations and policy emphasis—for the forthcoming year; departments make their budget requests on the basis of the guidelines.

Budget manual A booklet prepared by the budget office that includes, at a minimum, the budget calendar, the forms departments need to prepare their budget requests, and a description of the budget process.

Budget reserves Money accumulated for future purposes—e.g., to deal with unforeseen circumstances or to replace buildings or equipment.

Building improvement reserves Money accumulated for deferred maintenance, renovations, and repairs to government-owned facilities.

Capital assets Things the local government owns that cost a considerable amount of money and that are intended to last a long time—e.g., buildings, land, roads, bridges, and water treatment plants. Also known as **fixed assets**.

Capital budget A spending plan for improvements to or acquisition of land, facilities, and infrastructure. The capital budget (1) balances revenues and expenditures, (2) specifies the sources of revenues, (3) lists each project or acquisition, and (4) must ordinarily be approved by the legislative body.

Capital improvements plan (CIP) A list of capital projects for a period of time, usually five years, by department. The CIP may list anticipated revenues to pay for the projects.

Capital outlay Spending on fixed assets; generally, such acquisitions cost more than a specified amount (e.g., $5,000) or are intended to last more than one year.

Capital projects funds Governmental funds established to account for resources used for the acquisition of large capital improvements other than those accounted for in proprietary or trust funds.

Cash basis of accounting A method of accounting in which revenues are recorded only when cash is received and expenditures are recorded only when payment is made. Since payments for goods and services can be delayed to the next fiscal year, cash on hand can result in an inaccurate picture of the financial condition of a fund. To be in conformance with generally accepted accounting principles, local governments must use the accrual basis, rather than the cash basis, of accounting. *See also* **accrual basis of accounting**.

Cash flow The net cash balance at any given point. The treasurer prepares a cash budget that projects the inflow, outflow, and net balance of cash reserves on a daily, weekly, and monthly basis.

Causal modeling *See* **econometric modeling**.

Change order A change in the design or specifications of an approved capital project; change orders often increase the cost of a project.

Chart of accounts A chart that assigns a unique number to each type of transaction (e.g., salaries or property taxes) and to each budgetary unit in the organization. The chart of accounts provides a system for recording revenues and expenditures that fits the organizational structure.

Comprehensive annual financial report (CAFR) Usually referred to by its abbreviation, this report summarizes financial data for the previous fiscal year in a standardized format. The CAFR is organized by fund and contains two basic types of information: (1) a balance sheet that compares assets with liabilities and fund balance and (2) an operating statement that compares revenues with expenditures.

Contingency account An account set aside to meet unforeseen circumstances; this type of account protects the local government from having to issue short-term debt to cover such needs.

Debt service Annual principal and interest payments that the local government owes on money that it has borrowed.

Debt service funds One or more funds established to account for expenditures used to repay the principal and interest on debt.

Debt service payment reserves *See* **reserves for debt service payment**.

Default Failure to make a debt payment (principal or interest) on time.

Deterministic projection techniques Revenue projection techniques that rely on a simple mathematical formula. In the case of solid waste revenues, for example, the formula may be the monthly charge per household times the number of households in the jurisdiction. Also known as **formula-based projection techniques**.

Disbursement Payment for goods or services that have been delivered and invoiced.

Earmarking Legal limitations on the revenue from fees, licenses, taxes, or grants, which determine how the funds may be spent. Many state and federal grants are earmarked for particular types of projects. Earmarked revenues are frequently accounted for in special revenue funds.

Econometric modeling A revenue projection technique that assumes that the yield from a particular revenue source, such as the general sales tax, is affected by a number of factors, such as per capita income, inflation, and population change. Historical data are used to estimate the weights for each predictor, and a statistical model is developed that determines the effect of the various predictors on sales tax yield. Also known as **causal modeling**.

Economies of scale The cost savings that usually occur with increases in output. If the number of units increases, fixed costs are divided among more units, and the ratio of units to fixed costs will result in lower costs per unit.

Encumbrance Budget authority that is set aside when a purchase order or contract is approved. The encumbrance assures suppliers that sufficient funds will be available once the order

is fulfilled. Encumbrances are also known as **obligations**. *See also* **purchase order**.

Enterprise fund A separate fund used to account for services supported primarily by service charges; examples are water, sewer, golf, and airport funds.

Enterprises Government-owned services, such as utilities, that are supported primarily by fees rather than by tax revenues.

Entitlement program A program in which funding is allocated according to eligibility criteria: all persons or governments that meet the criteria specified in law receive the benefit.

Equipment replacement reserves Reserves designated for the purchase of new vehicles or operating equipment as existing equipment becomes obsolete or unusable.

Executive budget A proposed budget put together by the chief executive or his or her designees for review and approval or modification by the legislative branch.

Executive budget hearings Hearings that occur after an initial review by the budget office and that provide an opportunity for departments to explain their requests to the chief executive and the budget staff.

Fiduciary funds Funds that account for resources that governments hold in trust for individuals or other governments.

Financial report *See* **comprehensive annual financial report**.

Fiscal note A statement added to proposed mandating legislation estimating the full cost of the mandate to local governments. By requiring state lawmakers to calculate the costs that mandates impose on local governments, fiscal noting is intended to restrain state lawmakers from initiating unfunded mandates.

Fiscal year A designated twelve-month period for budgeting and record-keeping purposes.

Fixed assets *See* **capital assets**.

Formula-based projection techniques   *See* deterministic projection techniques.

Full-time equivalent (FTE)   The number of hours per year that a full-time employee is expected to work. If there are two workers, each of whom works half that number of hours per year, the two workers together equal one full-time equivalent.

Fund   A self-balancing set of accounts. Governmental accounting information is organized into funds, each with separate revenues, expenditures, and fund balances.

Fund balance   The difference between a fund's assets and its liabilities. Portions of the fund balance may be reserved for various purposes, such as contingencies or encumbrances.

General fund   The major fund in most governmental units, the general fund accounts for all activities not accounted for in other funds. Most tax-funded functions—such as police and fire protection—are accounted for in the general fund.

Generally accepted accounting principles (GAAP)   Uniform minimum standards used by state and local governments for financial recording and reporting; established by the accounting profession through the Governmental Accounting Standards Board (GASB). At the federal level, accounting standards are established by the Federal Accounting Standards Advisory Board.

General obligation (GO) bond   A bond that is backed by the government's unconditional ability to raise taxes. GO bonds are also known as *full-faith-and-credit bonds* because of a government's unconditional pledge to repay the debt using whatever revenue-raising capabilities are at its disposal. *See also* revenue bond.

Governmental Accounting Standards Board (GASB)   The body that sets accounting standards specifically for governmental entities at the state and local levels.

Grant   A payment of money from one governmental unit to another or from a governmental unit to a not-for-profit agency. Grants are often earmarked for a specific purpose or program.

Home rule   A limited grant of discretion from a state government to a local government, concerning either the organization of functions or the raising of revenue. Without home rule, local governments are restricted to whatever functions, organization, revenue policies, and borrowing restrictions are specified by the state government.

Impound   To restrict spending; impoundments are generally at the discretion of the chief executive.

Income elastic revenue   Revenue that increases or decreases at a greater rate than the economy expands or contracts; general sales tax revenue is an example.

Incremental budgeting   A budgeting process in which precedent determines how funds will be allocated among departments and programs. Under incremental budgeting, increases in allocations usually occur in small increments over past levels.

Independent auditor   An accounting firm (or, occasionally, a state or local official not associated with the local government) who reviews the comprehensive annual financial report and compares it with a sample of financial transactions in order to certify that the report represents accurately the fiscal condition of the governmental unit.

Informed judgment   A method of projecting revenues that relies on the judgment of experts. Also known as a **professional guess**.

Infrastructure   Basic public investments such as streets, storm drainage, water and sewer lines, streetlights, and sidewalks.

Interdepartmental order (IDO)   An internal request between departments for goods or services, usually initiated by a department head. An IDO automatically authorizes reimbursement for the internally provided goods or services.

Interfund borrowing   A transfer of money from a fund that has a surplus to a fund that has a temporary revenue shortfall.

Interfund transfer   The transfer of money from one fund to another in a governmental unit. Interfund transfers usually have to be approved by the governing body and are normally subject to restrictions in state and local law.

Interim financial reports Quarterly or monthly comparisons of budgeted with actual revenues and expenditures to date. These reports provide decision makers with an early warning of impending expenditure overruns or revenue shortfalls.

Internal rate of return (IRR) A criterion used to calculate the desirability of capital projects. The rate of return from the project should be higher than the cost of capital to pay for the project.

Internal service funds One or more funds that account for the goods and services provided by one department to another within government on a cost-reimbursement basis. Departments that use internal services (e.g., data processing) may have a line item in their budget for such services.

Legislative budget hearings Hearings on the budget proposal. The term is applied to two different types of hearings: (1) work sessions in which staff present the proposed budget to the council and (2) formal public hearings.

Legislative budgeting A budget process in which the council or a council committee receives requests directly from departments and pares them back; the executive branch has a minimal role in legislative budgeting.

Line-item budget A budget format in which departmental outlays are grouped according to the items that will be purchased, with one item or group of items on each line. *See also* **objects of expenditure.**

Line-item veto A rejection by the executive of one item or group of items in a line-item budget.

Mandate A requirement from a higher level of government that a lower level of government perform a task, perform a task in a particular way, or perform a task to meet a particular standard, often without compensation from the higher level of government.

Marginal cost The additional cost of providing service to one more resident or consumer. Once capacity is reached, additional service capacity

must be funded, and marginal cost increases substantially.

Modified accrual basis of accounting A form of accrual accounting in which (1) expenditures are recognized when the goods or services are received and (2) revenues, such as taxes, are recognized when measurable and available to pay expenditures in the current accounting period. *See also* **accrual basis of accounting, cash basis of accounting.**

Net present value (NPV) A method used to calculate the economic desirability of capital projects. NPV uses a discount rate to take account of the discrepancy between the present costs of undertaking a project and its future stream of benefits. The greater the NPV of a project, the more economically attractive it will be.

Objects of expenditure Items to be purchased in an operating budget. The line items in a budget are sometimes called objects of expenditure. *See also* **line-item budget.**

Obligation *See* **encumbrance.**

Operating budget That portion of a budget that deals with recurring expenditures such as salaries, electric bills, postage, printing and duplicating, paper supplies, and gasoline. The operating budget may be a separate document from the capital budget, or a consolidated document may be prepared that has one section devoted to operating expenditures and another to capital expenditures. Taken together, the operating and the capital budgets should equal the total amount of spending for the fiscal period. *See also* **capital budget.**

Operating deficit The amount by which this year's (or this budget period's) revenues are exceeded by expenditures for the same period. An operating deficit does not take into account any balances left over from prior years that may be used to pay off shortfalls.

Pay-as-you-go financing A method of paying for capital projects that relies on current tax and grant revenues rather than on debt.

Pay-as-you-use financing The use of debt rather than current revenues to pay for capital outlays.

Payback period The time that it will take to recover the funds invested in a project. The payback period is used as a criterion to evaluate and compare capital project proposals: a shorter payback period is more desirable.

Payments in lieu of taxes (PILOTs) Money transferred from enterprises into the general fund; the principle underlying such transfers is that the government would have received the equivalent amount in taxes had the service been provided by a privately owned firm. PILOTs are one means of determining how much money is appropriate to transfer from a public enterprise to the general fund.

Performance budget A budget format that includes (1) performance goals and objectives and (2) demand, workload, efficiency, and effectiveness (outcome or impact) measures for each governmental program.

Performance measures Indicators used in budgets to show, for example, (1) the amount of work accomplished, (2) the efficiency with which tasks were completed, and (3) the effectiveness of a program, which is often expressed as the extent to which objectives were accomplished.

Planning, programming, budgeting systems (PPBS) A budget reform that links budgeting with planning and evaluation on a program-by-program basis. The aim of PPBS, now generally known as **program budgeting**, was to introduce more formal economic analysis into budget deliberations: under PPBS, the benefits and costs of each program were determined, and funds were allocated to those programs providing the greatest net benefits.

Productivity The cost per unit of goods or services, holding quality constant. Productivity increases when the cost per unit goes down but quality remains constant or increases.

Professional guess *See* **informed judgment.**

Program budget A budget format that organizes budgetary information and allocates funds along program rather than departmental lines. A program is a set of activities with a common goal. *See also* **planning, programming, budgeting systems.**

Public hearing An open meeting regarding proposed operating or capital budget allocations, which provides citizens with an opportunity to voice their views on the merits of the proposals.

Purchase order An agreement to buy goods and services from a specific vendor, with a promise to pay on delivery. *See also* **encumbrance.**

Rainy day funds Revenue stabilization reserves that provide resources when tax revenues temporarily decline (as the result of a recession, the loss of a major taxpayer, or other similar circumstance).

Regressive tax A tax that is relatively more burdensome on lower-income households.

Rescission A reduction in the approved budget during the current year. Rescissions are executive-branch decisions.

Reserves for debt service payment Reserve accounts used to provide funds in the event revenues are insufficient to repay the principal and interest on debt coming due in the current year; generally for revenue bonds.

Reserves for unforeseen contingencies Funding for nonrecurring, unanticipated expenditures; the funds protect the local government from having to issue short-term debt to cover such needs.

Revenue bond A bond backed by revenues from the project that the borrowed money was used to create, expand, or improve. Also known as a *limited pledge bond* because of the conditional backing given to repayment of the debt. *See also* **general obligation bond.**

Revenue stabilization reserves *See* **rainy day funds.**

Salary savings The reduced expenditures for salaries that result when a position remains unfilled for part of a year or when a more senior employee is replaced by a newer employee at a lower salary.

Special revenue fund A fund used to account for revenues legally earmarked for a particular purpose. For example, if revenues from a hotel/motel occupancy tax are earmarked for tourism and convention development, a hotel/motel tax fund would account for the revenues and expenditures associated with such purposes.

Sunset review A periodic review, generally near the end of an agency's funding cycle, that gives policy makers the opportunity to redirect the agency's purpose and funding level.

Target-based budgeting A budget process in which departments are provided with a maximum level for their budget requests. The budget office requires separate justification for proposed spending levels that exceed the target.

Tax expenditures Abatements, partial or full exemptions, tax credits, deductions, or other forgone tax revenues.

Time series analysis A revenue projection technique based on averaging trends in prior years.

Transfer *See* interfund transfer.

Trust fund A fund established to receive money that the local government holds on behalf of individuals or other governments; the government holding the money has little or no discretion over it. Examples include employee pension funds and taxes collected for other governments.

Unified budget A budget that consolidates all revenues and expenditures for all funds. The purpose of a unified budget is to report accurately the full amount of governmental revenues and expenditures for the budget period.

Unreserved fund balance Money left over from prior years that is not committed for other purposes and can be allocated in the upcoming budget.

Veto The power of an elected chief executive to override all or a portion of an act or ordinance passed by the council. The council typically has the power to overrule the executive's veto by an extraordinary (e.g., two-thirds) majority. The executive's power to veto legislation is specified in the state constitution or in the local government's charter. In some cases, veto power is limited to an ordinance in its entirety; in the case of the budget, the executive may have the power to veto specific lines in a line-item budget. *See also* **line-item veto**.

Zero-base budgeting A budget process that requires departments to prepare decision packages representing various service levels and rank order them. Departmental rankings are then merged across the whole governmental unit to form a single, ranked list. Funding goes down the list until the money runs out.

Name index

Subject index

**Budgeting: A Guide for
  Local Governments**
Composition by:
  EPS Group, Easton, Maryland
Cover design by:
  Lauren Erdman
Printing and binding by:
  United Book Press, Inc., Baltimore, Maryland